CHILD
ADVOCACY

Psychological Issues and Interventions

CHILD ADVOCACY

Psychological Issues and Interventions

GARY B. MELTON

University of Nebraska
Lincoln, Nebraska

PLENUM PRESS • NEW YORK AND LONDON

Library of Congress Cataloging in Publication Data

Melton, Gary B.
  Child advocacy.

  Bibliography: p.
  Includes index.
  1. Children's rights—United States. 2. Children—Legal status, laws, etc.—United
States. I. Title. [DNLM: 1. Child advocacy. WA 320 M528c]
HQ789.M44 1983   305.2'3'0973   83-2255
ISBN 0-306-41156-3

© 1983 Plenum Press, New York
A Division of Plenum Publishing Corporation
233 Spring Street, New York, N.Y. 10013

Printed in the United States of America

Foreword

The details of the history of child advocacy have been vividly described in an article by Takanishi (1978). In reviewing her work and that of others, four historical phases in child advocacy can be identified:

1. The first period was the evolution of the concept of childhood as a distinct and separate developmental stage. Ariès (1962) has described how the concept of childhood as a period different from adulthood did not evolve philosophically until the sixteenth century. It was only after that time, through the influence of Rousseau and other philosophers, that childhood was seen, at first romantically, and later more realistically, as a special time for growth and learning, with unique styles and mechanisms.

2. It was not until the nineteenth century, however, with the rapid rise of science and major socioeconomic changes that a formal effort was made to identify and try to meet children's needs. A number of organizations specifically devoted to children arose and attempts to help children in ways consistent with the developing knowledge became a major social issue. Initially, the interest was in children's health with infant mortality, child labor, and safety as paramount issues. Although socioeconomic factors initiated the change (children's labor was no longer economically necessary), a basic humanistic philosophy underlay this phase. Major dedication to alleviating the pain and injury done to children who were helpless to defend themselves and who were being deprived of opportunities for growth became the goal. To accomplish this, political action was necessary. Although not labeled as advocacy, political forces were mobilized to bring about important legislative action (e.g., passage of child labor laws). But on the whole, the thrust was single-issue oriented rather than a general, broadly based philosophical or social movement.

Nevertheless, the issues that arose in phase two became symbolic of significant change in the social responsibility regarding children. What finally resulted was the initiation of national thrusts, such as the White House Conferences on Children starting in 1909 and the establishment of the Children's Bureau in 1912—the latter mandated to collect statistics and develop a strategy aimed to improve the conditions of children in the United States.

3. The third phase can be characterized by the rise of institutional status for child advocacy and the more general recognition for child advocacy as a social movement. These were derived from the United Nations Declaration in 1959 of the Rights of Children and the White House Conference in 1960 which listed the rights of children. Both these documents generated further interest in a much broader conception of children's needs and of the social structures necessary to meet them. It was out of this background that the 1969 Joint Commission on the Mental Health of Children for the first time in United States history defined a concept of "child advocacy." In the volume *Crisis in Child Mental Health: Challenge for the Seventies,* "child advocacy" was conceptually separated from both the delivery of services and the lobbying for specific individual issues (as had occurred in the early part of the century). The definition, which bears repeating, was:

> The child deserves an advocate to represent him and his needs to the society in which he lives, an advocate who will insist that programs and services based on sound child development knowledge be available to every child as a public utility— the promotion of national, state, and community responsibility and initiative in developing comprehensive and systematic programs of prevention and treatment, in increasing the accountability of those who minister relevant programs, and in coordinating and organizing resources for supportive, effective, and coordinated programs for our children and youth. (Joint Commission, 1970, p. 9)

Since 1969 there have been a number of books and articles on child advocacy and many individuals have been identified as child advocates. Indeed, Sweden has recognized the institutional need for child advocates by designating ombudsmen as a significant social role.

But the most important contribution of this third historical phase was the development of both conceptual models and empirical bases for the child advocacy field. Thus, in addition to the political and humanistic thrusts that formed the basis of earlier historical periods, there also arose greater concern with conceptualizing and studying the basic assumptions of child advocacy and their implications. The value of such conceptual and empirical elaboration served not only to legitimize the area but also removed it in part from the often ephemeral, personal, or political realm, adding a a base of knowledge that could remain as a permanent contribution to future understanding and planning.

Over the last decade at least three issues have surfaced in the child advocacy field: What is the role of the professional and what is the role of the parent as a child advocate? In what way are the problems of children's rights consistent with or in opposition to parents' rights and how can these be reconciled? What are the implications of an advocacy program based on a philosophy of child liberation as compared to one based on a paternalistic and protectionistic philosophy? The answers to these questions are highly complex and will take many years to be answered.

In 1970, the Joint Commission on the Mental Health of Children recommended a national advocacy structure with advocacy units at local, state, and federal levels. Unfortunately, this national program of child advocacy organizations was not implemented. What did evolve, however, in a few states such as Massachusetts, were small child advocacy centers or task forces that have had some success locally but minimal impact on a national level.

In addition to conceptualization, over the last decade a large body of data has been collected on attitudes toward children, the structure and organization of children's services, the role of the professional, and the effectiveness of various mental health programs. As society's responsibility for children has increased, there also has been greater concern with integrating the fragmented programs of employment, nutrition, education, recreation, and health.

But institutionalizing the concept of child advocacy has not been enough. What seems clear is that an ideology favorable to children in the United States is lacking. The socialist countries have invested a great deal in children because they believe that they can mold a "new man" for the next generation. Scandinavian countries have invested in children because of an underlying deep philosophical commitment to assisting the helpless and powerless. Whether or not a child advocacy structure can be developed in the United States without an underlying and constructive ideology of the value of children (other than as consumers) has yet to be seen.

4. Children historically have been most vulnerable to socioeconomic changes in the United States. In the late 1970s and early 1980s the economic situation has worsened. As a result, in a fourth phase, there seems to be a slowing of interest and concern in general and with child advocacy in particular. Children, unable to be a force in the political system, have fallen easy victim to reduced resources while other groups with greater political influence have been heard and given priority. For example, the 1980 White House Conference on Children and Youth was canceled as a national conference and was organized instead as a series of individual state conferences. Funds for children's programs have been reduced markedly. Discussion of children's needs and ways to meet these needs has dramatically abated.

Despite these changes, however, child advocacy as an area remains a significant historical event that will continue to have profound impact on the organization, structure, and development of children's services on a national scale well into the future. One of the contributions to this brighter future is Dr. Melton's current volume.

Dr. Melton's book is a comprehensive review of child advocacy, for it integrates the historical, humanistic, political, theoretical, and empirical aspects of the field, placing all these elements within an ecological framework. Thus, it broadens the field further than have others. As the boundaries between professional functioning and social action become more narrow and as we begin to evolve an inevitable national child, youth, and family policy (as has taken place in many industrialized countries) based on integrated scientific data derived from many fields—law, anthropology, social work, sociology, psychology, psychiatry, education—Dr. Melton's volume, ranging from theory to grass-roots political action, will be seen as a significant contribution toward stemming the tide of retreat by continuing to raise our consciousness and showing how we must mobilize our resources to improve the quality of life for our children and youth and, in that way, the quality of life for all future generations.

MILTON F. SHORE, PH.D.
Associate Chief
Mental Health Study Center
National Institute of Mental Health

Acknowledgments

Undoubtedly the most rewarding aspects of writing a book come near its completion. There is the obvious reward associated with the crystallization of one's ideas on paper, especially when, as is the case with this volume, the topic is one of substantial social import. Beyond the sense of accomplishment that comes with the completion of a book about a topic about which one feels deeply, though, the end of a writing project brings the opportunity to thank publicly some of the people who have contributed to the development of the ideas in the book.

Let me begin this pleasant task by thanking several colleagues who reviewed all or part of the manuscript: Alden Abbott, Gerald Koocher, Milton Shore, Ross Thompson, and Lois Weithorn. The manuscript is stronger as a result of their comments.

Several student assistants at the University of Virginia contributed their energies to library research which was useful in providing background for some of the issues discussed in this volume. Thanks are due Karen Bisset, James Faubion (who coauthored Chapter 9), Daniella Levine, and Irwin Shur.

Chapter 2 was based upon my doctoral dissertation at Boston University. The assistance of my dissertation committee (Gerald Koocher, Frances Grossman, and Verne McArthur) in formulating this research is gratefully acknowledged.

Chapter 7 was enriched by the accounts of experiences or observations of Washington children's lobbyists by a number of persons who graciously consented to an interview: Barbara Bode, Laurie Flynn, Helene Gerstein, Ellen Hoffman, Margaret Jones, Mary Lopatto, Mary Roberts, and Nancy Tague.

I owe particular thanks to two individuals who have contributed to the development of my thinking on the topics presented in this volume. Gerald Koocher has been both mentor and colleague in child advocacy efforts. William Malamud supervised part of my internship in 1975-1976 at Boston University School of Medicine and the Massachusetts Office for Children and helped me to integrate these disparate experiences into a concept of clinical advocacy.

During the writing of this volume I have been fortunate to have worked in two settings that were quite facilitative of the effort. Much of the first half of the book was written while I was a member of the faculty at the University of Virginia's Institute of Law, Psychiatry, and Public Policy. The Institute's director, Richard Bonnie, was supportive both in providing research assistants and other resources and in helping me to learn to "think like a lawyer." The University of Nebraska-Lincoln's Department of Psychology has been an equally collegial place in which to work.

More personally, I am indebted to my wife Julie and my daughter Jennifer for their understanding when the final writing stretched into evenings and weekends and indeed for all that we share.

Finally, my parents, Harold and Marion, taught me respect for children through their example. It is to them that this book is dedicated.

GARY B. MELTON

Contents

CHAPTER 1

Children's Rights

THE FOUNDATION OF CHILD ADVOCACY

Particularly since the call by the Joint Commission on the Mental Health of Children (1970) for "child advocacy," there has been a social movement on behalf of children. Child advocacy is indeed a social movement, an effort to enhance the status of children. It is more than simply the provision of direct services to children or doing "nice things for them." Rather, child advocacy represents an attempt to increase the responsiveness and accountability of social institutions affecting children. Whether the intent is to increase children's self-determination or to enhance the social, educational, and medical resources to which children are entitled, child advocates have as their mission social action *on behalf of* children. Like earlier "child-saving" movements, the current advocacy movement has had at least two basic assumptions. First, it is assumed that children are in a state of dependency that leaves them vulnerable to abuse by caretakers. By law, social custom, and in some cases the developmental incapacity of the child, children are subject to a "benign oppression" which renders them essentially powerless (Koocher, 1976b). Even if caretakers are not malevolent in their intentions, their actions may not be in children's best interests through ignorance or simply as a result of complex competing pressures. Furthermore, even if the caretakers are both competent and primarily concerned with their children's interests, the realities of "the system" may make it impossible for them to fulfill their children's needs. Simply put, "mothers cannot do it all" (Hobbs, 1975, p. 225). In such an instance, there is a need for an advocate to support the interests of the child.

Secondly, it is assumed that the fulfillment of basic needs is especially important in childhood (see Westman, 1979, for a detailed exposition of this view). Only when children are provided basic resources will they be enabled

1

to exercise choices that then will provide the opportunity for self-actualization throughout the life span. Given children's dependent status and the state's interest in their developing skills to enable them to function as independent adults, historically the state has borne the responsibility of ensuring that at least some minimum of physical and psychological care is available to them. Within such a view, formalized in the state's parens patriae power, children's *needs* may become conceptualized as children's *rights*. Many child advocates have taken as their mission the fulfillment of these rights, which they typically have perceived as quite broad. Thus, child-advocacy groups such as the Children's Defense Fund (e.g., Edelman, 1981) have been active in fighting for the recognition of rights to adequate health care, education, and so forth.

It should be noted that such a view may bring "child-saving" advocates into conflict with other child advocates who conceptualize their primary goal as "liberating" children and recognizing rights to increased self-determination for them. This conflict within the child advocacy movement will be analyzed later in this chapter (see also Mnookin, 1978a) and indeed will arise in many contexts throughout the book. Edelman (1981) has starkly phrased the issue from the perspective of advocates with a child-welfare or child-saving orientation:

> The Children's Defense Fund is not a children's liberation group. Our goal is not to stress children's rights against the family or their playing adult roles at younger and younger ages. Rather, we focus on children's rights to and needs for fair and decent treatment from a range of external institutions—schools, health, mental health, juvenile justice, and child welfare systems—and rights to the necessities of human development. We disagree with those who focus simply on an expansion of procedural rights for children without also paying attention to children's needs, which involve the provision of adequate family, job, and income support as well as supportive services. (p. 113)

Nonetheless, while deemphasizing the significance of childhood as special or different, even the "kiddie libbers" have advocated their position on the basis of "needs," albeit a quite different analysis of what those needs are.[1] Thus, Holt (1974) has suggested that increasingly treating children like adults (i.e., recognizing rights to work, travel, maintain privacy, etc.) would help children "to be more informed, competent, and independent" (p. 279) as well as allow each child to fulfill his need "to feel that he is a human being in his own right" (p. 147). Indeed, Holt's volume *Escape from Childhood* is subtitled "*The* Needs *and* Rights *of Children*" (emphasis added). Further-

---

[1] A liberationist position can, of course, also be advocated on the basis of respect for personal autonomy, independent of an analysis of children's needs.

more, Holt's advocacy efforts (see especially Holt, 1974, Chap. 28) are clearly conceptualized as an adult's efforts on behalf of children to change the behavior and attitudes of other adults.

Thus, regardless of the level of libertarianism present in a particular child advocate's conceptualization of what child advocacy is, there is a recognition that significant change on behalf of children—meeting children's rights and needs, whatever they are—will require adult action. At this point children clearly are in a largely dependent position, whether because of law and custom or because of their immaturity, and need adults as their advocates to see that their needs are met.

Assuming the validity of such an assumption, a technology of child advocacy needs to be developed. Child advocacy frequently has rested on platitudes and polemics (essentially, "be nice to kids") without a careful analysis of (a) what children's needs and rights are and (b) how these goals might be most effectively met. Knitzer's (1976) analysis of the confusion as to the implications of the Joint Commission's call for child advocacy is still largely on point. This book represents an initial effort to apply social science research and theory to the development of advocacy techniques. In addition, I will examine the contributions that psychologists have made, or might make, to resolution of questions of public policy concerning children. Thus, the approach employed is primarily empirical. We shall first briefly examine, though, the ethical and political issues implicit in the advocacy movement's assumptions.

WHAT ARE CHILDREN'S RIGHTS?

Webster's definition of a "right" emphasizes the concept of a "just claim." That is, rights are a form of *entitlement*. Even if they are unfulfilled, they are not (at least in theory) dependent on the benevolence of powerful people and institutions. As Friedman (1977) argued, a right is "a claim that (if it is truly a right) *has* to be granted. Individuals are taught that authorities have no right to withhold a right. If a matter is in the discretion of authority, then the claim is not a right" (p. 74). To continue with Friedman's line of reasoning,

when blacks demand full equality on the basis of the Fourteenth Amendment, they are not in theory asking whites to *grant* them equality but to stop their incursions on rights that in some ethical or legal sense inhere in the words or the spirit of the Constitution, though, in fact, they have never had full objective reality. (p. 75)

One may in fact go further and argue for natural rights based on requirements for human dignity and arguably accruing to individuals as persons, even if these rights are not recognized in law. Such "rights" derived from ethical imperatives are fully developed in the tradition of Lockian classical liberalism exemplified in the American Declaration of Independence and the French Declaration of the Rights of Man.

Only within the past 15 years has it become clear that children do in fact have rights under the United States Constitution. Not until the case of *In re Gault*[2] in 1967 did the Supreme Court make clear that children were "persons" within the meaning of the Fourteenth Amendment and accordingly were entitled to its benefits. Since then, the Court has made clear that "the Bill of Rights is not for adults alone" and has acknowledged constitutional rights for juveniles to limited freedom of expression,[3] due process in school suspension[4] and delinquency proceedings,[5] equality of educational opportunity,[6] access to abortions[7] and contraceptives,[8] and so forth. With Head Start, Medicaid, the Education for All Handicapped Children Act, and other social legislation, at least the rudiments of statutory rights to education, health care, and adequate nutrition and housing have also been established for children.[9]

The arguments raised in support of recognition of such rights typically have had as a partial basis the idea that they are grounded in natural law. The premise is that justice demands fundamental liberties and protection to all participants in society (Rawls, 1971). Furthermore, it is argued that, as persons and as future participants in society with human capacity for moral behavior, children are entitled to basic human rights. Nonetheless, it is clear that, while their personhood may be judically recognized in some contexts, children still are not "as equal as people" in other contexts. Thus, they do not have all of the same rights as adults to due process when they are accused of crimes (although they are entitled to those procedural rights that are "fundamental" to due process);[10] unlike any other citizens, they reasonably may be subject to corporal punishment by state authorities (in the public

---

[2]387 U.S. 1.

[3]Tinker v. Des Moines Independent School District, 393 U.S. 503 (1969).

[4]Goss v. Lopez, 419 U.S. 565 (1975).

[5]In re Gault, *supra* note 2.

[6]Brown v. Board of Education, 347 U.S. 483 (1954).

[7]Bellotti v. Baird II, 443 U.S. 622 (1979); Bellotti v. Baird I, 438 U.S. 132 (1976); Planned Parenthood of Central Missouri v. Danforth, 438 U.S. 52 (1976).

[8]Carey v. Population Services International, 431 U.S. 678 (1977).

[9]There is some indication, however, that the Supreme Court will refrain, on federalism grounds, from enforcing broad, vague mandates to the states to provide services. *See* Pennhurst State School v. Halderman, 451 U.S. 1 (1981).

[10]McKeiver v. Pennsylvania, 403 U.S. 528 (1971).

schools).[11] Similarly, unlike adults, children can be "volunteered" for psychiatric hospitalization by third parties (i.e., their parents or guardians),[12] and their access to employment, as well as "bad influences" (such as pornography[13] and alcoholic beverages[14]), can be limited simply on the basis of age, provided that a legitimate state interest outweighing the minor's liberty interest can be demonstrated. Particular restrictions on expression of constitutional rights may be placed on "immature" minors; thus, requirements of parental notice when immature minors seek abortions are constitutionally permissible.[15]

Much of the lack of clarity concerning the rights that children do have emanates from the fact that recognition of *independent* rights for them disturbs the traditional concept of inviolability of parent–child and, to a large extent, school–child relationships except under the grossest threats to the child's health and safety. The courts traditionally have supported the notion of the sanctity and privacy of the family[16] and have been reluctant to disturb *parents'* rights to socialize their children as they see fit.[17] While this assumption originally may have been grounded in economic interest, its ethical basis lies in an assumption that parents and children have interests that are essentially unitary. Goldstein, Freud, and Solnit (1979) have, for example, argued that children are more or less helpless and require seemingly omnipotent parents to foster adequate impulse control and socialization (for a similar view not based on psychoanalytic theory, see Baumrind, 1980). Thus, they conclude, children "require the privacy of family life under guardianship by parents who are autonomous" (p. 9). In their view, the child's liberty interests are essentially equivalent to those of the parents:

> We use the phrase "family integrity" . . . to encompass the three liberty interests of direct concern to children (parental autonomy, the right to autonomous parents, and privacy). (Goldstein, Freud, & Solnit, 1979, p. 9, footnote)

The validity of the assumption of unitary interests is clearly questionable in many instances (see generally Melton, 1982a). Indeed, Goldstein et al.'s assumption of children's need for autonomous parents lacks any clear empirical base and may be effectively refuted by research suggesting psychological

---

[11]Ingraham v. Wright, 403 U.S. 651 (1977); Baker v. Owen, 395 F. Supp. 294 (M.D.N.C.), *aff'd without opinion,* 423 U.S. 907 (1975).

[12]Parham v. J.R., 442 U.S. 584 (1979).

[13]Ginsberg v. New York, 390 U.S. 629 (1968).

[14] *See generally* Wechsler (1980).

[15]H.L. v. Matheson, 450 U.S. 398 (1981).

[16] *See, e.g.,* Griswold v. Connecticut, 381 U.S. 479 (1965); Parham v. J.R., *supra* note 12.

[17] *E.g.,* Wisconsin v. Yoder, 406 U.S. 205 (1972); Pierce v. Society of Sisters, 268 U.S. 510 (1925).

harm of overemphasis on privacy and parental autonomy in child-rearing practices (Garbarino, Gaboury, Long, Grandjean, & Asp, 1982). Regardless, however, of the validity of this general claim, it seems clear that there are particular instances in which children and parents have identifiable separate interests. For example, in *Wisconsin v. Yoder,*[18] the Supreme Court upheld the right of Amish parents to exempt their children from compulsory school attendance beyond the eighth grade on grounds of religious freedom. In a dissent, however, Justice Douglas argued eloquently that the critical interests under consideration were those of the children and not the parents. As Douglas argued,

> If he [the student] is harnessed to the Amish way of life by those in authority over him and if his education is truncated, his entire life may be stunted and deformed. The child, therefore, should be given an opportunity to be heard before the State gives the exemption which we honor today.[19]

In such a case, the interests of parents and children are clearly at least potentially in conflict. Furthermore, even if they agree in the end, their interests are different, the principal point to be made here. Further complicating matters is the fact that the State itself has distinct, complex, and somewhat contradictory interests in supporting family life, individual liberty, and the socialization and education of minors to be productive adults.

Failure to recognize the multiplicity of interests involved and their independence, or at least partial independence from one another, leads to continuing confusion concerning what children's rights really are. For example, one of the earliest cases in the children's rights area was *Meyer v. Nebraska,*[20] a 1923 Supreme Court decision that struck down a Nebraska law prohibiting instruction in foreign languages as violative of the Fourteenth Amendment's protection of individual liberty. The decision is unclear, however, as to whose liberty interest was vindicated: the child's, the child's parents', or the teacher's. One need not go back so far to find unclarity in court opinions concerning whose rights are at stake. For example, one of the cases that seemed to establish clearly that children were indeed "persons" for purposes of constitutional analysis was a 1969 case *(Tinker v. Des Moines Independent School District)*[21] in which the Supreme Court held that school suspensions for wearing black arm bands in protest against the Vietnam war were unconstitutional

---

[18]406 U.S. 205.
[19]*Id.* at 246.
[20]262 U.S. 390 (1923).
[21]*Supra* note 3.

infringements on freedom of expression. Constitutional rights, Justice Fortas wrote, are not "shed . . . at the schoolhouse gate."[22] Nonetheless, as the dissenters in *Tinker* pointed out, one of the plaintiff children was 8 years old; their parents were antiwar activists.[23] It is unclear accordingly whether *Tinker* really stands for *children's* freedom of expression in school. The facts of the case lend themselves almost as easily to an analysis of *parents'* rights vis-à-vis state authority.

Complicating the definition of children's rights further is the fact that advocates frequently contend that children have not only the same natural rights as adults but other rights that accrue from their developmental needs. This argument is in keeping with the assumption noted earlier that it is especially important to meet the needs of children so that they might be able to exercise choices later as adults. The basic human rights of the child are argued to be different from those of the adult because different resources are necessary to meet fundamental needs of the child. Although we may agree that society bears an obligation to provide such basic protection, there is nothing approaching consensus on the definition of those rights. For example, education certainly is requisite to full adult functioning in a high technology society and it is sometimes argued that there is a natural right to education. Indeed, the United Nations Declaration of the Rights of the Child, enacted unanimously by the General Assembly in 1959, provides for a right to a free education. Furthermore, in terms of constitutional law, the Supreme Court has cited due process as necessary in school suspension cases, because "the State is constrained to recognize a student's legitimate entitlement to a public education as a property interest which is protected by the due process clause" of the Fourteenth Amendment.[24] This interest was based on an acknowledgment that allegations of misconduct resulting in suspension could "seriously damage the students' standing with their fellow pupils and their teachers as well as interfere with later opportunities for higher education and employment."[25] Nonetheless, the Court has held that education is not a "fundamental right" explicitly or implicitly guaranteed by the Constitution.[26] Moreover, even if there is a basic right to education, the limits of such a right are not self-evident. What content has to be included in a curriculum to fulfill such a right? Must all of the "special needs" of the child be met? Does a right to education

[22]*Id.* at 506.
[23]*Id.* at 516.
[24]Goss v. Lopez, *supra* note 4, at 574.
[25]*Id.* at 575.
[26]San Antonio Independent School District v. Rodriguez, 411 U.S. 1 (1973).

mandate *compulsory* education and the lack of a right to decide the nature and quality of education a child obtains? If the state does not have control over such decisions, does the right belong to the student or does it belong to his or her parents? How much "academic freedom" does the teacher have to define the quality and quantity of education required? An example of the issues involved in Bikson's (1978) contention that the child has "intellectual rights" to a stimulating educational environment that would facilitate curiosity, creativity, and active participatory learning for children of all social classes and intellectual ability levels.

One may ague that the state need not provide the resources necessary for a child's attaining his or her potential, but that it does bear the obligation to ensure a benign environment for those for whom it has responsibility as parens patriae. Thus, Judge Judd contended in the *"Willowbrook"* decision that due process demands "protection from harm" of those in the state's care.[27] Such an argument is a conservative one based on the premise that it is a travesty of due process to place mentally retarded persons in a more repressive environment than criminals. Although apparently a narrow criterion, the protection from harm criterion is an open-ended one that, if carried to its logical extreme, would pave the way for recognition of a broad right to treatment and entitlement to a whole network of services as a means to escape the harms that might result from not providing such services (Melton, 1978a). Halpern (1976), for example, has suggested that protection from the mental harm of institutionalization implies a right to treatment in the community. Thus, even a narrow definition of rights of dependent persons still leaves unanswered questions of "Protection from what harm?" and "Protection by whom?" There is additional ambiguity concerning whether the standards of care for children under state guardianship, such as handicapped children in state facilities, should be much higher than those for children living at home. That is, how much responsibility does the state have for meeting the needs of children entrusted to their parents? Even for children directly in state care, the right to treatment is still not clear, at least on constitutional grounds (see Ehrenreich & Melton, in press).[28] Statutory requirements for necessary educational services, including "related services" such as psychotherapy, to meet handicapped children's special education needs[29] come close to a legal requirement

[27]New York State Association for Retarded Children v. Rockefeller, 357 F. Supp. 752 (E.D.N.Y. 1973).
[28]The Supreme Court has explicitly reserved judgment as to whether such a right exists. O'Connor v. Donaldson, 422 U.S. 563, 573 (1975).
[29]Education for All Handicapped Children Act, Pub. L. 94–142, 20 U.S.C. §§ 1401–1461.

to meet children's individual developmental needs, at least when children require special services to remediate educational deficits. Even this societal commitment to children is controversial, however, and at this writing, there are reports that the Reagan administration intends to repeal regulations requiring local school systems to draw up plans for meeting the special educational needs of individual, handicapped children. (For an interesting exchange on a related issue, see the debate by Ellis, 1979, and Roos, 1979, on the limits of state responsibility in educating and caring for severely and profoundly retarded children.) The broad question remains: how much does society owe its children, both ethically and legally?

ATTITUDES TOWARD CHILDREN'S RIGHTS

Given the varying conceptions of children's rights, it would seem important to identify attitudes of various interest groups toward children's rights if one is to change public policy on behalf of children. Consistent with the discussion at the beginning of this chapter, Rogers and Wrightsman (1978) have hypothesized that such attitudes fall broadly on two dimensions, nurturance and self-determination. That is, some of the rights advocated for children involve protection and provision of the goods and services necessary for self-actualization and quality of life (e.g., the right to an education). Other proposed or extant rights involve determination of one's own fate and freedom from coercion and government intervention (e.g., the right to choose among educational alternatives, including the right not to attend school). At its extreme, the self-determination orientation is represented by the "children's liberationists" (Farson, 1974; Holt, 1974) who contend that children have "the right to do, in general, what any adult may do" (Holt, 1974, p. 19). Conceptually, one can advocate "positive" or "nurturance" rights and still not favor "negative" or "self-determination" rights of children or vice versa. Nurturance rights tend to be based on a paternalistic belief that the state must respond to children's particular needs and interests. Self-determination rights are based on a belief that adult civil liberties should be extended to children. More basically, "nurturance" and "self-determination" perspectives tend to be rooted in differing concepts of the nature of childhood and of children's capacities and, accordingly, of their level of vulnerability, a point to be developed in detail in Chapter 9. It should be noted, however, that a mixture of nurturance and self-determination attitudes is not necessarily inconsistent and, indeed, in some instances logically may follow. For example, although one generally may favor children's rights to self-determination, it is consistent with such a position to favor sufficient "nurturance" so that children in fact have a range of options for development of their skills to a degree to which they feel that they in fact have the capacity to make decisions (including decisions to seek advice when helpful or necessary). Thus, children's liberationists may still advocate broad social welfare entitlements. Where they are likely to depart from the child savers is in the latter group's tendency to support interventions for children's "own good" regardless of whether such "help" is requested. Of course, an advocate also might choose to follow a "pure" ideology of libertarianism or of paternalism.

Factor Structure of Rights Attitudes

In general, Rogers and Wrightsman's (1978) hypothesis of two major factors in attitudes toward children's rights has been confirmed by their work on their Children's Rights Attitudes Scale, a Likert-type questionnaire of items drawn from "bills of rights" that various individuals and organizations have suggested for children. Further support for the nurturance/self-determination typology was garnered in research described on children's concepts of their rights, described more fully in Chapter 2. In that research (Melton, 1980a), children themselves were asked to respond to 12 vignettes about conflict situations in which children might assert a right. (The entire interview protocol is printed in the Appendix to this volume.) Children's responses were scored twice, once for level of conceptualization and once for attitude toward children's rights. Attitude scores were based on whether the child favored assertion of a right by the child in the vignette. Concept scores were based on the degree of social awareness and principled thinking underlying the child's reasons for his or her position, regardless of whether he or she espoused a right for the character in the vignette. The scoring system and its rationale are discussed in detail in Chapter 2. Interrater reliability of scoring was satisfactory. Item-by-item agreement between two psychology graduate students who served as coders was 76.7% for the concept scale and 85.4% for the attitude scale.

There was high internal consistency within respondents in scores on the scale measuring level of conceptualization of rights. It is suggested that the concept scale does in fact measure a way of thinking about rights that is stable across a variety of situations involving conflicts between persons of varying social status or between individuals and institutions. All 12 vignettes loaded on a single factor, eigenvalue = 4.908, accounting for 40.9% of the variance.

More specifically, the correlations among items were generally highly significant. The one exception involved a vignette concerning a child's refusal of medical treatment (Item 4), which also had the lowest loading on the general factor, $r = .456$. The physician may in fact be the strongest authority figure depicted in any of the items, which also include conflicts with school principals, teachers, parents, store managers, and so forth. It may be that the trust that both children and adults often find it necessary to place in their doctors makes the concept of a right seem less salient in such an instance (see Lewis, 1983, for a discussion of physician/child relationships). Even Item 4, however, correlated significantly with 5 of the 11 other items.

There was a high correlation between total scores on the concept scale and the attitude scale, $r = .665$, $p < .001$. Children who used more mature reasoning concerning rights also were more likely to perceive children as having rights. However, in keeping with Rogers and Wrightsman's formulation of attitudes toward children's rights in their research with adult groups, the internal structure of the attitude scale appeared to be considerably more variable than that of the concept scale in the present study (see Table 1). The three factors identified in scores on the attitude scale are not easily interpretable in psychological terms, but the first two factors may reflect self-determination and nurturance orientations respectively. It is thus suggested that attitudes toward children's rights among children themselves are differentiated along dimensions similar to those previously confirmed by Rogers and

Table 1. Rotated Factor Matrix for the Attitude Scale

Item[a]	I[b]	II[c]	III[d]
1. Access to school records	.487	−.063	.340
2. Determine own custody	.172	.602	.167
3. Choose own courses	−.064	.211	.605
4. Refuse medical treatment	−.001	−.154	.667
5. Medical treatment when unable to pay	−.043	.813	−.222
6. Free press	.528	.264	.259
7. Access to public park	.460	.084	−.159
8. Right to vote	−.574	.370	.339
9. Right to work	.365	.166	.652
10. Right to privacy (diary)	.692	.138	.270
11. Due process in school discipline	.653	.312	.005
12. Access to treatment without parental consent	.327	.731	.193

[a]Each vignette is listed in full in the Appendix.
[b]Eigenvalue = 3.061.
[c]Eigenvalue = 1.522.
[d]Eigenvalue = 1.402.

Wrightsman with adult samples. Factor I might involve a self-determination orientation in that all except one of the items loading on it (1, 6, 7, 8, 10, and 11) clearly involve confronting a more powerful individual (i.e., teacher, principal, parent, or older child) and asserting a right on some ground of personal entitlement or privilege. Mitigating to a certain extent against such an interpretation is the high negative loading on the factor by an item (No. 8) that concerns whether children should be able to vote, $r = -.574$. While not involving interpersonal conflict in the same way that the items that load positively on the factor do, Item 8 clearly involves a child's determining his or her own fate, albeit in a more indirect fashion. It is of course also plausible that Factor I primarily involves response to interpersonal conflict.

Factor II appeared to involve a nurturance factor. Loading on it was the item (No. 5, right to treatment even when unable to pay) that most directly involves a nurturance right. The other two items (2 and 12) that loaded on Factor II are ones that are phrased in terms of self-determination but to which many children responded in terms of nurturance. Item 2 concerns a child's right to choose with whom he or she will live if his or her parents divorce. Children frequently responded to that item not in terms of an individual's being able independently make decisions that have a major impact on his or her life but rather in terms of prevention of harm to the child if one parent is abusive or neglecting. Similar reasons were frequently given in response to a vignette (Item 12) about a child's being able to seek medical or psychiatric treatment without parental permission. That issue also frequently was perceived in terms of the protection of the child from the harm that might come to him if a serious condition went untreated (see Melton, 1978a, for a more extensive discussion of responses to this item).

Factor III includes the vignettes that the children tended to perceive as the most farfetched. Three of the four items on which the mean responses were most in opposition to self-determination by the child in the story have a high loading on this factor. They include: No. 3, right to select one's own curriculum, $\overline{X} = -.40$, $r = .605$; No. 4, right to refuse medical treatment, $\overline{X} = -.60$, $r = .667$; No. 9, right to work, $\overline{X} = -.01$, $r = .652$. The other vignette in which children tended to perceive themselves as lacking the maturity for self-determination was No. 8, right to vote, which loaded moderately on Factor III, $\overline{X} = -.32$, $r = .339$.

Factors Affecting Attitudes

Given the dual factor structure of attitudes toward children's rights, systematic group differences might be expected on the basis of the degree of adherence to concepts of competence and autonomy of the child, "liberalism" and social-welfare orientation, and general approval of civil liberties. Rogers and Wrightsman (1978) administered the Children's Rights Attitudes Scale (CRA) to four different groups in the Nashville area: high school juniors and seniors, undergraduate education majors, undergraduates in liberal arts, and adults enrolled in weekend and summer continuing education classes. This finding may be indicative of a previously reported tendency of participants in research on attitudes toward civil liberties generally (discussed later in this chapter) to disapprove of expression of specific civil liberties. Americans' attitudes toward civil liberties are not positive generally and their attitudes toward children's self-determination may be reflective of those broader attitudes. It also may be that children (on the CRA scale, aged 10 to 14) are viewed as incompetent and properly dependent. In a replication varying the ages on the CRA, Parks (1980) found, not surprisingly, that positive attitudes toward self-determination increase as the age of the child in question increases. In terms of the age group on the original CRA (10–14), "apparently, we are more willing to try to make the dependent status of children more comfortable than we are willing to grant children freedom" (Rogers & Wrightsman, 1978, p. 67). It should be noted, though, that compared to other groups, the high school students favored self-determination rights more strongly and nurturance rights less strongly. It may be that many adolescents experience the paternalistic child-saving stance as oppressive.

In general, research on adults' attitudes toward civil liberties suggests that there is consensus among Americans on broad democratic principles, such as freedom of speech. That consensus, however, breaks down when opinions are sought about specific applications of these principles, such as tolerance of a Communist's giving a speech (Erskine & Siegel, 1975; Prothro & Grigg, 1960; Wilson, 1975; Zellman, 1975). Views of childhood (see Chapter 9) clearly color responses to both the Melton and the Rogers/Wrightsman scales so that research on attitudes toward adult civil liberties may not be directly applicable to them. Nonetheless, it is important to note that both scales involve specific applications of rights. Different results may have been obtained if the questions had been phrased in terms of broad rights for children rather than specific expressions of rights.

Although it is a hypothesis that is as yet untested, it seems logical to assume that attitudes toward civil liberties for adults are correlated with attitudes toward children's rights. In general, democratic beliefs have been correlated more highly with education than any other demographic variable (Montero, 1975; Prothro & Grigg, 1960; Wilson, 1975; Zellman, 1975). Prothro and Grigg (1960) found, for example, that regional and income differences in democratic beliefs disappeared when controls for educational level were added. Erskine and Siegel (1975) suggested that increased tolerance for minorities over the previous two decades is related to increased levels of education. Supportive of such an interpretation is a Kohlbergian analysis by Zellman (1975). She argued that the elite status associated with high levels of education results in "active participation and involvement with rules and conflict resolution [which] has been found to produce both more rapid cognitive development and, ultimately, a more mature moral ideology"(Kohlberg, 1969) ." Thus elites, who think and act more, would be expected to be at a higher state of moral development" (Zellman, 1975, p. 47).

A similar argument is that college "broadens horizons." By exposing students to a variety of ideas, it is thought to increase tolerance. It is also is argued that college increases a sense of universality, as is implicit in the concept of rights, by inducing a value on ordered, logical systems of thought. Therefore, favoring "free speech" except for Communists is thought to create more dissonance in educated individuals than in those with less experience in academia.

It is quite possible, though, that the causality in the education–libertarianism relationship is at least partially in the opposite direction. That is, "open" personalities may be more likely to find education tolerable, and a self-selection factor may be at work. Montero (1975) reached such a conclusion in his study of support for civil liberties among a cohort of high school graduates and college students:

> Each year those students who are least disposed to accept the impact of the university's incongruent experiences tend to drop out, leaving in college those who readily accept them. If this process occurs systematically, each succeeding college class will have a larger percentage of highly libertarian individuals than the preceding class, a prediction generally confirmed in this and earlier studies. (p. 134)

Consistent with such a view, Zalkind, Gaugler, and Schwartz (1975) found personality variables to correlate significantly with civil liberties attitudes even with education and other demographic variables held constant. Specifically, flexibility, independence, and self-reliance related positively to libertarian attitudes, while there were low but statistically significant negative correlations of such attitudes with anomie and external locus of control. Similarly, Zellman and Sears (1971) found attitudes of fifth through ninth graders toward free speech to be related to the level of their "divergent thinking self-esteem." That is, confidence in one's own ability to generate and entertain novel ideas is positively related in both children and adults to tolerance for free speech.

Of relevance to child advocacy is the implication of the personality research that libertarian attitudes are related to the degree of threat that new or deviant ideas impose on an individual. Zellman (1975) has argued, for example, that the tendency to support abstract democratic principles while opposing the concrete application of those principles is related to the greater threat that is posed by the actual *expression* of a principle, particularly by persons whose beliefs threaten the modal value system. It is conceivable that for many adults the idea of a child's having rights poses a particular threat, especially if an adult feels insecure in his or her parenting skills or bases his or her parenting style largely on assertion of authority. If one lacks confidence in what he or she has to say, expression of ideas by someone perceived as dependent and small may seem particularly threatening. Insofar as children's rights conflict with parents' rights, many adults may experience children's rights as a threat to their personal freedom. Such threats have been observed to raise a high degree of reactance (Brehm, 1966) or arousal. These threats would probably be particularly potent, given that freedom in child-rearing and family privacy are highly valued in our society. The implication is that success in increasing sensitivity to the rights and needs of children is likely to be related to the degree to which the threat to authoritarian adults can be minimized.

A clear example of this problem is Feshbach and Feshbach's (1976, 1978) proposal that family privacy should be reformulated to provide for more societal review of child-rearing practices (for a similar view, see Garbarino et al., 1982). Starting from a premise that punishment, especially physical punishment, has been shown to be detrimental to children, the Feshbachs have advocated opening these practices to review, at least on a circumscribed basis. Their argument is as follows:

A barrier of secrecy surrounds parent socialization practices and, more important, prevents effective communication of alternatives to parents whose children can benefit most from such communication. Recently, in some states and communities this wall of secrecy is being scaled. School personnel are now requested to make public the frequency with which specific disciplinary procedures are applied for specifically designated infractions. Certainly we do not expect or advocate that the family be placed under legal and administrative strictures similar to those to which schools are subject. However, we do advocate greater access in regard to the disciplinary practices that families employ. That is, we think it a reasonable proposition that professionals involved with children's welfare, such as pediatricians, educators, and psychologists, be given the right to ask parents what strategies of discipline are customarily used in interactions with his or her child. And equally reasonable is the expectation of a parental response to such an inquiry. (Feshbach & Feshbach, 1978, p. 170)

The Feshbachs' proposal is a relatively innocuous one involving voluntary disclosure to "unofficial" confidants. Nonetheless, it is likely that such an attempt to monitor and ultimately change disciplinary practices would arouse considerable reactance. Although the Supreme Court's wisdom in deciding that corporal punishment in the schools does not constitute "cruel and unusual punishment"[30] is dubious (see Bersoff & Prasse, 1978), the Court majority were undoubtedly accurate in their assessment that physical punishment is condoned and even supported by the American public. For example, most psychologists report the use of spanking in their own families (Anderson & Anderson, 1976), despite an official statement of the American Psychological Association's Council of Representatives (1975) in opposition to corporal punishment. Given the ubiquitousness of the practice and the value placed on family privacy, it is likely that any attempt, even a relatively uncoercive one such as that advocated by the Feshbachs, to alter disciplinary practices would raise considerable and emotional opposition that might have the effect of discrediting any later attempts of the advocate to deal with other issues. It is quite possible, for example that the renewed law-and-order mentality in many schools is partially a response to the threat posed by "experts'" attempts to modify traditional school hierarchies and disciplinary practices.

It is important for advocates to identify in advance issues that are likely to arouse emotional conflicts and, more specifically, to predict which groups are likely to be on a particular side of the issue. Feshbach and Tremper (1981) have made an initial attempt in this regard to gather normative data as to ages at which there is popular support for self-determination in particular contexts. Mothers and adolescents in the Los Angeles area were asked to specify ages they believed appropriate for minors to participate in a given decision and to be the one to make the decision. Attitudes across groups were similar; therefore, only the findings from the initial study of mothers will be reported here. Not surprisingly, mothers were prone to approve of increased decision making as children grow older and of earlier ages for participation in decision making than for full power of consent. By the time a child is 12 years old, the majority of mothers were willing to permit the child to participate in four-fifths of the decision areas sampled. (Decision areas assessed included: medical and psychological treatment, school attendance and placement, custody, birth control, abortion, sex education, clothing purchases, and television viewing.) Over 75% of the mothers sampled supported child participation by age 15 in all areas except school attendance. However, giving the

[30]Ingraham v. Wright, *supra* note 10.

child responsibility for decisions in the areas included in the survey is delegation of authority that in most instances parents feel should not be made before the child is at least 15. At that age, at least two-thirds of mothers sampled are willing to allow minors power of decision making with regard to custody, research participation, special education, and psychological treatment. Least approval was given for 15-year-olds making decisions about school attendance and abortion. The Feshbach and Tremper data suggest that the most resistance can be expected to proposals that would result in significant alteration of authority in school. Although there is an unsurprising resistance to increased access to abortions, there also is less resistance than might be expected to decision making by adolescents on sexual topics, particularly regarding sex education. Furthermore, there is openness to children's being involved in major decisions (e.g., custody) at preadolescent ages. Advocates seeking to increase self-determination by children might begin by focusing efforts on increasing participation in decision making by children without pushing initially for full power of consent, especially in emotionally-charged areas.

SOCIAL WELFARE ORIENTATION AND CHILD SAVING

Given the existence of two factors in attitudes toward children's rights, espousal of self-determination (civil liberties) for children would not necessarily be related to advocacy of nurturance rights. Although one can argue that they are intertwined (i.e., education, health, etc. are necessary for a realistic opportunity to make choices), support for nurturance rights would appear to involve support for social welfare programs generally. For example, in a report that was widely reviewed in the popular press, the Carnegie Council on Children (Keniston, 1977) proposed a "policy for children and families" that amounted to a plea for basic social and economic change in the society as a whole. The principal recommendations included proposals for government work programs to achieve full employment, redistribution of income through income support programs, and so forth. Although it is possible to justify such programs on the basis of provision of more adequate home environments for children, support for liberal or radical economic change clearly involves different premises than support for individual freedoms alone.

Complicating the matter further is the fact that nurturance by definition involves *protection*. As such, advocacy for nurturance rights for children inevitably involves decisions about what children *should* have and do. There is clear potential for advocacy of one's own economic and political interests (even if not consciously done in self-interest) in such a way as actually to limit the choices of the children whom one claims to represent. Indicative of this problem is the fact that many of the "reforms" that have been proposed recently by child advocates are programs to undo reforms advocated by earlier, presumably well intentioned child savers (Takanishi, 1978). For example, the attention of child advocates often has been focused in recent years on drastically changing or actually closing institutions that earlier advocates worked hard to establish in the hope of providing treatment to children they believed in need of it. Similarly, advocates now frequently argue that child labor laws have effectively hamstrung adolescents' achieving occupational experience and training; essentially they have hurt the very group that they were designed to protect.

Some argue, therefore, that child advocacy movements should be analyzed in terms of the interests that are directly represented within them. Exemplary of such an approach is Platt's (1977) analysis of the "invention of delinquency" by turn-of-the-century child savers. Platt argued that child saving represented a kind of middle-class maternalism that was involved in protecting youth in the midst of economic change. The child savers took an individualistic approach to salvation of youth from what was perceived as the sordid life of the inner city and the immigrant classes. Consequently, rather than attacking power and privilege, the child savers sought to alter "the normative behavior of youth—their recreation, leisure, education, outlook on life, attitudes to authority, family relationships, and personal morality" (Platt, 1977, p. 99). Rather than taking a stance of advocacy of political and economic change to enhance the position of working-class families, the child savers advocated "therapeutic" approaches aimed at increasing the adaptation of the poor to middle-class norms. Thus, while benevolently motivated, child saving had a clear social-control component and a goal of increasing order and stability in the culture. Furthermore, it resulted in repression rather than liberation of youth by redefining criminal behavior to include "undesirable" behavior (status offenses) and by removing due-process procedures from juvenile criminal (delinquency) proceedings.

Professionals should not be assumed to be immune from acting in self-interest or in defense of prevailing economic and social interests. Levine and Levine (1970) have demonstrated convincingly that professional ideologies and practices tend to reflect the prevailing political climate. Thus, in conservative periods, emphases are placed on individual "pathology" and strategies of individual change. On the other hand, during periods of social change, more emphasis is placed on changes in the social structure. Even during such left-ward swings, however, social programs often reflect the belief of the majority of Americans that "God helps those who helps themselves" (Feagin, 1972). There is considerable evidence that people tend to perceive the world as just and to rationalize even chance rewards and punishments as deserved (Lerner, 1980). As Ryan (1971) has pointed out, many programs have been based on an assumption that the poor are responsible for their plight. Thus, energy is expended in "compensatory education" for "culturally deprived" children rather than in pursuit of structural change in social and educational institutions. Such an emphasis on understanding of social ills and institutional failures in terms of individual faults leads potentially to a self-fulfilling prophecy of agency failure in providing for "difficult" children. Inaction and even destructive action can be rationalized on the basis of the client's personal shortcomings. I have previously described a case (Melton, 1977a) that aptly illustrates the destructive influence of victim-blaming on an individual level:

> Prior to his psychotic break, Joe had been in the state system about four years as a delinquent without ever having a real commitment made to him in the form of a long-term treatment program. In that time not even a social history was gathered. The consulting psychiatrist rationalized this by saying that the omission was to be expected because Joe's mother is "aloof." Another psychiatrist suggested that the system may in fact have driven Joe crazy through its lack of treatment and a few grossly inappropriate interventions along the way. The consultant replied that the state bore no responsibility for Joe's condition because "you can't hurt a schizophrenic." (Melton, 1977a, p. 29)

The need to protect agency interests (often at the expense of the child's interest) may assume paramount significance for other reasons as well. As Polier (1975) noted in her impassioned statement on the "professional abuse of children," children and their families frequently are confronted with fragmented services, the disposition of which is at the "all but unchecked discretion" of individual professionals. The temptation is to avoid the difficult problems and to succumb to "the seductive lure of focusing increasingly in discrete ways of improving the quality of professional services to a smaller and smaller segment of those most in need" (Polier, 1975, p. 359). As McGowan (1978) has noted, contemporary professionals typically are employees of bureaucracies, and a principal motive is to preserve the bureaucracy and one's place in it. For example, despite a general acknowledgment of the importance of primary prevention and community interventions in enhancing positive mental health, many community mental health professionals spend the greatest portion of their time delivering traditional psychotherapeutic services to individuals simply because they easily generate income for the agency. Similarly, labels often are placed on children as the result of a single screening because of the demands of Medicaid and other third-party payers for a diagnosis (Children's Defense Fund, 1978). On a larger level, professional self-interest may interfere with significant policy changes on behalf of children. In a perceptive analysis of the demise of the Children's Coalition, a short-lived coalition of child-oriented lobby groups, Steiner (1976) suggested that such groups almost inevitably were destined to fail because of the conflicting agenda of the specific lobbies (see Chapter 7). For example, although two of the most influential lobbies for children's services, the National Education Association and the Child Welfare League, obviously have particular stakes in enhancing the status and opportunities of their members, such agenda can interfere with support for nonprofessional programs, such as family day care homes.

The position of professionals in advocacy for individual children and for classes of children is complicated by the frequent unclarity of responsibility. Koocher (1979) has discussed the relevance of Latané and Darley's (1968) research on "diffusion of responsibility" for child advocacy. Latané and Darley's classic research on the willingness of bystanders to help in a crisis showed that involvement is less likely to occur the greater the number of people who are present at an event. As Koocher put it,

> It is as though each individual were waiting for another more competent, more assertive, or more involved person to act. Where these "others" are to come from, no one knows. In the mental health fields we have our supervisors, administrators, and plenty of red tape to diffuse responsibility for acting when we wish to do so. (1979, p. 95)

Furthermore, professionals often feel uncomfortable with "politics" and unprepared to deal with the vicissitudes of interagency conflicts. When a child's particular needs "fall through the cracks" of agency mandates, professionals can find many reasons to avoid taking responsibility. It is important to note that, besides not addressing the needs of the child, such a stance can in the long run be a very costly one. The case of John H., a five-year-old atypical child, is exemplary:

> In addition to bizarre, autistic-like mannerisms, John had been diagnosed as having moderate psychomotor retardation and multiple congenital anomalies. However, he had some social awareness and occasionally made good eye contact. Hence, he was considered "workable." Nonetheless, Mrs. H. had a number of problems of her own and openly admitted that she was unable to cope with John. Mrs. H. had been a chronic alcoholic and depressive, and she had made a number of suicide attempts. She had few supportive relatives or friends, and Mr. H. had left the home after John was diagnosed at age two years. Becoming aware that she might abuse John, Mrs. H. asked her welfare worker to place him in a foster home or residential school after he completed a summer camp program. Then, in part

through the advocacy of the Association for Retarded Citizens, a plan was developed to place John in a foster home. He was placed in three different homes in the course of about a month and was finally returned to Mrs. H. without any warning. In the meantime, Mrs. H., expecting no longer to have to care for John, had moved into a tiny two-room apartment. John was in no program at all, and Mrs. H. was forced to send his two-year-old sister to stay with various relatives and Alcoholics Anonymous (AA) members. Mrs. H. herself was getting no support, and she could not attend AA meetings because she could not find a babysitter for John.

By this time, a very humorless comedy of bureaucratic errors had ensued. A vast array of agencies were involved: the local Department of Public Welfare (DPW) office, the DPW Homefinders, Group Care, and Protective Service units, a private child welfare agency, another foster-home placement agency, a mental health center, the Association for Retarded Citizens, the public schools at the local, district, and system-wide levels, a behavior-modification training program, a clinical nursery and the developmental disabilities unit of which it was part, and a hospital developmental disabilities clinic. Despite all of this professional manpower, nothing was being done and often for very silly reasons. For example, a referral to the Group Care unit was returned because the proper form was not enclosed, and no one followed up on it. After this nonsense continued for almost two months, four of the agencies involved independently of one another called OFC [the Office for Children, a state child advocacy agency] in an effort to have something done about the situation. Thus, the tasks which I had were "only" to assign responsibilities for serving John and his family and then to monitor implementation of the plan. (Melton, 1977a, pp. 27–28)

Because of no one's taking an active role of coordinator and advocate for John and his family, there was a waste of thousands of dollars in professional time as well as tremendous human cost to John and his family.

Even if the professional is willing to expend the energy (and perhaps take the risk) to be responsible for advocacy on behalf of a child, there remains a question of the legitimacy of that action. There is frequently not a clear delineation of ultimate responsibility for a child's well-being. Does it belong to the state, the parents, or the child himself? Thus, there is diffusion of responsibility not only because of conflicts among agency mandates but also because of ambiguous and conflicting responsibilities and interests. For example, when a minor seeks treatment independently, a health professional's responsibility is unclear. Becoming actively involved with a child client in such an instance may place the professional in legal jeopardy even though he or she believes action to be necessary in the child's interest (see Ehrenreich & Melton, in press). The issues are particularly complex in the mental health field, given the value-laden and social-control aspects of psychiatric intervention, even when the clinician believes a child to be in real distress.

There is the potential for value conflict if the parent believes mental health intervention to be of potential harm rather than benefit to the child. One such case involved Wanda, a 15-year-old Honduran girl who had come to an adolescent clinic in a Northeastern city ostensibly to inquire about her boy friend who attended a therapeutic school there. It soon became obvious that Wanda was seeking help for herself. "I feel I'm all mixed up, and I want someone to straighten me out." The clinicians who met Wanda felt that she was subject to a schizoaffective disorder and that she was actively decompensating. She was markedly depressed, and she had expressed much suicidal and homicidal ideation. There was a paranoid quality to much of her ideation, and she perceived the world as filled with "evil spirits," perhaps a family myth. Wanda initially resisted informing her parents of her visit to the mental health center, but she had no qualms about such disclosure on her second visit. While Wanda's parents permitted home visits, they attributed her behavior to silly American ways and felt no need for mental health intervention. Her beliefs, paranoid by the clinicians' standards, were consistent with the family's spiritualism. (Melton, 1978a, p. 201)

In addition to the unclarity of parent-versus-professional legitimacy of authority with respect to children, there is ambiguity about the role of the child himself. Child advocacy is unique in the sense that the "oppressed" must depend upon the "oppressors" (i.e., adults) to advocate for them. Hence, children may have advocates who argue positions that their supposed constituents themselves oppose. Almost by definition, child advocates assume a paternalistic stance of "knowing what's best" for children. The conflicts may be quite emotionally charged. For example, a 1978 issue of the *Journal of Social Issues* contained a provocative exchange about whether children mainifesting "gender disturbance" should be subject to psychotherapy (against their will but "in their best interest"). Rosen, Rekers, and Bentler (1978) argued that such children should be treated regardless of the children's own goals because of future and present discomfort that "deviant" behavior will bring them in the context of their peers. On the other hand, Morin and Schultz (1978) strongly contended that there is a need for support and advocacy on behalf of those children who are developing a gay identity and lifestyle:

From our developmental perspective, the rights issue needs reframing: It's a question not of the rights of children but of the rights of adults that children become. That is, we regard a gay identity and life style as a positive option for adults, an outcome with certain developmental requirements. Unless and until these developmental needs are met, the right of adults to be gay is a hollow right. (p. 140)

Beyond these clear ethical and political dilemmas, there is the general problem that adults may not be able to look at issues from the position of the child. Child advocacy is essentially "cross-cultural" and entails the difficulties inherent in an attempt to express the viewpoint of people whose view of the world may be quite different from one's own. The temptation (perhaps legitimately) is to work from the perspective of what the child's interest *should* be, as an adult sees it. The role-taking problem cited here is present in "pure" developmental research as well as in its applications. Speier (1973) has argued persuasively that studies of childhood typically are designed from an "adult ideological point of view." Thus, developmentalists have focused on socialization, the process by which a child becomes an adult. The process of interaction within children's own culture has been largely ignored. The result is that it becomes difficult to perceive the child's interests from his point of view.

> For example, a mother sees two boys in the living room at home. She chides them for making a mess or for roughing around indoors instead of outdoors. To her they are dirt-makers or trouble-makers or noise-makers, or whatever else might appropriately label their behavior. But to the boys, they are building model airplanes, or wrestling, or the like. The definition they give to their own activity is not contained within the practical definitions the mother gives to them. She must attend to their actions in a way that corresponds to her duties and responsibilities as mother and housekeeper. The relevance of viewing their activity is determined by her own household activities rather than by the children's activities. In fact, it seems to be the case that for adults, anything children do between, say, the ages of one and ten, can be characterized as play. Now, surely that is not what children always recognize and treat as their own constitutive definition of what they do, if we are going to be objective about it. That is, two children might be having a conversation on the grass while two onlooking mothers can speak of them as "playing nicely together." (Speier, 1973, pp. 146–147)

Essentially, we need to be concerned not only with enhancing the child's potential as an adult but also with recognizing the child's current experience of the world and supporting growth within the world of childhood.

Problems of "Informed Consent"

To the extent to which the child's direct participation is valued in setting the agenda for advocacy (or even seen as his right), problems of "informed consent" arise, particularly when "case advocacy" on behalf of the individual children is involved. The most obvious issue is the question of competence to make such decisions. This may not be as problematic as it appears on first glance. Adolescents usually are able to handle complex information as well as adults. Even elementary-school children often make reasonable decisions and usually can comprehend the relevant factors in given decisions (see the reviews in Melton, Koocher, & Saks, 1983; especially Weithorn, 1983). Even assuming competence, however, there is still a question of whether it is reasonable to expect consent to be freely given by a child. As Keith-Spiegel (1976) put it in her discussion of such issues, children learn to 'obey thy father and mother'—and anyone else bigger than you are" (p. 56). They learn at a very early age that failure to acquiesce to adults' requests is likely to result in punishment. From a different perspective, it may be that *dissent* from adults' recommendations by some youngsters is "involuntary." For some adolescents, such actions may be developmentally appropriate anticonformist judgments that are in their own way as conformist and unreasoned as unquestioned obedience by young children (Grisso & Vierling, 1978). In a different context, Grisso and Pomicter (1977) have shown that juvenile suspects' maintaining silence in police interrogation is related to age. The tendency of late adolescents to exercise this right more frequently than younger juveniles is probably related to developmental phenomena in understanding of rights (see Chapter 2). It may also be a function, however, simply of heightened negativism during that age period. Given the existence of such an age trend, the advocate is faced with the dilemma of whether to accept adolescents' dissents to his well intentioned interventions at face value, particularly if the dissents would appear to result in harm to the prospective clients. At its root, we return to the question of self-determination versus nurturance rights. Protection of the child implies some intrusion into his privacy and diminution of his autonomy, even if "for his own good."

THE SOCIAL SCIENTIST'S ROLE IN CHILD ADVOCACY

Perhaps the most general conclusion that may be reached from our discussion thus far is that some degree of caution must be exercised in advocacy. Although inaction and the harm that may result to clients from diffusion of responsibility are often ethically indefensible, it is important to assess the "environmental impact" of an intervention on a given system (see Koocher, 1979). In situations that, as we have seen, almost inevitably involve conflicts of interests and perhaps of rights, there is seldom a clear unilateral effect of an intervention. Rather, as discussed more extensively in Chapter 3, there usually is a complex interplay of forces within a system. It is often not possible to predict all of the consequences of an intervention. At the very least, though, professionals who assume an advocate's role are obligated to review carefully the probable results and to identify points of uncertainty.

I have argued elsewhere (Melton, 1978b) that, whenever professionals become invooved as "experts" in a dispute, the parties have a right to expect the rudiments of due process. That is, they should expect to be treated fairly. In keeping with the mandate for fairness, advocates have an obligation to identify their clients. Furthermore, it is important that they recognize the limits of their expertise, pragmatically to maintain credibility and ethically to provide the bases of sound policy. An excellent example of what *not* to do is Goldstein, Freud, and Solnit's widely cited argument for courts to go *Beyond the Best Interests of the Child* (1973) in deciding custody battles. Although many of their recommendations were intuitively clinically sound, Goldstein et al. ignored the empirical literature on adoption and foster care, extrapolated from clinic populations without attention to control groups, derived causal conclusions from correlational data, based generalizations on single case studies, etc. (see Katkin, Bullington, & Levine, 1974). They also ignored some of the long-range effects of their recommendations. For example, in the interest of enhancing "psychological parenthood," Goldstein et al. advocated elimination of split custody and visitation rights. They even argued for drawing straws to settle difficult cases. In so doing, they ignored "the potential escalation of tensions because of the deprivation felt by the losing parent and the loss felt by the child. The child might also have intensified guilt feelings because of the legal rejection of one parent and the fulfillment of oedipal wishes" (Melton, 1978b, p. 190). Thus, despite the influence that their book ultimately has had on both judges and scholars (Crouch, 1979), Goldstein et al.'s policy analysis was strikingly incomplete, even from a psychoanalytic perspective.

This caveat is not to suggest, however, that social scientists have nothing to contribute to questions of policy involving children. We really do not know, for example, the psychological impact that court involvement has on children. If children are to be accorded greater status in the courts, then we need to know more about their understanding of the legal process. It may be that "due process" for children really is different than for adults, at least in some circumstances.

In any case, it is important that "hard data" be obtained to support recommendations and that reservations are stated if in fact the existing data are equivocal or nonexistent. Indeed, part of the weakness of Goldstein et al.'s work was that they confused their clinical intuitions with "science." Although these intuitions are not totally without worth, it is important to recognize their limitations relative to data gathered more systematically with attention to control of extraneous variables. Essentially, fact must be separated from hypothesis, and value assumptions must be clearly stated.

In the following chapters, we will examine some possible contributions of the social sciences to child advocacy and suggest questions for research. We also will look at the practical problems in dissemination and application of this knowledge.

The Consumer's Point of View

CHILDREN'S CONCEPTS OF THEIR RIGHTS

As discussed in Chapter 1, there are a number of factors that affect adults' attitudes toward children's rights. Questions of what really constitutes "rights" to which children are entitled aside, those attitudes probably will reflect the rights that are finally fulfilled for children. In practical terms, adults decide the degree of autonomy that children may exercise and the adequacy of conditions for self-actualization to which they are exposed. Nonetheless, questions remain concerning what children *themselves* think about their rights. One of the reasons that the child advocacy movement's goals have been so variously defined is that those goals have represented the opinions of adults of different ideologies about what *they* believe to be important to children. Child advocates may assume the same paternalism as ostensibly less child-oriented adults. It is interesting that, prior to the research reported in this chapter, no one had bothered to ask children about their views of their rights.

What children think about their rights is more than an academic question. First, given the extent to which the child advocacy movement purports to involve consumer advocacy, one needs to know what the consumer thinks. Secondly, it is important from a legal viewpoint to know what children think about their rights because of the relevance of that concept to any meaningful participation in a defense of their own interests. In a "lawyer's request for aid," Wald (1976) argues that, "from a legal perspective, children's rights inevitably mean children's participation" (p. 5). Such participation raises questions of the limits of children's competence to pursue due process for themselves, including assertion of legal rights. Wald vividly described the range of questions raised:

> On a more personal note, I have often wondered, when I was representing a child in a delinquency or neglect proceeding, what it meant for me to go up to a 9- or

10-year-old and say, "I'm your lawyer. Here I am; tell me what to do. What do you want me to do in representing you?" What do the children think of me? What do legal rights mean to them? What are the long-term consequences for a child of being told you have a lawyer, you have rights, and we are going to defend you in court? Does this give children a sense of self-esteem, of controlling their own fate, a sense of powerfulness? Or does it leave them bewildered? How are children different who have gone through such proceedings? (p. 5)

CHILDREN'S LEGAL STATUS

Changes in the law and legal practice have highlighted these psychological questions about children's understanding of their rights and their place in the political system. Under common law, children under the age of 7 were considered doli incapax and not responsible for their actions (i.e., the "defense of infancy"). Older children (7 to 17) also were considered incompetent unless the state proved them doli capax. Although one may question the use of these age criteria themselves, the question was moot until the Supreme Court decision in the case *In re Gault.*[1] Prior to that decision, juvenile courts in their role of parens patriae were considered protective rather than adjudicative, and they were assumed to represent the "best interests of the child" regardless of the child's ability to represent himself. In the *Gault* decision, however, the Supreme Court recognized that "neither the Fourteenth Amendment nor the Bill of Rights is for adults alone," and several fundamental procedural rights were held to apply to juveniles in delinquency proceedings. They included right to notice of the charges, right to counsel, right to confrontation and cross-examination, and the privelege against self-incrimination. Juvenile courts were transformed from "kangaroo courts"[2] to more formal adversary proceedings. Juveniles' ability to participate in their defense became a live issue. In addition to the questions raised by Wald about children's understanding of legal representation, the *Gault* decision brought several other questions to the surface about children's capacities. For example, although recognizing "special problems" with self-incrimination by minors,[3] the Court still maintained the possibility of a waiver of constitutional rights by the child and his parents. It stated that any waiver of rights must be "know-

[1]387 U.S. 1 (1967).
[2]*Id.* at 28.
[3]*Id.* at 55.

ing and intelligent,"[4] an expectation that may be unrealistic in view of recent research suggesting that, relative to adult defendants, juvenile respondents are unlikely to understand *Miranda* rights as applicable to themselves (Grisso, 1981; Melton, 1981c).[5] The Court also assumed a unity of interest between parent and child[6] that often is not present (Lefstein, Stapleton, & Teitelbaum, 1969).

Questions about reasonable expectations of children are not limited to delinquency proceedings. For example, Massachusetts law requires the consent of any child over the age of 12 in adoption proceedings.[7] One may question whether the age standard is sound. More generally, it would be helpful to know the meaning to children of their participation in decisions about their own custody. Do children in fact believe that they *really* have a say in these decisions when their opinions are sought, as is in fact required in many jurisdictions (Siegel & Hurley, 1977)? In a provocative article in which he claimed that children should not be "as equal as people," Arthur (1968) argued that court appearances may be too stressful and that children are too susceptible to influence there anyway. Therefore, he proposed that "out-of-court statements made by children pertaining to their relationship with their immediate family should be admissible as an exception to the hearsay rule" (p. 208). Similar assumptions have led to laws in most states that permit judges to hear children's testimony in closed chambers (Siegel & Hurley, 1977). We need to know how valid Judge Arthur's assumptions are.

Similar questions about children's ability to assert rights in disputes involving their parents and the state were raised by the Supreme Court's decision in *Wisconsin v. Yoder*.[8] The Court ruled in this case that Amish parents could exempt their children from compulsory school attendance after the eighth grade. Citing developmental research about the moral and intellectual abilities of 14-year-olds,[9] Justice Douglas argued in a minority opinion that they should be able to assert their right to a public school education even if their parents disagreed. Had Douglas's views prevailed, there would have been interesting and difficult problems concerning the contexts, if any, in

[4]*Id*. at 55.
[5]*But see* Fare v. Michael C., 442 U.S. 707 (1979). In *Fare,* a sobbing, poorly educated 16-year-old boy was held to have competently waived the privilege against self-incrimination, despite the facts that he believed his attorney really to be a police officer and that the police interrogators had denied his request to see his probation officer.
[6]The Court referred to rights as belonging *both* to Mrs. Gault and to her son.
[7]Mass. Gen. Laws Ann. ch. 210 § 2 (1973).
[8]406 U.S. 205 (1972).
[9]*Id*. at 245–46, n.3.

which competent voluntary decisions could be elicited.[10] What would it mean to an Amish 14-year-old to tell him that he had the *right* to decide whether to stay in school or to seek a waiver of compulsory education on grounds of religious freedom, an assertion already made by his parents and supported by his church and culture?

In some cases the courts have attempted to take developmental factors into account in determining the limits of minors' liberty by invoking a "mature minor rule" in which the minor, regardless of chronological age, can make a decision if he or she understands its consequences and the action is for the minor's benefit. This kind of criterion has been applied in Supreme Court decisions involving the right of minor women to abortions.[11] One still needs to know, however, how to determine maturity, a question that the Court has not yet addressed.

Although an understanding of rights is not sufficient for competent exercise of rights in the various contexts discussed in this section, it is probably necessary. For rights to be meaningful, children presumably need to know, at a minimum, both what a right is generally and what specific rights are available to them. Otherwise, legal recognition of children's rights, at least of self-determination rights, is probably moot. The present investigation, an initial study of children's concepts of their rights, was designed to begin to gather data to address these issues.

REVIEW OF THE LITERATURE AND HYPOTHESES

Within the present study, it was hypothesized that children's perception of themselves as having just claim to rights is a function of both developmental factors and social class. Research on moral development by Piaget (1932/1965) and Kohlberg (1964, 1976) has shown that young children regard rules as "sacred and untouchable," eternal, and emanating from parental or divine authority (see Lickona, 1976b, for a review of this literature). Children holding such morally absolutist views would not be likely to challenge parental or

---

[10]These problems were in fact raised in a case in which Douglas's views were applied to a determination of whether a mother could deny surgery to her son on religious grounds. In re Green, 448 Pa. 338, 292 A.2d 387 (1972). *See* Mnookin's (1978b, pp. 75–76) provocative questions about the problems in determining how to solicit Ricky Green's views and then how to weigh them.

[11]H. L. v. Matheson, 450 U.S. 398 (1981); Bellotti v. Baird, 443 U.S. 622 (1979); Planned Parenthood of Central Missouri v. Danforth, 428 U.S. 52 (1976).

other authority and assert rights for themselves. Rights also imply a measure of universality that would require diminution of egocentricity to the extent that the child has at least partial respect for others. Piaget's perspective is that a sense of social justice is derived from the egalitarian peer relationships of middle childhood. Furthermore, as children develop cognitively, they would be more likely to differentiate among those things that they are privileged to have and those things that are theirs by right as well as rights that have been unfulfilled.

Such changes in conceptualization probably are dependent upon having experienced rights as well as upon cognitive differentiation and abstraction. To lower-class children in our society, "rights" may, in fact, be accurately perceived as dependent upon the whim of benovolent authority. Perhaps realistically (in terms of rights that remain unfulfilled), lower-class youngsters could be expected to be less likely than their more affluent peers to perceive themselves as having rights to self-determination and self-actualization. The political socialization literature indicates that lower-class children tend to have global, undifferentiated views of government, particularly as personified by the president and policeman. They tend not to perceive government as being responsive to their needs or themselves and their parents as not having any significant impact on the system (Greenstein, 1965; Hess & Torney, 1967; Liebschutz & Niemi, 1974).

The restricted social mobility of lower-class children also may have negative implications for the development of principled thinking in general. For example, drawing from historical examples and cross-cultural research, Garbarino and Bronfenbrenner (1976) argued that "morally mature and independent judgment and behavior are facilitated by a pluralistic, as opposed to a monolithic or anomic, socio-psychological human ecology" (p. 80). Essentially their theory is that, in order to develop abstract, unconventional ethical reasoning, one must at least be exposed to alternative points of view. Similarly, Kohlberg (1976) and Selman (1971) have emphasized the importance of "role-taking opportunities" as sociocultural facilitators of moral development. Kohlberg (in preparation; cited by Kohlberg, 1976) and his associates have in fact found low social class to have a retarding influence on moral development cross-culturally. In the only previous research directly studying the relationship between rights attitudes and social class in children, Zellman and Sears (1971) found that social class was positively correlated with tolerance for free speech. As noted in Chapter 1, there are analogous results among adults. It has been suggested that social elites are more likely to espouse civil liberties because of their greater experience with rules and conflict resolution

(Zellman, 1975). In other words, in keeping with Kohlberg's formulation, the *opportunity* for decision making and role taking in social situations can be expected to facilitate moral development. This opportunity is perhaps often unavailable to economically disadvantaged groups.

Specifically, the present study tested the hypothesis that children's concepts of their rights can be expected to develop along a progression of three levels of reasoning similar to those postulated by Tapp and Levine (1974) in their theory of legal development. Within the current study, the following sequence of development of concepts of rights was predicted:

1. Children in their egocentrism might perceive all that they have and do as representative of a right bestowed by a benevolent authority. Young children can be expected to have difficulty differentiating between an "is" and an "ought." In the child's mind, if someone is able to do or have something, then it is by right. Only the concrete reality is salient. A corollary to this belief is a conviction that big ("full grown-up") people have more rights (because they are able to do more things) and that children have rights only if adults allow them.

2. A less global approach may be taken in which rights are seen as part of a system of laws enacted by and potentially changed by people. Rights still might be confused with privileges, however, and reasons for them may be derived from "conventional" notions of role expectations necessary for orderly and beneficial social functioning.

3. Rights may be conceptualized on a higher plane of ethics and "natural law" in which they are seen to be part of basic requirements for maintenance of human dignity and individual freedom. Within this framework, then, one may adhere to a system of rights not recognized in law or by social convention.

In essence, the hypothesized sequence of development is toward the realization that rights may exist theoretically even if unfulfilled or not present in statutory law. The following hypotheses were presented:

Hypothesis 1: The order of development of concepts of rights would be in keeping with the three-level formulation described above. That is, children in higher school grades would be likely to give higher level responses than children in lower school grades.

Hypothesis 2: Children from high social classes would be likely to give higher level responses than less affluent children.

Hypothesis 3: Children in higher school grades would be more likely to espouse fulfillment of a right by children than would children in lower grades. That is, older children would be more likely to have positive attitudes toward children's rights.

Hypothesis 4: Children from high social classes would be more likely to espouse fulfillment of a right by children than would less affluent children.

METHOD

The hypotheses described above were tested in semistructured interviews of 90 first, third, fifth, and seventh graders from the Boston area during spring, 1978. Forty of the participants (10 per grade) were selected randomly from a high income professional community west of Boston (High-SES). Forty other children were selected from a poor and working-class suburb close to Boston (Low-SES$_1$).

These two groups differed on more dimensions than social class alone. Although the High-SES youngsters were almost exclusively from Caucasian "mainstream" families, the Low-SES$_1$ children were mostly from bilingual families (Portuguese and Spanish-American) or families of Italian descent. In addition, the school climates were markedly different for the two groups. For example, the High-SES school administration welcomed the study and teachers were very interested in learning more about ways of facilitating a sense of self-determination for their pupils. On the other hand, the principal of the Low-SES$_1$ school introduced the researcher to his teachers as follows: "This is Mr. Melton. He wants to learn what children think about their rights. They can't read. They can't do math. But everyone wants to know about their rights." Thus, any differences in rights concepts and attitudes might be the result of school climate, independent of social class. It should be noted, however, that such differences are highly correlated with social class (Moos, 1976). Restrictive, traditional schools are likely to be part of the lifestyle of lower-class families. In order to try to identify idiosyncratic school effects, a group of 10 seventh graders from Boston itself (Low-SES$_2$) was added to the sample. Seven of these participants were black.

The interviews consisted of two parts. First, each child was asked a series of general questions designed to gather normative data about children's ideas about rights:

What is a right?
Who has rights?
Do children have rights? What rights?
Should children have rights? What rights?

Second, a series of 12 vignettes in which a right might be asserted by a child was presented to each child. An example of the vignettes, all of which are included in the Appendix, follows:

> Joe knows that he has a chart in the school office, and he wants to know what it says about him. The teacher told Joe that he is not allowed to see his own chart. Should there be a rule or a law that the teacher can keep Joe from seeing his own chart? Why?

The child's response to each vignette was scored on a simple positive-neutral-negative scale as to whether he or she espoused expression of a right by the child in the story (attitudes toward children's rights). In addition, each response was scored for the level of conceptualization it represented. That is, each vignette was scored on a three-point scale corresponding to the formulation presented earlier in this chapter. To recapitulate, Level 1 reasoning involves an emphasis on obedience to authority and a belief that "he who can, does." Level 2 reasoning emphasizes a criterion of fairness and maintenance of social order. Youngsters using Level 3 reasoning rely on abstract ethical principles (e.g., free speech, right to privacy, etc.).

RESULTS AND DISCUSSION

Effects of Maturation and Social Class

Maturational factors accounted for much of the variance in children's concepts of and attitudes toward their rights. Thus, Hypotheses 1 and 3 were confirmed at high levels of significance.[12] First graders, regardless of class, tended to give Level 1 responses in which rights are perceived as based on what will be allowed by authority. Older children tended to give Level 2 responses in which the existence of a right is based more on criteria of fairness

---

[12]The quantitative data and statistical analyses have been reported elsewhere. *See* Melton (1980a).

and competence. Regardless of class, the modal third grader was also able at least to give an example when asked, "What is a right?" Even seventh graders, however, tended to give Level 2 responses to the vignettes rather than Level 3 responses based on abstract ethical reasoning. Such a finding is consistent with what might be expected on the basis of research on cognitive development. Although beyond the Level 1 point of defining rights as what one can in fact do, Level 2 reasoning still is based on maintaining fairness and order in the here-and-now social situation. It is only when children have achieved formal operational thought that they can be expected to conceptualize abstract principles of rights that may exist only hypothetically.

Although cognitive ability is necessary, it is not sufficient for a sense of potential for self-determination and self-actualization. As predicted in Hypothesis 2, social class accounted for a highly significant proportion of the variance in children's concepts of their rights. Low-SES_1 children tended to achieve Level 2 reasoning several years later than the High-SES youngsters, who gave predominantly Level 2 responses by third grade (see Table 2).

In keeping with Hypothesis 4, there was a similar shift toward positive attitudes toward children's rights by third grade in the High-SES sample but not until fifth grade in the Low-SES_1 sample (see Table 3). There was, however, an unpredicted tendency for the lower-class early adolescents to have more positive attitudes than their more affluent peers. Thus, there was not a significant main effect by social class. There are several possible explanations for this finding, which needs to be investigated further.

First of all, the finding may be representative of a transition from Level 2 to Level 3. Frequently, abstract ethical reasoning was mixed with the fairness criterion. There is freedom of the press, but it is not nice and printing "disruptive" statements in the school newspaper will embarrass the principal. In keeping with this idea, it may be that "middle-class morality" has been internalized by the time a child reaches early adolescence in the High-SES

Table 2. Mean Scores on Concept Scale[a]

	Grade			
	1	3	5	7
High-SES	12.9	20.4	22.2	22.4
Low-SES_1	14.3	15.7	18.6	22.1
Low-SES_2	—	—	—	19.3

Note. Possible range: 12–36.
[a] $n = 10$/cell.

Table 3 Mean Scores on Attitude Scale[a]

	Grade			
	1	3	5	7
High-SES	−2.5	+2.7	+3.7	+4.5
Low-SES$_1$	−2.3	−0.9	+4.5	+6.5
Low-SES$_2$	—	—	—	+4.1

Note. Possible range: −12 to +12.
[a]n = 10/cell.

subculture. It has been argued that middle-class schools do a more efficient job of socialization than overtly repressive lower-class schools because they inculcate the rules by which the system operates (Kozol, 1975). Thus, it may be that High-SES adolescents have the potential for abstract views of rights but reject them because they are not consistent with reality.

It is also noteworthy, as discussed later in this chapter, that High-SES adolescents sometimes identified with the authority figures in the vignettes. Thus, mildly negative views toward children's rights actually may represent a positive view of entitlement and self-determination for *themselves* as a privileged class.

Finally, it is possible that the unpredicted interaction, which was only marginally statistically significant (p = .076), may have been a chance finding. More data should be collected, including data from older adolescents, to learn if the finding is replicable in a larger sample.

Content of Children's Concerns about Rights

Children generally gave at least tacit recognition to the concept of universality of rights if they had any understanding of rights at all. Of the 75 children who gave a response to the question "Who has rights?," 60 responded, "everybody" or "the people." However, several of the youngsters qualified their answers ("everybody practically") or indicated that the answer was true in theory but not in reality. Specifically, in this part of the introductory section and the subsequent questions, it was frequently volunteered that "kids don't have that many rights" and that realistically their rights are fulfilled in terms of the "limits" that adults set. Some of these qualifications placed on rights seemed to be less reflective of a philosophical understanding of social constraints placed on children or other groups than of the concrete thinking of elementary-age children. The phenomenon is similar to that described in Level 1 within the current research: that which one can do is by right. For example, one High-SES third grader said that everyone has rights except "babies and mental people, people who have problems, like if they're deaf or blind or something." When asked why he said that those people did not have rights, the boy replied, "Well, they don't have the right to speak well or hear or see or something."

Although most children acknowledged the universality of the idea of rights, several children perceived rights as belonging only to people in authority. Exemplary of this viewpoint was the response of a High-SES third grade boy:

> Some people have rights to like take projectors from the library, and Mr. H. [the school principal] has the rights about the school, and Mrs. J. [the librarian] has rights about the library. And the President has rights about the country, or the king or queen.

Some older children thought, however, that rights should be restricted not because of position but because of competence. In this view, analogous to Level 2, rights should belong to those who earn them or "who can use them correctly."

In terms of the kinds of rights children perceived as actually or legitimately belonging to them, even among seventh graders, civil liberties rarely were mentioned, although three seventh graders did cite a right to express one's opinions. Nurturance rights were also generally not salient, except for one High-SES fifth grader, who felt that children have a right to honest television advertising. Rather, children tended to cite global freedom from restraint: children have rights to "do things" or "do what they want." More specifically, the modal response was right to recreation (to play, watch television, go for a walk, etc.), particularly in the younger age groups. It is perhaps true that many of the day-to-day issues that arise between parent and child at that age concern rules about going out, watching television, etc. It is also true that playing is in fact what children can do and, therefore, in their minds is by right. Children did, however, frequently qualify even this right in terms either of a rule of reason (i.e., one can't stay out after 2 A.M.) or of family or school rules. An example of the latter thinking comes from the response of a High-SES first grader: "I think that kids should really have the right to play or do whatever they want on Sunday after church, unless we have to go somewhere."

The relatively restrictive school climates of the Low-SES schools seemed to have an impact on the kinds of concerns students had about rights. When one Low-SES$_1$ seventh grader was asked if children have rights now, he replied. "No, not really. Oh yeah, like when you ask to go to the bathroom they mainly say yes." Another Low-SES$_1$ student also mentioned going to the bathroom as a right that children have. In the Low-SES$_2$ group, three seventh graders mentioned freedom from fear as a right that children have. One boy commented: "They should be allowed to move about freely and not be tense . . . Like some kids walk around tense. A kid threatens him and says, 'I'm going to beat you up.'" A Low-SES$_2$ girl emphasized the need for more comfortable teacher–pupil relationship: "In school the teachers shouldn't get on their backs if they make a mistake."

Perhaps again reflective of the reality of constraints of children's self-determination or simply of a misunderstanding of the concept of rights, eight children at various ages felt that children have a right to be good, "follow orders," and do chores such as taking out the garbage. Representative of these responses was that of a High-SES first grader who said that children have a "right not to do stuff like not hitting or punching or slapping or doing stuff without asking their mother."

Younger children tended to perceive rights (as reflected in the vignettes) in terms of Level 1 ideas. That is, they perceived rights as being bestowed at the whim of people in authority or of the concrete reality of the situation. They were very sensitive to relative power of individuals, and they freqeuntly pointed out who was the "boss" in a particular situation, down to the care-taker in a part (Item 7). In keeping with the political socialization literature, the police and the president frequently were mentioned as the ultimate arbiters. One High-SES first grader, for example, said that a panel of the police, Jimmy Carter, and George Washington should decide whether children should be allowed to vote. Even when at first glance first-grade children seemed to espouse rather mature views of rights, they usually came to the point of citing authority. The response of a very bright High-SES first grader to Item 9 (right to work in a grocery store) was particularly striking:

> Yeah. (?) Because she's a kid. (?) Yeah, and she has a right to do that. (?) Because everybody has rights. She could tell the President to shoot the grocer and get one that's more friendly.

Similarly, young children were attuned to the possibility of punishment as an important factor in their views about rights. A Low-SES$_1$ first grader's response to Item 6 was typical: "When the principal says something, that's what you have to do. Else you have to go in there [the office] again." Another representative example was a High-SES first grader's ideas about whether children should be able to vote (Item 8):

> No way. (?) Because it's a dumb question. (?) Because grown-ups should be able
> to vote and not the kids. (?) It's the law. If a kid did, they would probably be in
> big trouble.

As noted previously, children began to give predominantly Level 2 responses by the time that they reached third grade in the High-SES group and by late elementary school in the Low-SES$_1$ sample. Particularly salient to these children were concepts of fairness or competence. In terms of the fairness notion, children were concerned not with making decisions according to ethical principles but rather according to general rules of order. Thus, preventing a child from seeing his records could be justified, in the thinking of a child at Level 2, on the basis of the teacher's having a reason (perhaps avoiding embarrassment to the child) but not just on the basis of the teacher's authority as a person who can give rewards and punishments. Similarly, children sometimes argued that principals should not censor school newspapers on the basis that the story might be interesting rather than that children have a right to express themselves. Children frequently suggested compromises: print one story in favor of the school rules and one in opposition, and everyone will be happy. This reliance on a criterion of fairness extended even to decisions having serious impact on someone's life. For example, a High-SES seventh grader gave this reason for providing treatment to an injured child whose parents cannot afford it:

> Because it's really not fair to the family if they don't have much money to let the
> kid die or be really ill. The government should pay for it.... If it keeps on happening, there won't be anyone left to pay for it.

Incidentally, many of the High-SES children had a difficult time conceptualizing not having enough money for medical care. They often wanted to ignore the dilemma and simply said that the parents could get a "mortgage" or write a check. When they did acknowledge there was an issue, some of the High-SES children (most notably the sons and daughters of physicians) identified with the doctor and cited his "rights" to be paid and avoid trouble. One seventh grader was particularly adamant:

> No, if his parents can't afford it, that's his problem. The doctor can't help him if
> his parents can't afford it. (Anything to do with his rights?) Yes. (?) If the doctor
> does not know his parents well and only works for people who can pay for it, he
> shouldn't have to get tangled up in that mess. The doctor has rights, too.

Explanations based on criteria of competence were very common and fairly obvious. Thus, children at this level cited the child's lack of math skills in his not being able to work, his not listening to speeches, his not being able to vote, his not knowing about diseases, his not being able to decide whether to accept medical treatment, etc. A variant of this logic, which represents a transition from Level 1 to Level 2, was the idea that the authority figure should be able to decide the fate of children because he is in authority and, therefore, he must be competent. In other words, principals know how schools should be run and, therefore, they are best able to make decisions within the schools.

Level 3 responses were not very common even among the seventh graders in the High-SES sample. In fact, the highest single score on the levels-of-conceptualization scale was 28 or an average score per vignette of 2.33. High-SES seventh graders sometimes did seem almost to reach principled reasoning but to be held back by negative or ambivalent attitudes about the expression of rights. The following responses to Item 6 is a good example of the kind of conflict that the items seemed to evoke:

> There's two sides to it. Here's the first side. There's freedom of the press. In the school newspaper you're supposed to print what's happening and what you think. If you can't print it, why have a newspaper? Then, the other side from the principal's point of view: If one kid says it, then everybody is going to come up to the principal and try to get the rules changed even though they're still good. (How would you resolve it?) I'd say you couldn't. (Anything to do with rights?) Well, maybe in a town newspaper you could write but not in a school newspaper. (?) Well, I gotta give you a example. Last year these kids thought that—There was a big auction, and all the people in the school donated things. It was for buses to go on a camping trip. We raised more than we needed. So the kids got up a petition that it should go to us, and the teachers said it should go to the other grades that didn't go on the camping trip. And the kids had to stay after school because they didn't listen to the teachers explain. That's probably what would happen if Mark complained—everybody would. (?) I don't think they should have had to stay after school, but it was kinda dumb. We had a good deal. It was only about $35 for the whole week. We had a deal. It was really kinda selfish. They didn't want the money to go to the other kids.

Thus, as discussed earlier, the reality even for youngsters in an "open" progressive middle school may be that expression of rights is not tolerated. Their views about children's rights reflect this reality. To some extent, one may argue that bolstering a sense of self-determination may be setting a child up for trouble. Perhaps it is more sensible to work directly in changing "the system" to allow children such expression.

IMPLICATIONS FOR PUBLIC POLICY AND EDUCATIONAL PRACTICE

As is the norm in social science research, there is little directly applicable to public policy. That is, although the present study indicates children's concerns and concepts about rights, the decision about whether children should be allowed to exercise those rights is ultimately a political and ethical question and not a scientific one. With that caveat in mind, however, one may speculate on possible implications of the study for public policy.

One clear implication is that it is ludicrous for children under the third grade to waive rights because they do not know what the word means. Clearly the state must assume the role of parens patriae in both civil and criminal actions involving young children and ensure that waivers of rights by parents or guardians are in fact "in the best interests of the child."

It also appears that children often have the cognitive capacity to exercise rights and perhaps function as "mature minors" at least in a limited way earlier than they frequently are thought to be able. Such functioning may of course be unrealistic given the social constraints placed upon children's expressions of autonomy. Furthermore, that children can define and conceptualize rights does not imply that they can exercise them maturely; indeed, competence might be expected to vary across types of rights, given varying complexity of decisions and varying socialization concerning the appropriateness of asserting rights in various contexts. The present study indicates only that children cross the threshold of some understanding of what a right is at a rather young age.

The results do not imply that children would wish to exercise civil liberties even if they had the right to do so. In general, although able to apply at least Level 2 reasoning to issues involving civil rights, children did not include such rights in their comments about which rights children should have. It may be, of course, simply that having those rights seemed too inconceivable to come to mind. When asked about specific vignettes involving due process, free press, or self-determination for children, older children (at least third grade) tended to indicate positive attitudes toward such rights.

It appears that curricula about rights, particularly those belonging to children, could be meaningfully instituted as early as third grade. I would argue in favor of such a program for two reasons. First, children now have rights to due process in delinquency preceedings and, in many courts, in civil proceedings. For example, children's own wishes in custody proceedings are now an important factor in many courts, although children's rights in such cases are still limited. At any rate, preparation needs to be made for reasoned exercise of rights. For example, Grisso (1981) found that most juveniles in detention understood their right to silence, in terms of being able to describe the following statement from the *Miranda* warning: "You do not have to make a statement and have the right to remain silent." However, when asked if they had to "talk" on a judge's instruction, about 60% said "yes." Apparently, the juveniles still believed the "right to silence" to be a priviledge granted and potentially revoked by the authority. Thus, although they superficially understood the term, it could be argued that the waiver of the right to silence in such an instance would not be "knowing and intelligent."

Secondly, regardless of children's current legal standing, one can argue that rights are a cornerstone of a free society. Within that political framework, it makes sense to help children to develop toward principled views of rights. Too frequently "civics" courses, which usually are not taught until secondary school anyway, dwell on the process by which a bill becomes law, for example, and neglect the ways in which individuals come into contact with the political system on a daily basis. It is clear from the current research that vignettes of the type used in the interviews are "discussable," even by elementary school children. There is at least one social studies series, the Xerox Public Issues Series (Cutler & Schwach, 1975; Oliver & Newman, 1968; Pearson & Cutler, 1975), that has attempted to deal with such topics as rights in school suspensions, rights with regard to dress in school, rights in delinquency proceedings, etc. The Xerox curriculum is appropriate to a fifth-grade level or higher. With some imagination, it probably could be extended downward to third and fourth grades.

Prior to instituting such curricula, however, it may be necessary to educate teachers about rights. In a study of attitudes of teachers and education students toward civil liberties, Weiser and Hayes (1966) found that two-thirds agreed that "the government should prohibit some people from making speeches" and more than two-thirds did not believe in the right of free petition. Pluralities favored allowing police to give suspects the "third degree" and to censor books and other materials they found objectionable. A majority of the teachers surveyed favored establishment of a legal requirement that teachers sign an oath renouncing the Communist party. Although children were quite willing to discuss issues about their rights, it might be that some of their teachers would effectively quash such discussion as "disruptive." Therefore, interventions aimed at enhancing principled views of rights ideally would be directed first at adults, particularly professionals who work with children (school administrators, teachers, attorneys, and mental health professionals).

Although this discussion has been concerned primarily with the educational and legal systems, research on children's rights potentially has relevance to the mental health system as well (Grisso & Vierling, 1978; Melton, 1981a). For example, this study may provide data useful in helping to determine the age at which children are competent to seek or reject treatment independently of their parents. It also would be intriguing to use the measures developed in the present study as an outcome measure in the psychotherapy research. It has been argued that the mental health system sometimes is used as a social control mechanism designed to eliminate the "right to be different" (Kittrie, 1971). For children, the issue is particularly pointed in that they frequently are unwilling participants in psychotherapy and their participation is demanded because their interests are at variance with parents or the law (Bing & Brown, 1976; Koocher, 1976a). One may question in such instances whether the "bottom line" of treatment of the child is conformity or self-actualization and perception of the potential for self-determination. It would be interesting to learn if psychotherapy results in a change in rights attitudes and concepts in either direction.

In summary, there are ethical and political issues in direct application of the findings of this study to public policy, but it does help to clarify when children meaningfully can assume or waive rights. Such data have relevance to the educational, legal, and mental health systems in terms of both current policies and potential new curricula and other interventions having to do with children's rights. Perhaps of equal importance, this study suggests the usefulness of talking with children about their concerns before embarking on advocacy efforts. "Children's issues" in fact can span broad social issues, as suggested by the references to freedom from fear by the seventh graders in the Low-SES$_2$ school.

CHAPTER 3

Human Ecology and Child Advocacy

As discussed briefly in Chapter 1, helping services for children have tended to fluctuate between individual, exceptionalistic approaches and community approaches to intervention (Levine & Levine, 1970). Intrapsychic factors in behavior tend to be emphasized during periods in which the political climate swings to the right. Thus, during conservative periods, individuals tend to be perceived as responsible for their plight, and interventions are aimed at changing the individual's psyche. Even during "liberal" periods, assumptions about behavior and interventions may have overtones of victim-blaming (Ryan, 1971), although they are more likely to have at least a superficial objective of social reform. The approaches to be discussed in this chapter are "ecological" in the sense that they preclude just looking at psychodynamics or just looking at the social system while ignoring the individuals within it. Rather, they involve a focus on the *fit* between a child and his environment. Child advocates (at least those whose views tend at least in part toward "nurturance") are interested in creating a system in which, given the child's current state of development, his psychological functioning is likely to be enhanced (see Hobbs, 1975). This approach obviously requires sensitivity to both the needs of a particular child or a particular class of children and to the response of the environment to these needs. Where the fit is less optimal or perhaps even less than adequate, attempts may be made to bring the system into equilibrium by interventions directed at both the child and the social institutions with which he or she has direct or indirect contact.

Indeed, as Rappaport (1977) has pointed out:

> The ecological paradigm ... can be applied as a means to adjust persons to environments or environments to people, hut also allows for the possibility that neither solution is adequate, and that entirely new environments, created by, and in the control of, people who are different from the mainstream are desirable. (p. 23)

Thus, advocates may in some instances perceive a need for what has been called the "creation of settings" (Sarason, 1972). In those cases, the work is not simply to reform existing institutions or to treat the individual. Rather, the advocate's job is to work toward creation of new environments responsive to the families within them. To use a large-scale example, Bronfenbrenner (1974a) has discussed the possibility of incorporating such concepts from other cultures as "park-aunties" and "children's palaces" in order to deal with the problem in our culture of breakdown of extended family networks.

Child advocacy as it is conceptualized here is a positive endeavor. Rather than "curing" or "treating" "pathology," it is aimed at fostering adaptation. Again, the child and the other elements of the system must accommodate to one another. To borrow concepts from psychoanalytic ego psychology, the effort here is to provide at least an "average expectable environment" (Hartmann, 1939/1958) in which the child's own sense of mastery and competence (White, 1959) is developed. The emphasis is one provision of sufficient resources to allow the child to make a successful adaptation.

Before conceptual issues are discussed further, it may be useful to consider a current example of the problems of exceptionalistic approaches that ignore the system as a whole. Public Law 94–142[1] is a recent piece of social legislation that is likely to require major changes in the educational system before it is fully implemented. Briefly, it mandates local school systems to provide whatever services a child must have in order to meet his or her special educational needs and to do so with as little segregation as possible. Contrary to some misinterpretations (for example, Silverman, 1979a, 1979b; reply by Melton, 1979), Pub. L. 94–142 does not *necessarily* require "mainstreaming" but it certainly does carry a mandate to eliminate unnecessary segregation of handicapped children. As a result, regular classes now include, at least for part of the day, children who formerly received homebound instruction or who were placed in special classes or simply excluded from school. Often these children are "dumped" into the mainstream with little preparation for the situations that they may encounter for the first time. Where there is preparation, it tends to be in terms of building the child's own social and academic skills. Indeed, an Individual Educational Plan, a requirement under Pub. L. 94–142, should specify progress a child needs to make before placement in a less restrictive education program prototype. Such preparation of the child certainly makes sense; building skills is after all the purpose of education.

The problem, however, comes with exceptionalistic approaches that con-

---

[1]Education for All Handicapped Children Act, 20 U.S.C. §§ 1401–1461.

ceptualize the child's needs simply as a reflection of his or her objective medical condition and neglect ecological factors. Behavior that is considered deviant or upsetting or representative of a disabling condition in one social setting may not be noteworthy in another (see, for example, Mercer's 1973 study of factors in the labeling of mental retardation). Furthermore, preparation of the child without simultaneous preparation of his new classroom environment is likely to result in a failure for the child. For example, the "normal" children in the regular classroom may not understand their new classmate's disabilities and as a result may respond with avoidance or defensive teasing (Bergmann & Freud, 1965; Wright, 1960). They need to be prepared for interacting with their handicapped peer in order to facilitate a relationship that enhances rather than impairs his or her psychosocial development. A number of new techniques and materials for education about handicaps are available (Melton, 1977b, 1980b). Such interventions may have transfer to other situations in which children interact with people who are different.

Similarly, regular class teachers need to be prepared for teaching handicapped students. Teachers may perceive the presence of such children as an additional, time-consuming burden for which they have little professional training (Paul, Turnbull, & Cruickshank, 1977). In such an instance, the child may be resented and at the very least receive few benefits from being placed in a regular classroom. Incidentally, the teachers' sense of lack of support may be very realistic. Sarason (1971), for example, noted the common perception of teaching as a job that is accompanied by loneliness. Teachers usually have limited contact with adults during the day; they are essentially on their own. In addition, few school systems have given much attention to the specific issue of providing necessary training of regular class class teachers for educating handicapped children.

The latter observation of the teacher's lack of support for herself brings us to another point. So far the discussion has been concerned primarily with the child's "microsystem" (Bronfenbrenner, 1977). That is, we have considered the connections among people in the child's immediate setting (e.g., the teacher, the child's peers, and the child himself). It is often useful to consider "exosystem" influences as well. The handicapped child's adjustment to the regular classroom is likely to be related to the strength of administrative supports for the teacher as well as other external factors, such as pressures placed on the teacher by parents of the children and school board decisions about purchase of special equipment. Attempts to "prepare" the teacher without attention to these factors are likely to miss the point, just as isolated preparation of the handicapped child does.

An example of the influence of such external factors on the child's adjustment was described by Rogeness, Bednar, and Diesenhaus (1974). In a school
in which they consulted, the school size was reduced by half. Seemingly as a
result of the greater intimacy, staff satisfaction increased and teacher turnover
was reduced. What is most interesting here, however, is that reported behavior problems among pupils decreased. Such a decrease is consistent with earlier, more systematic observations of the effects of school size on sense of satisfaction and degree of participation (Barker & Gump, 1964).

As essentially a correlational observation, the study by Rogeness et al. of
course has problems of subjectivity in analysis of the line of causality.
Although a description of the rehabilitative process in a noneducational setting (a prerelease program for adult offenders), Sarata and Reppucci's (1975)
article entitled "The Problem is Outside" gives more compelling evidence for
the linkage among exosystem factors, staff satisfaction, and client behavior.
The program studied underwent a period of staff uncertainty related to a possible loss of funding, another program's being moved into the same building,
and a visit (perceived as an intrusive visit) by a representative of the deputy
commissioner. Compared to preceding and following periods of program stability, residents demonstrated more aggressive behavior and scored higher on
a measure of Machiavellianism during the period of staff uncertainty. Similar
negative effects on client behavior of external factors resulting in organizational instability have been reported by Boling and Brotman (1975) in a discussion of a fire-setting epidemic in a state mental hospital.

SUPPORT SYSTEMS

A related concept that has been useful in assessing the nature of a child's
ecosystem is that of "support systems." Caplan (1974) has been particularly
influential in the application of this concept. Borrowing from the work of
Vickers (1971), Caplan has defined support systems as "continuing social
aggregates that provide individuals with opportunities for feedback about
themselves and for validations of their expectations about others, which may
offset deficiencies in these communications within the larger community context" (1974, pp. 4–5). Essentially, as Caplan conceptualizes it, a support system attends to an individual's personal needs for reward and comfort and for
information about his performance in the community.

The existence of such supports for a child is particularly important in
terms of learning information-processing strategies as well as of meeting basic

emotional needs (see, for example, Reiss, 1971). Cochran and Brassard (1979) have analyzed the developmental implications of personal social networks. They suggest that parents' social networks have direct influences on the child's cognitive development, independent of indirect effects through support for and shaping of the parents' child-rearing skills. Cognitive abilities directly affected include: perceptual differentiation,[2] skills required in goal-oriented tasks, representational thinking, and cognitive receptivity or openness to new intellectual stimuli. The child's social development may be further affected at least in the following areas: attachment, independence behavior, experiences with social roles, child-rearing attitudes and behaviors, and self-concept. In short, the child with few resources learns relatively few ways of approaching problems and of resolving "life-crises," another Caplanian concept. Support systems provide both a sanctuary when stressors become too intense and cues for selection of strategies to deal with stress. Support systems help in mobilizing the individual to deal with the crisis, sharing and diffusing the stress, and providing extra "supplies" to be used in weathering the crisis.

The concept of life-crisis is important in that it provides a focus for prediction of times when a child or a family is particularly likely to undergo a period of stress. At such points the provision of supplies is especially important (e.g., entering school, birth of a sibling, divorce of parents, etc.), and opportunities are presented for primary prevention. It is important to note that life-crisis may involve either positive or negative events. Essentially, any major change or "psychosocial transition" is presented as entailing a crisis when a strong support system is helpful (Marris, 1974). Thus, many "normal" phases in the development of a child and his or her family present stressors that may expectably create disequilibrium but which also provide opportunities for the development of strengths (Erikson, 1964). Child advocacy is important in providing or bolstering the support systems necessary for such positive outcomes.

There is considerable empirical evidence for the significance of support systems in preventing child or family disturbance. Perhaps the most well conceptualized body of literature concerns ecological factors in child abuse. Garbarino (1977; Garbarino & Crouter, 1978; Garbarino & Sherman, 1980; Garbarino, Gaboury, Long, Grandjean, & Asp, 1982) has been particularly

---

[2]Cochran and Brassard argue that variety of social stimuli fosters perceptual differentiation:

> Our rather straightforward suggestion is that members of the social network provide the child with practice, first in discriminating facial features and then in differentiating among differing interactive styles. In the Piagetian sense the members of the social network may provide the moderately conflicting and contrasting experiences which upset the cognitive equilibrium enough to permit movement to a higher stage of cognitive development. (Cochran & Brassard, 1979, p. 607)

persuasive in arguing that social isolation is a key variable in fostering child abuse. His contention is that lack of adequate support systems is the catalyst that translates other predictor variables (e.g., poverty, inconsistent parenting style, difficult temperament of the child) into abuse. The feedback function of support systems is viewed as particularly important in providing child care expertise and external controls for parents under stress. Social networks also provide access to child care itself and social and economic resources to alleviate stress.

Several studies have corroborated a strong correlation between social isolation and abusiveness. Abusive parents have been found to be less likely than nonabusers to belong to organizations, have a telephone, have relationships outside the home, etc. (see, for reviews, Garbarino & Crouter, 1978; Gelles & Straus, 1979). Parenthetically, although the absence of social supports is conceptualized as itself a factor in child abuse, it should be noted that the isolation may be a reflection of parental behavior styles rather than causative of them. Thus, isolation is perceived as a psychodynamic expression of the "cycle of abuse":

> Perhaps part of the problem is that abusive parents do have trouble turning to others for help, in trusting others to *want* to help. They tend to be isolated, without friends and without confidants. In a crisis they seem to feel they must struggle alone; asking for help represents failure. It may well be that, just as children they accepted their parents' unrealistic expectations of them, now as adults they have unrealistic expectations not only of their own children but also of themselves. (Kempe & Kempe, 1978, pp. 20–21)

Even this psychodynamic formulation, though, may be extended to a need for development of social supports, at least within a therapeutic relationship.

> [A] factor is that no effective "lifeline," or line of communication to sources of aid, exists at the moment of crisis. This factor is most important. Lifelines to call for help are essential to all of us. Since abusive parents cannot rely on each other for rescue in moments of crisis, outside lines have to be developed quickly in treatment. Clearly, one cannot easily change parents' emotional backgrounds or twenty-year histories of deprivation, nor can one help them to see their children as loveable; but one can provide for rescue and the beginning of crisis management. (Kempe & Kempe, 1978, p. 24)

In Garbarino and Crouter's (1978) own work, a number of social indicators have been found to be predictive of incidence of child abuse in a community within a multiple regression paradigm. Economic factors[3] alone con-

---

[3]"Economic factors" in this instance refer to the percentages of families in a community with incomes over $15,000 per year and of families with incomes under $8,000 per year.

tributed 62% of the variance, $r = .79$. Variables related to neighborhood stability also were found to be significant. Garbarino and Crouter believe that the correlation between social class and abuse rates is a "true" one, not the function of a reporting bias. (For further evidence on this point, see Pelton, 1978.)

Nonetheless, Garbarino and Crouter found marked differences by social class in the sources reporting child abuse and neglect. Suspected cases of abuse within lower-class families tend to be reported by "distant" sources, such as social welfare or health agencies, while cases among middle-class families tend to be reported by "close" sources (relatives, friends, or neighbors). There are no differences between institutional and noninstitutional reporters, however, in correlations between socio-economic variables and reporting rates. Garbarino and Crouter argued that this finding tends to refute the allegation of class bias by agency professionals in reporting child maltreatment. From Garbarino's point of view, differences in rate of abuse among different demographic groups are reflections of differences in the quality of life. Those families that then do become engaged in abuse are those which are most isolated. That the reporters of lower-class abuse are likely to be distant is viewed as a reflection of the pervasive drain experienced by families in lower-class families. The resources necessary to provide the feedback mentioned earlier are unavailable. Support systems simply are overworked by the constant strain and may not function adequately. The result is a breakdown of the monitoring function:

> Community standards used in defining inadequate and unacceptable child care are lower in the most socioeconomically distressed areas. Put more directly (and bluntly), in the informed opinion of field-workers, patterns that would be judged abused or neglectful in more affluent areas are likely to be accepted (with resignation perhaps) in less affluent areas. (Garbarino & Crouter, 1978, p. 611)

Such an interpretation implies a need for construction or replacement of supports that will mediate family stress in poor communities. The recommendation in turn implies intrusion into existing family and community social systems. Garbarino (1977) has proposed a reversal of "the cultural sanctity for privacy in extreme form," in part through the establishment of "intrusive monitoring networks, particularly among populations prone to abuse, i.e., those exposed to high stress, unstable parenting and communities, and those having difficult children" (p. 573). The ethical issues raised by such a strategy are obvious, particularly when the invasions of privacy are applied discriminatively to particular communities. These monitoring systems are perhaps less offensive, however, when they are based on natural helping networks, the strengths already existing within a community. From a positive viewpoint, ecological interventions also may be understood as providing families with the resources to overcome stress and function independently and productively. Garbarino argues that families should not be able to have so much privacy that they become isolated. (Perhaps the more basic issue, though, is the need to eliminate the stressors that combine to make isolation particularly pathogenic.)

Garbarino's mentor, Urie Bronfenbrenner, has written even more extensively about the importance of supportive family networks in child development. In one frequently cited paper, Bronfenbrenner (1974b) attributed a rampant feeling of alienation among youth to rapid changes in American family structure. Family structure has changed markedly with striking increases in the number of one-parent families, families, particularly of preschoolers, in which both parents work, etc. Most pernicious from Bronfenbrenner's point of view are social changes that have isolated children and their families:

> the fragmentation of the extended family, the separation of residential and business areas, the breakdown of neighborhoods, zoning ordinances, occupational mobility, child-labor laws, the abolition of the apprentice system, consolidated schools, supermarkets, television, separate patterns of social life for different age groups, the working mother, the delegation of child-care to specialists (p. 54).

These social changes are perceived as having a side effect of reduced supports for children and families.

Bronfenbrenner (1974a) has strongly advocated social science research in "real-life" settings on issues of public policy. He has been particularly concerned with examination of external influences, such as those listed above, on the development of the child. For example, Bronfenbrenner has been interested in the effects on children (hypothesized to be positive) of changes in the parents' work schedule. What are the effects on children of one or both parents' working only part-time? What are the effects on children and families of "flexitime" strategies in which workers create their own work schedules? Attention to such seemingly far-removed settings in the ecology of the child is thought by Bronfenbrenner to be particularly important in establishing a national family policy.

THE QUALITY OF LIFE

One approach to the development of empirical bases for national child development policies has been to attempt to gather broad data on the quality of life in American children. In his presidential address to the American

Orthopsychiatric Association, Brim (1975) contended that there is a need for data that may serve as "social indicators of the state of the child." These indicators would involve time-series data, analogous to leading economic indicators, which would provide a sense of changes in the well-being of children and the social conditions surrounding them. These macrostructural data may provide the bases for defining carefully the problems with which child advocates should be concerned on a "class" level. Social scientists would appear to have a particular contribution to make in developing valid indicators of the quality of life.

In a related paper, Zill and Brim (1975) have speculated on the kinds of specific data that would be useful as childhood social indicators. For example, data are needed on the demand for child care services and on the child care arrangements actually used. Data on use of health and mental health services by children, incidence of various medical conditions, educational achievement, etc., would be helpful in policy development. Perhaps of most interest, Zill and Brim argued that it is important to gather survey data about children's own perceptions of their environments and experiences in order to identify factors in their subjective quality of life (see Melton, 1982a).

Such a national survey of children aged 7 to 11 was in fact conducted by Zill and his associates in the fall of 1976 (Foundation for Child Development, 1977). Although the findings from this study are too extensive to report here, it may be useful to review briefly some of the concerns raised about the quality of children's lives. Probably the most disturbing finding in the survey was the large proportion of the sample who reported a fear of violence in their communities. Age was not a correlate of these reports; therefore, they are unlikely to reflect irrational childhood fears. Nearly one-third of girls and about 20% of boys reported fear of what might happen when they go outside. These fears may be well founded. According to interviews with parents, about 20% of the sample live in neighborhoods where there are "undesirable people in the streets, parks or playgrounds, such as drunks, drug addicts, or tough older kids."

In terms of family life, the vast majority of children expressed satisfaction with their families. At the same time, more than 80% of children said that they worry about their families and the figure rises to near-unanimity in families that were described by the mother as "not too happy." It is noteworthy that children in these families were three times as likely to have been in a fight at school during the past week as children in families that marriages were described as happy.

Most children said that they like school, but it also seemed clear from the data that school is stressful for many of them. About two-thirds reported anxiety about tests in school and shame when they make mistakes in school. A majority of the children agreed that "I sometimes feel I just can't learn."

In regard to their neighborhoods, children had more negative perceptions than their parents. Only about 30% of the children, as opposed to about 60% of their parents, described their neighborhood as a very good place in which to grow up. Primary sources of dissatisfaction were inadequate places to play and crime and bad behavior.

The import of the survey findings for public policy is not clear, although they do suggest that social concerns not identified as "family issues" (e.g., crime) often may in fact be directly related to the well-being of children. Thus, advocates for a sound "family policy" actually may find themselves concerned with social policy in general (Keniston, 1977). For any who still have an idyllic view of childhood, the survey also indicates the profound stressors associated with most of the settings in which children spend their time.

What is most significant about the FDC survey, though, is that it provides a baseline for examination of changes in the quality of life of American children. Zill et al. seem to have made a good beginning in establishing broad indicators of the quality of many of the social institutions affecting children. Similar efforts in terms of adult social indicators might provide a better ecological picture of the ways in which these institutions interact.

ECOLOGICAL ASSESSMENT

Just as child advocates need macrostructural measures of the quality of life in planning advocacy on public policy issues, assessment of the ecology of an individual's life is important in decisions about case advocacy. One way to begin to formulate the ecological imbalances within the life of an individual might be to assess the person's own impressions of the quality of his or her life. In so doing, it would be important to attempt to measure perceptions of one's life within as many potentially significant contexts as possible (family, school, neighborhood, work, etc.). Blau (1977) has developed such an individual quality-of-life inventory for adults, but no comparable standardized inventory exists for children.

Alternatively, an individual's ecology might be assessed by gathering perceptions of a setting by all of the participants within it. By this more global approach to the settings of which a child is a part, the advocate might begin to develop hypotheses about relative strengths of social support at various points in the child's life. Some researchers in social ecology, especially Moos and his colleagues, have used this approach of assessing shared perceptions of relationships, orderliness, etc., within a setting as a technique for describing its ecological characteristics. Most notably for our purposes, such a measure (the Classroom Environment Scale) is available for assessing the social climate of specific classrooms (Moos & Trickett, 1974; Trickett, 1978).

Both of these approaches potentially may contribute valuable information for both research and applied purposes. However, to the extent to which both purport to provide a comprehensive assessment of the environment, their practical utility is limited in two important ways. First, although probably providing valid indicators of individuals' experience of a given setting, the Blau and Moos measures do not directly assess social *processes*. They do not give clear information about the interpersonal dynamics within an institution or of exosystem influences on it. Thus, broad measures of environmental perception may indicate the social quality of a setting and thus give a sense of whether there is a need for an intervention. Combined with traditional clinical data about an individual child, the environmental-perception instruments may provide the advocate with a sense of the degree of fit between the child and his or her environment. However, the environmental-perception measures give little sense of where to focus an intervention or of the nature of the intervention to be used.

Second, and more significant from an ecological point of view, the environmental-perception measures do not give an indication of the *interactions* within a system. As implied in the disucssion of factors in mainstreaming, external factors may be key influences in the success of mainstreaming for a particular child. Conceivably, pressures put on regular classroom teachers because of some apparently unrelated reason could have an ill effect on the handicapped child. By the same token, any intervention on behalf of the child is likely to have effects of varying magnitude on other units of the system. The interactions are at the heart of ecological explanations of behavior. The complexity of causality considered by ecologically oriented psychologists is the feature that distinguishes their approach from unidirectional "S-R" and intrapsychic approaches to behavior. Conceptually, then, environmental-perception inventories that do not touch the multidirectional flow within a system are lacking as measures of the social ecology.

From an applied perspective, lack of information about interactions leaves the advocate ignorant about probable "side effects" of an intervention. There is some danger in well-intentioned advocates' zealously pursuing a given intervention without attention to its "side effects." Koocher (1979) has argued that advocates should prepare the psychosocial analogue of an "environmental impact statement" before pushing for a particular change. As he conceptualized the problem, there are two issues: the responsibility to act and the need for responsible action. As discussed in Chapter 1, there is likely to be some tendency to avoid dealing with the ambiguous, conflict-laden situations that may surround a child. While such avoidance may be costly to the child, once the commitment is made to act, care should not end. "Doing something" is not sufficient. Action without careful attention to its likely consequences ultimately may have negative effects on the child himself or on other parts of the system.

For example, I argued in Chapter 2 that children should be educated about their rights with the goal of fostering a sense of efficacy about entitlement. At the same time, though, it was noted that the majority of teachers (and probably parents as well) have negative attitudes toward application of civil liberties. An educational intervention might result in children's asserting rights in situations in which adults in authority do not recognize such rights. Thus, children may be inadvertently "set up" by a rights-education program to be punished. The obvious point here is that there is a need to evaluate carefully *where* and *how* to intervene. Changing the child (in this instance, almost "organizing" children) without attention to the repercussions of such an intervention within the system may create more serious problems than it solves. Parenthetically, in this example, the advocate obviously would need to engage somehow in "consciousness-raising" of school personnel and the community as a whole as well as of children themselves.

Potentially harmful side effects are particularly likely when the advocate and the other adults in the child's life have different value systems. On an individual level, Koocher (1979) presented a dilemma commonly faced by clinicians. The dilemma described is one in which a child is brought by her rigidly moralistic parents to a psychologist for treatment of "symptoms" that appear quite normal, such as a dislike of wearing dresses rather than pants. The psychologist is faced with several options, all of which bear some risk of either accepting the parents' designation of their daughter as a "patient" or of increasing behavior to which the parents are likely to respond punitively. Careful assessment is needed of the probable side effects of each of the interventions the clinician might make.

When one moves to the level of community interventions, the potential for turmoil resulting from value conflicts becomes still greater. To give one politically charged example, it has been frequently observed that Appalachian persons tend to be rather passive and nonverbal (Gotts, 1980; Looff, 1971).

Assuming for the moment that this observation is valid, an advocate might attempt to intervene to induce more assertiveness in children in the region and to foster a sense of control over their fate. On the other hand, it might be that the community itself does not perceive such a need and in fact perceives the changes desired by the advocate as undesirable. The community might argue (perhaps accurately) that an attack on the cultural value of obedience to authority would disrupt an extended-family system that they have found important. Intervention may in fact still be justified (perhaps even ethically demanded) because of the increase in alternative choices that the advocate believes would be perceived by the children as they grow older. In the process of designing the intervention, though, the advocate must endeavor to develop sufficient data to be able to select a strategy that will reduce harmful side effects for the child and his or her community.

At the risk of belaboring the point, it is worthwhile to note that many of our current social reform movements are in part efforts to undo the work of earlier child-savers (see Takaniski, 1978). The pre-*Gault* juvenile court was perceived as more capricious and violative of due process than protective. Institutions are perceived as warehouses resulting in deterioration rather than habilitation. Special classes are perceived as programs of last resort rather than of choice. One may argue with some validity that the implementation of these earlier reforms was more pernicious than the concepts behind them. With adequate funding, the institutions perhaps would not have grown into the inhuman places that many of them became. It also is unrealistic to expect perfect prediction of the consequences of a reform. Nonetheless, the point here is that the advocate is ethically obligated to note the limits of his or her knowledge (American Psychological Association, 1981, Principle 1) and to diagnose as carefully as possible the nature of the need and the consequences of meeting the need in a particular way. In the end, the situation often is not simple, and the advocate must make a judgment as to relative costs and benefits. For example, although the mainstreaming of handicapped children may result in increased academic achievement and perhaps better social adjustment in the long run, it also is likely to cause at least a short-term drop in self-esteem (Dibner & Dibner, 1973). Ultimately, in such a situation (with "all other things being equal") a decision must be made as to which change has more ethical significance. In short, the "value judgment" must be made.

As is probably clear by now, there is no standardized or "cookbook" method of performing an accurate ecological assessment. To a large extent, the advocate must rely on his or her own sense of local justice and "clinical intuition" and on confirmation of his or her judgment through consultation with other advocates and the "clients" whom the advocate purports to represent.

A Framework for Evaluation

Although still not explicitly dealing with interactions within an ecosystem, Davidson and Rapp (1976) have suggested a "multiple-strategy model" of child advocacy that may provide a framework for a thorough evaluation. The strength of their model is that it includes recognition that evaluation must go beyond the client's needs to the resources and defeats of the system.

The Davidson-Rapp model begins the process of advocacy with a phase of primary assessment (see Figure 1). There are two key elements in the initial assessment: assessment of unmet needs and assessment of needed resources. This phase involves descriptions both of the gaps in the system and of possible ways of filling these gaps. Davidson and Rapp empasized the importance of multiple sources of data collection in making these assessments. Although arguing that "the client or the client group must be the primary director" (p.

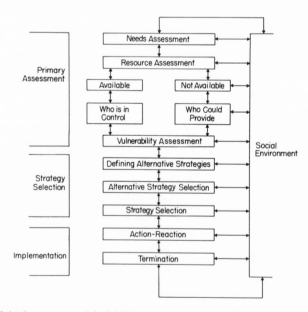

Figure 1. Multiple-strategy model of child advocacy as developed by Davidson and Rapp (1976). (From "Child Advocacy in the Justice System," by W. S. Davidson & C. A. Rapp, *Social Work,* 1976, *21*(3), 228. Copyright 1976 by the National Association of Social Workers, Inc. Reprinted by permission).

228), they suggested gathering opinions about unmet needs of youth from whoever is likely to have special knowledge of the situation in a given community: parents, educators, employers, and so forth. This information-gathering process requires some awareness of the parties who are most likely to be aware of "the inside" of a system, including persons outside the professions. For example, some school janitors serve as "natural helpers" and have a clear sense of the state of well-being of the students. Similarly, in Garbarino and Sherman's (1980) study of neighborhood factors in family well-being, mailmen were recruited to give impressions of particular neighborhoods. It should be noted here that the selection of sources of data is again based on the advocate's intuitively "knowing" the key persons or groups in a system. There is no "hard" methodology in identifying, for example, the natural helpers in a system.

The assessment of the resources needed also requires sensitivity and some degree of creativity as well as knowledge of the research literature of the factors involved in various needs and problems. Davidson and Rapp emphasized thinking beyond the obvious resources to generate and evaluate alternative possibilities for meeting a child's needs. As they put it, "this phase of assessment will include such multiple tactics as interviewing, brainstorming, investigative reporting, and legal research" (p. 228). In this process, one must be problem oriented rather than discipline oriented.

In addition, the advocate must avoid the trap of deducing the resources needed from the child's diagnostic label. Although most services are established on a categorical basis, such approaches rarely meet the needs of an individual child or even a particular community or group. To give an obvious example, a common experience in agencies whose sole mission is child advocacy is to receive requests to help obtain a program for a particular child. Suppose that a caller seeks help in obtaining a residential school for a retarded child. I have often observed well-intentioned but clinically naive advocates immediately enter a fight with a school system or other agency to obtain a particular type of program for the child without ever evaluating if it is the *best* type of program to meet the child's needs. Often the advocate does not even attempt to learn the degree of the child's retardation or the particular skills that he or she needs to master. Clearly, the label of "mental retardation" alone gives minuscule information about needed resources. Thus, sophistication about more traditional "clinical" as well as "social-systems" approaches to diagnosis and treatment is needed. Zealous pursuit of an intervention without a careful formulation of needs runs the risk of winning the battle but failing to help the child.

After the advocate, in conjunction with his or her client, has formulated the child's needs and ways in which those needs could be met, assessments become directed toward acquiring data helpful in selecting strategies of acquiring the needed resources. Initially, the advocate identifies who is in control of these resources or, if not available, who could provide them. The focus of the evaluation then moves to this individual, group, or institution. Specifically, the advocate is then interested in what Davidson and Rapp term the "assessment of vulnerability." To what kinds of positive appeals or aversive contingencies might the target be responsive? Davidson and Rapp perceptively listed a sample series of specific questions that will aid in answering the broader question of the target's vulnerability:

1. Does the target have an ideology that would resist or encourage the provision of the resource for the client?
2. Is there any relationship between the advocate and the target?
3. Does the target view the relationship as positive or negative?
4. What are the target's self-interests?
5. To whom is the target most responsive—supervisors, taxpayers, consumers, legislators, or pressure groups?
6. How accessible is the target?
7. Does the target have direct control over the provision of needed resource or is the target only one part of the decision-making process? and
8. Does the target have many potential allies and how influential are they? (p. 229)

The answers to these questions are then used to develop the strategies to be used in obtaining the needed resources. Examination of such aspects of the situation as the target's alliances may be helpful in making predictions of the likely side effects of a given strategy. Davidson and Rapp's sample list of questions gives a clear sense of the structural points of vulnerability of the target. Knowing the strength and quality of connections among elements of the system is useful in prediction of the reverberations of an intervention across the system and identification of points of access to the target. As such, Davidson and Rapp's evaluation guidelines provide a beginning toward evaluation of system interactions. A clear point is made that assessment in a vacuum of a child's "objective" needs is insufficient for planning an effective intervention.

In addition to the structural, essentially "sociological" questions that Davidson and Rapp suggested in assessing the target's vulnerability, it is important to consider points of psychological "vulnerability" as well. Bureaucrats have psychodynamics, too! A caveat is in order here, however. Particularly when a case is not going well, it often is tempting to perform an "armchair psychoanalysis" of the opponent and to speculate on the ways in which his or her neurosis is interfering with the work. For example, a recalcitrant bureaucrat's nitpicking adherence to a strict interpretation of regulations without regard to a client's interests may be understood as a manifestation of the bureaucrat's obsessive-compulsive or perhaps passive-aggressive character structure. Although that hypothesis may be correct, it well may be that the bureaucrat is simply "holding the line" on a directive from his superiors to avoid encumbering the agency. Thus, what is *experienced* as a "personality conflict" is in reality largely a policy dispute. Simply trying to "use psychology" on the offending bureaucrat probably will not address the problem.

Even when the root problem is a policy or structural matter, however, the participants' experiences of the dispute do become significant in formulating the current situation and ways of changing it. Furthermore, there are instances in which a participant's personal history and psychological needs predispose ("overdetermine") a particular course of action. For example, one Social Security employee tended to require extraordinary documentation by parents who had applied for Supplemental Security Income (SSI) on behalf of their handicapped children. As it turned out, the employee was himself handicapped. He apparently had pulled himself up "by his bootstraps" with little support and he seemed to be dealing with his anger by placing his child-clients into a situation in which they would have to recapitulate his own history. Although it would be unrealistic and inappropriate for the advocate to "treat" the employee, addressing his concerns about the need for economic supports for handicapped persons while acknowledging his achievements and the difficulty of his own struggles might have reduced his resistance to providing help for others. Essentially, the advocate should analyze the parties' interests—both institutional and personal—and attempt to identify bases on which an alliance may be formed on behalf of a particular child or group of children.

The Case of John H.

Social-psychological variables, particularly the interpersonal or small-group dynamics among participants, also should be considered in strategy selection. (See O'Neill, 1981, for a particularly creative application of small-group research to the work of community organizers and consultants.) The case of John H., described in Chapter 1, is exemplary of the usefulness of such an analysis. In that case an atypical four-year-old boy had come into contact with a myriad of agencies, but he and his family were receiving no services despite his alcoholic, depressed mother's active request for help (specifically, foster care) and her fear of abusing John because of her own desperation.

Based on our conversations with all of the agencies' representatives involved, it was clear that blame was centered on Mrs. Brown, the H. family's case-worker in the local office of the Department of Public Welfare. The general perceptions were that Mrs. Brown should have coordinated the case, that she was negligent in not doing so, and that she was incompetent. At the same time, Mrs. Brown openly acknowledged to us that she felt helpless and ill prepared to deal with John's case. A rather elderly lady, she had been a pay-ment and assistance worker for many years. After a career of filling out forms and handing out checks, she suddenly had been converted into a "generalist" because of DPW "decentralization" of social service functions to local offices. Rather than being a villain, Mrs. Brown herself was a victim. Without addi-tional training, she had been placed into a position that she had not sought and in which she simply could not cope.

It was clear that John and his family had multiple serious needs: special educational services for John, companionship and social supports for Mrs. H., day care for John's sister, a stable home for John, adequate housing for the family, and so forth. It also was clear that a meeting of all of the agencies involved was necessary to delineate responsibilites, one of which was case coordination and monitoring. After thinking through possible strategies for obtaining these services (apart from resolving the policy issues raised by the case), we decided that the agency best able to assume the coordinator role was a private social services agency that had a child-protection contract under DPW. This agency, which was perceived favorably by all of the participants (including Mrs. H.), had the capacity to provide most of the needed resources itself, provided that it was given permission to do so by DPW.

The question then became one of how to maneuver toward such a result. At this point a formulation of the dynamics of the group of agency represen-tatives was important. It was predictable that an initial undirected review of the situation would become an exercise in the other participants' scapegoating Mrs. Brown and venting their anger. It also was predictable that Mrs. Brown again would present herself as helpless to deal with the situation, a response that was likely to elicit still more expressions of anger and frustration.

Assuming that the sequence of events would in fact follow our analysis, we made plans to intervene after Mrs. Brown asked for help. At that point, as the "expert" guardians of the child's interests, we would acknowledge the shared frustrations of the group and support their altruistic intentions. Our comments would resemble the following:

> It sounds as though everyone has invested a great deal of energy on behalf of John and his family. This case is so complex, though, that we're probably not going to

get anywhere unless one agency can really take over and deliver a package of services for the H. family. One worker just can't do it.

We then would conclude that it seemed as though the private agency (previously minimally involved in the case) had the resources to carry out the treatment plan, which itself was not in dispute. Attention then would be called to the protective-services contract that would enable such involvement and provide a way out of the shared dilemma.

The meeting went as predicted. Initially, alliances were formed against Mrs. Brown and the focus was on her failures rather than on the group's task of implementation of the treatment plan. After Mrs. Brown asked for help, however, we were able to enter the meeting with support for all of the participants' positive intentions. As leaders who had not previously allied with any of the agencies in particular but who now allied with all of them in general, we were able to present a solution with which the participants quickly agreed. In this instance, a supportive conciliatory strategy was selected to build on the positive motives of the participants.

Although this meeting illustrates the utility of a psychological slant to the advocacy process, it also is exemplary of the danger of approaching assessment too "clinically." Careful assessment of a situation's psychological elements without consideration of the structural and policy elements may leave one unprepared. Although there was quick agreement among the participants with our plan, an unexpected obstacle developed equally quickly. The DPW Protective Services supervisor expressed ignorance (real or feigned) of the existence of his agency's contract with the private agency. The underlying issue appeared to be the supervisor's reluctance to consider a case in which the child himself was "disturbed" as a protective case despite Mrs. H's fear of abusing John and evidence for neglect. His position was that, given John's own special needs, the case was purely one for the Department of Mental Health.

At that meeting and thereafter, we and the other agencies involved began using "official" channels, such as a state interdepartmental team on children's issues, to confront the supervisor and his own supervisors with the relevant statutes and regulations. With this administrative and legal support, perceptible changes occurred in Protective Services intake policies, at least in the short term. On this issue, unlike the general problem of implementing the treatment plan, it was felt that a more confrontational adversarial strategy was necessary. The DPW administrators' primary motive seemed to be avoidance of setting a precedent that might result in the agency's assumption of an additional financial burden. There did not seem to be a basis for formation of an alliance. (Alternatively, a long-range strategy might be to acknowledge the pressures of DPW administrators and form an alliance to lobby for a more generous Protective Services budget.)

Furthermore, the hostile affect that an adversarial strategy is likely to engender (Davidson & Rapp, 1976) was a less troublesome possible side effect on the issue of Protective Services policies than in the case of the implementation of the treatment plan for John H. In the latter case, confrontation might have resulted in a superficial agreement but with a probability of sabotage or at least passive resistance to full implementation. Essentially, John ultimately might have been worse off as a result of being placed in the middle of an agency battle. It was important to reduce the possibility of recriminations against the H. family. On the other hand, confrontation on the policy issue presented less risk of a personalized dispute concerning the client.

CONCLUSIONS

To summarize, an ecological model of behavior is a parsimonious conceptual base for child advocacy. The advocate is concerned with enhancing the fit between children and their environments. This work may move the advocate's focus to social institutions in which children themselves usually are not directly involved but that still affect children. Thus, the ecological model teaches advocates that they must be concerned with interacting effects among institutions and individuals. There is no single straightforward way of identifying or predicting these interactions. Nonetheless, it is clear that, both in assessing problems and planning strategies, the advocate needs to look beyond the immediate situation and to think in terms of reverberations within and among systems.

CHAPTER 4

Social Interventions with Children

In Chapter 3, the potential usefulness of ecological theory in conceptualizing child advocacy and interventions on behalf of children was discussed. A corollary to this conclusion is that purely individual treatments without attention to intervention in the social context are likely to miss the mark. This chapter is devoted to a review of various modes of intervention when children do not "fit" within their ecosystem. As conceptualized here, the process of advocacy itself can be "therapeutic." At the same time, however, just doing something for or to a child ostensibly in his or her best interests does not constitute child advocacy. Rather, child advocacy is distinguished from other interventions said to be in children's best interests by the emphasis on increasing the accountability and responsiveness of social institutions affecting children.[1] For example, psychotherapy might be a useful intervention for a particular child, but psychotherapy as usually practiced would not constitute child advocacy. This distinction will be explored in detail in Chapter 5, with particular attention to the use of child advocacy as a "clinical" intervention. The purpose of this chapter is briefly to review various social approaches to serving children (without claiming that they are techniques of child advocacy). The literature on established forms of social interventions is instructive in developing techniques of and foci for child advocacy. Furthermore, delivery of direct services may serve as a base for advocacy.

CHILD THERAPY

It should first be noted that it is common for child psychotherapy, at least as currently practiced, to reach beyond the 50-minute weekly session. In a

[1] *See,* for example, the definition of child advocacy by Kahn, Kamerman, and McGowan (1972): "intervention on behalf of children in relation to those services and institutions that impinge on their lives" (p. 63).

national survey of child psychiatrists and clinical child psychologists, Koocher and Pedulla (1977) found that most child therapists do at least some consultation with their patients' teachers. Only 2% never did such consultations, and about one-fifth of the therapists surveyed consulted with teachers on all of their therapy patients. The mean percentage of cases in which there was school consultation (by therapists' self-report) was 63%. This involvement by therapists in the institutions of which their clients are a part is a welcome and perhaps recent phenomenon (Brooks, 1980). However, this entrée into the patients' "real world" is a very circumscribed one. The frequency of therapist–teacher contacts about a particular child ranged from zero to five per year, with the modal frequency being only twice a year (58.2%). Thus, while in child therapy there does not seem to be a professional prohibition against attempts to make the child's environment more supportive, this involvement is in fact quite limited. The interventions beyond the child's own therapy session are primarily with his family and then usually in separate sessions in the "child-guidance" model (Koocher & Pedulla, 1977).

Perhaps as a result of this isolation from the systems affecting the child, there is little evidence for efficacy of child therapy (Levitt, 1957, 1971). Although the effectiveness of adult psychotherapy also is controversial, there is particular reason to expect minimal impact of child therapy without other interventions. There are, of course, theoretical considerations (discussed in Chapter 3) that suggest interactions among social institutions to be important in understanding and treating children. There is also an important pragmatic consideration. Children obviously have less real autonomy than adults. Change in the child is unrealistic without accompanying change in the adults who have responsibility for him or her. If isolated change occurs in the child, it is likely to result in conflict and possibly punishment for the child.

Most of the outcome research currently available indicates that the "spontaneous remission" rate for defectors from child therapy is essentially the same as the improvement rate for children who complete a course of therapy (Levitt, 1957, 1971). About two-thirds of children with neurotic symptoms and about 55% of children with acting-out symptoms improve without treatment. Similar improvement rates have been reported for child therapy.

Problems of Current Outcome Research

It is interesting to note that Levitt's summary of the research did not stimulate the outcry and new body of research that Eysenck's (1952) similar revelation about adult therapy did. It is quite possible, as some critics (Barrett, Hampe, & Miller, 1978; Heinicke & Strassman, 1975) have noted, that the relatively simple question of "Does it work?" is the wrong question. Research aimed at attempting to understand the conditions under which psychotherapy *does* work (Bergin & Suinn, 1973; Gomes-Schwartz, Hadley, & Strupp, 1978) has been more productive, at least for adults. That is, interactions among types of therapists, types of clients, and types of therapies may obscure the overall effects of psychotherapy. In short, the relative dearth of research on child therapy may have left hidden those conditions under which therapy is effective for amelioration of the problems of troubled children.

Research on outcomes of child therapy is in fact quite limited. In Levitt's review in Bergin and Garfield's (1971) *Handbook of Psychotherapy and Behavior Change,* he noted that only 2.2% of the pages on therapy in the *Annual Review of Psychology* since 1950 had been devoted to work with children. Barrett, Hampe, and Miller's review in the second edition of Garfield and Bergin's (1978) *Handbook* showed little new research in the field.

There are a number of reasons for this lack of research on an intervention that is certainly widely practiced. First, the lack of research probably is reflective of the relative lack of attention and resources devoted to children.

Second, the trend in the sixties toward social change, and particularly preventive, social approaches to work with children, may have inhibited research on individual approaches. Indeed, as Barrett et al. (1978) speculated, many child psychologists may have found the negative results unsurprising for the reasons previously discussed. Therefore, they may not have felt the need to disconfirm Levitt's pessimistic summary of the literature.

Third, outcome research on child therapy is intrinsically laden with methodological difficulties and consequently is not reinforcing for "pure" researchers. In addition to the problems of evaluative research in general (e.g., selection of sensitive dependent variables, ethical issues in establishing a control group, etc.), there are special problems in attempting to determine the outcome of child therapy. Levitt (1971) enumerated three of these. There is the general problem of spontaneous remission. Careful controls are necessary to ensure that changes that are observed are not simply the result of maturation. There also is a problem that Levitt called "developmental symptom substitution." That is, emotional disturbance is expressed in different ways at various ages. A child thus may no longer display the behaviors that brought him or her to therapy (or placed the child in the control group), but there may be no real improvement. Finally, there is the variable focus of child therapy. If change occurs, did it result from the child's own therapy or that of his parents, or both?

In short, the existing outcome data on child therapy are not compelling evidence of its effectiveness. The failure to modify the social context of maladaptive behavior may be responsible in large part for the negative findings. At the same time, however, it is premature to say that child therapy does not work. More precisely, most of the complex interactions under which child therapy does work have not yet been specified. It is not clear from available data, for example, what kind of therapist would be most effective in treating a particular kind of child-client. What does seem clear, both intuitively and empirically, is that child therapy is most likely to enhance a child's development if efforts are made simultaneously to adapt the environment to the child's needs and to provide the child with specific skills that will aid him or her in creating a niche for himself or herself. Thus, some specific therapeutic programs with accompanying social interventions have proved successful. Most of the remainder of this chapter will be devoted to such interventions.

VOCATIONAL TREATMENTS

Perhaps the clearest and best documented examples of a "skills" approach to treatment have been programs aimed at enhancing general ego functioning of a youngster by providing him or her with skills useful in the world of work. Within our society a large part of one's identity clearly involves one's identity as a worker. As Erikson (1964) has pointed out, even in childhood one's sense of personal worth is in large part determined by his or her sense of "industry." In the eyes both of adult authorities and of the child himself or herself, one is esteemed according to his or her value as a worker, what one can *do*. Without the *competencies* necessary to be accepted or "fit" within a social system, "insight" is likely to be of little use.[2] On the other hand, development of social, academic, and vocational skills alone should have pay-off in the overall well-being of the child or adolescent. An increase both in matches with social expectations (and, therefore, in the probability of rewards) and in general ego strength and sense of active mastery would be expected. Given the percentage of waking hours that it consumes, it is not surprising that personal satisfaction throughout the lifespan is heavily influenced by the meaning one finds in work

---

[2]The concept of "learned helplessness" (Seligman, 1975) is relevant here. With a history of repeated failures, the youth cannot be expected to be mobilized in his or her own behalf. Only when he or she is pushed into experiences with mastery and positive reinforcement can such efforts be expected. One must learn that experiences need not be aversive or unrewarding. Bibring's (1954) concept of the "paralyzed ego" as a key element in depression is an analogous development in psychoanalytic theory.

(Sarason, 1977). Consequently, treatment programs that have proven successful in reaching youth alienated from and by society often have included a specific emphasis on building prevocational and vocational skills.

The Need for Social Change

The discussion thus far has emphasized helping the youngster to become competent within his ecosystem. It should be noted that successful vocational treatment programs also require a "systems change" in order to give youth opportunities for career development. As Shore and Massimo (1979) have noted, programs for "hard-to-reach" adolescents often have failed because, when a vocational element is included, it typically involves "meaningless" or "dead-end" jobs. Current official estimates of youth employment are 30% to 40%, with unemployment rates for minority youth soaring even higher.

Indeed, as Bakan (1971) has compellingly shown, a social function of child labor laws, compulsory education, and the juvenile court has been to place adolescents in a special dependent status shielded from productive work. It is arguable that adolescent "Sturm und Drang" did not even exist as a common phenomenon before the development of these social institutions (Bakan, 1971; Kett, 1974). Adolescents in this society have been placed in a lengthy period of conflict between adult and infantile roles.

This heightened dependency and isolation from work has been exacerbated by the American high school. There is usually no ready opportunity for trying out various occupational roles and developing work skills. At the least, schoolwork has been isolated from the experiences of the workplace. Grinder (1978) has described the situation well:

> The school has replaced the experiential learning that once took place in the family and workplace with the "student role" in which adolescents wait to be taught. The school has kept the classroom as its main mode of teaching, and as it has changed emphases in socialization from learning through experience to learning via instruction, it has reduced the student role to a passive one in which the adolescents are always in preparation for active work but never actually engaged in it. One consequence of separating learning from action and experience has been to segregate youth from adults. They have been removed from the labor market and their contacts with adult models in working situations has become highly limited. Moreover, the contact that they do have with adults ensues from highly specialized relationships, and they meet them less as persons than as technicians or specific subject-matter experts—as teachers, dentists, lawyers, doctors, garage mechanics, and so forth. (p. 554)

Thus, while vocational programs have an aim of changing the youngster, of making him or her more competent, the *implementation* of such programs usually will require intensive advocacy for institutional changes. Not only must jobs be created for youth (no small task in a recessionary economy), but to a large extent assumptions about the "proper" role for children and youth must be altered.

Vocationally Oriented Psychotherapy

An excellent example of a "real-world" adaptation of psychotherapeutic techniques is Massimo and Shore's (1963) vocationally oriented psychotherapy. The initial example of this program was a small demonstration project with only 10 boys in the treatment program. Consequently, its applicability on a large scale has yet to be proven,[3] and Massimo and Shore did not have to face the implementation problems encountered by more ambitious endeavors. Nonetheless, vocationally oriented psychotherapy is worthy of discussion for two reasons. First, it is exemplary of a skills-based intervention into virtually the child's whole lifespace. Second, Massimo and Shore have conducted follow-up evaluations over a period of 15 years that have documented the long-term effectiveness of a comprehensive vocationally oriented program in adolescence. This thoroughness of follow-up evaluation is almost unique. (For a follow-up of a delinquency program of similar time span, but with negative results, see McCord, 1978; commentary by Sobel, 1978.)

Participants in Massimo and Shore's demonstration project were suburban adolescent boys aged 15 to 17 who were of normal intelligence and nonpsychotic. They all had a history of antisocial behavior with "a reputation familiar to attendance officers, courts, or police." The treatment program began at a crisis point when the boy was expelled from school or dropped out. Initial contact was offered as a means of help in "getting a job." The initial focus of treatment accordingly was on expectations and attitudes in regard to work. After job placement, the focus shifted to job performance and problems encountered on the job. Thus, the therapy always was focused on events in the work situation.

Beyond the reality focus in an important sphere of the boys' lives, the most significant characteristic of the program was its comprehensiveness. Each boy had a single therapist who was available any time of day or night, often as many as 8 or 10 times per week. The breadth of involvement was

---

[3]Some of the War on Poverty programs (e.g., Job Corps, Neighborhood Youth Corps) were based on similar concepts, but they lacked both the comprehensiveness and the rigorous evaluation of Massimo and Shore's program. Furthermore, the meaningfulness of the job opportunities (for example, forestry camps for inner-city youngsters) was questionable.

such that it verged on what will be discussed later in this chapter as "clinical advocacy":

> Motility and action were emphasized. The therapist had no central office, and made frequent field trips when necessary. In essence, the therapist entered all areas of the adolescent's life. Job finding, court appearances, pleasure trips, driving lessons when appropriate, locating and obtaining a car, arranging for a dentist appointment, going for glasses, shopping for clothes with a first pay check, opening a bank account and other activities require this maximum commitment. (Massimo & Shore, 1963, p. 636)

The results of this intensive 10-month intervention were impressive. The treated boys showed improvements in academic achievement (Massimo & Shore, 1963), positive attitudes toward others (Shore, Massimo, Kesielewski, & Moran, 1966), and future orientation (Ricks, Umbarger, & Mack, 1974). Compared to controls, the treatment group had better employment and court records (Massimo & Shore, 1963).

These short-term gains started most members of the treated group in a positive direction that has been maintained well into their adult years. Conversely, most members of the control group have continued in maladaptive behavior. Follow-up evaluations have been conducted after two years (Shore & Massimo, 1966), five years (Shore & Massimo, 1969), 10 years (Shore & Massimo, 1973), and 15 years (Shore & Massimo, 1979). In general, the experimental group's adult adjustment has been quite superior to that of the control group in vocational, marital, legal, and educational areas. For example, the treated subjects have had more stable and higher status job histories.

It is unclear which aspects of vocationally oriented psychotherapy as designed by Massimo and Shore were particularly potent. Perhaps, however, the key element was the comprehensive attention to the boys' adaptation within their own social situations. That is, the ecological basis and comprehensiveness itself were particularly important. The authors themselves have implied that, at least for the "hard-to-reach" group for whom the program was designed, the program should not be "watered down" if it is to be effective (Shore & Massimo, 1979).

New Haven's Residential Youth Center

Another well-documented community-based comprehensive program with a primary focus on job counseling and training was the Residential Youth Center (Goldenberg, 1971). The RYC differed from Massimo and-Shore's vocationally oriented psychotberapy in several major respects, however. First, the participants were inner-city, lower-class, and probably even "harder-to-reach" than the group in Massimo and Shore's project. In fact, the 25 participants chosen for the demonstration project had been identified by New Haven agencies as the most "hard-core" in the community. They had extensive histories of institutional custody or treatment. Second, the RYC was obviously residential and group oriented. Third, the explicit focus of the program design was on the staff and not the residents. Goldenberg and his colleagues worked hard at the creation of a setting that was "horizontal" and staffed and managed by indigeneous paraprofessional counsellors. Indeed, the bulk of the volume describing the RYC (Goldenberg, 1971) concerns the staff's development. The horizonality of the RYC extended to staff–resident relationships as well. Residents were actively involved in the program's governance and were able to come and go more or less as they pleased.

Despite these differences, however, Goldenberg's and Massimo and Shore's programs had in common both program focus and, to a large extent, program technique. In both programs, therapists were available on call and became involved in "their kids'" lives in a variety of settings and many problem areas. Contacts were not limited to the office but rather occurred in the multiple settings in which the adolescents spent their time. In neither instance did therapists feel it an intrusion on their relationship to help a youngster to find a job or otherwise venture into "reality problems."

Even without positive results, the RYC would have been significant for the detailed study of the process of creation of a setting (see Sarason, 1972). The results that *were* obtained lend the probram still more significance. The experimental group had significantly better work attendance, job complexity, and wages. They were also less alienated and had a more positive world view. On follow-up after six months, their arrest rate and time spent in jail had decreased significantly (49% and 54% respectively). In contrast, the controls had experienced deterioration in employment record, psychological well-being (especially interpersonal trust), and arrest record and days spent in jail (22% and 84% increases respectively).

Taken in combination, the Massimo and Shore and RYC programs suggest that even "hard-core" youngsters can be reached when two key conditions are met: (a) the youth is taught skills to enable him or her to function in the workplace and the broader society and (b) of particular import in the present context, the "therapist" also functions as an advocate who helps the youngster to find a job and generally to increase the fit between the youngster and "the system."

EDUCATIONAL TREATMENTS

Similar to the skills orientation of the programs described in the previous section, a number of model programs have sought to improve maladjusted children's social and cognitive functioning through educational interventions (see, e.g., Zax & Cowen, 1976, Chapter 18). Of most direct analogy are those programs that have combined an educational, problem-solving approach to help the child to adapt to the environment with an attempt to restructure the child's environment to make the setting more conducive to his or her development. A frequently cited example of this genre of programs is Project Re-ED (Hobbs, 1966). Re-ED is an effort to treat seriously disturbed children through intensive education rather than psychotherapy. A group of residential schools, Re-ED is staffed primarily by teacher-counselors "who can handle mental health concepts and vocabulary and have the skills of an effective recreation leader, handyman, personal counselor, and parent substitute" (Zax & Cowen, 1976, p. 518). In addition, each unit of eight children has a "liaison-teacher" who stays in constant touch with the children's home schools prior to, during, and after their stay at Re-ED in order to ensure coordination with the home school environment and shaping of it to support the child's personal growth. Children educated for a brief time at Re-ED have in fact shown impressive improvement when they return to their communities (Weinstein, 1969; see review of unpublished evaluations by Weinstein in Zax & Cowen, 1976).

Re-ED has involved a relatively small number of quite disturbed children in a residential setting. The principles of emphasis on skill building and a blending of cognitive and affective education while shaping the environment have been demonstrated in a number of broader social contexts. In particular, there have been several intensively evaluated model educational programs designed to enhance mental health and prevent serious problems.

Rochester Primary Mental Health Project

Prevention programs can be conceptualized according to the point in the development of problems at which the intervention takes place. *Primary prevention* involves interventions designed to eliminate the conditions that might result in disturbance before such disorders actually occur. *Secondary prevention* consists of interventions aimed at alleviating disorders before they become serious; "early intervention" programs typically belong in this category. Finally, *tertiary prevention* involves efforts to halt the course of serious dysfunction and to minimize its effects. Tertiary prevention is a misnomer in that there really is nothing prevented. The disorder already exists; the task becomes one of rehabilitation rather than prevention.

Perhaps the most extensively researched educational treatment program is a secondary prevention program: the Primary Mental Health Project developed over the past two decades by Emory Cowen and his colleagues at the University of Rochester. There have been literally scores of articles describing and evaluating PMHP. A brief summary will be attempted here; the reader interested in a more detailed description of the program should see the monograph by Cowen, Trost, Lorion, Dorr, Izzo, and Issacson (1975). Cowen et al. used brief teacher checklists and brief psychological and social-work assessments to do mass screenings in order to identify ("Red Tag") children at risk in the primary grades in several Rochester-area school districts. This global Red Tag/Non-Red Tag judgment is in fact reasonably predictive of later school performance and general adjustment. One-third of Rochester children were classified as Red Tag, but more than two-thirds of these children later appeared (over an 11- to 13-year period) in the Cumulative Psychiatric Register of relatively more serious mental health contacts. Their school performance also was significantly poorer than that of non-Red Tag children, at least through seventh grade.[4]

Early detection is meaningless without an attempt then to intervene. Given the numbers involved, an efficient means of service delivery was needed. Cowen decided to train nonprofessionals—specifically, housewives—as "child aides" to work with the children identified as Red Tag. Professionals' roles shifted to personnel selection and training and to general consultation.

As PMHP expanded to numerous schools, the heterogenity of the program increased and opportunities for control groups decreased. Thus, methodological rigor was sacrificed to some degree in favor of service demands and results were not always consistent. However, taken in sum, the outcome research is impressive. Relative to controls and to pupils treated by college

---

[4]In their 1975 summary of their work, Cowen et al. did not address the difficult ethical problems raised by early detection programs. Does labeling as "Red Tag" in fact increase the probability of behaving as if there really is a serious problem present? Perhaps the best defenses to this argument are that (1) teachers already had identified the Red Tag as children doing poorly in school and that (2) untreated Red Tag children in fact do much worse over time than children who go through PMHP. Interestingly in terms of the former point, negative peer sociometric ratings at age nine were the best predictors of later psychiatric problems.

volunteers, Red Tag students involved in the aide program improved significantly more, according to teachers' ratings. Furthermore, there is evidence from interviews with mothers that these gains are sustained over several years.

Although early detection and use of nonprofessionals are the key elements in PMHP's secondary prevention efforts, another interesting element of the program, perhaps key to its implementation, has been the use of a "team" in the schools. In addition to the project staff (i.e., child aides, school mental health professionals, and university consultants), the teachers and administrators are actively involved in treatment planning for individual children and in seminars and consultation sessions. Although there are "political" aspects to this inclusion (i.e., PMHP founders were well aware of their status as "guests" on school turf), there were important conceptual reasons as well. Besides teachers' contributing valuable observations about the children, their participation has resulted in increased sensitivity to children's needs and increased skill in dealing with "different" children.

This integration of staffs was not without incident. In the early days of the program, some teachers felt uncomfortable about the aides' higher level of training in child development and about unclarity of divisions of role and authority. In some cases teachers responded to these concerns by limiting children's access to the aides. Because of these role-boundary problems, the term *child* aide (rather than *teacher's* aide) was ultimately adopted. Perhaps in part as a result of the teachers' eventual involvement and investment in the program, however, there were discernible changes in the climate of many of the participating schools. A number of principals commented about a new calmness in their schools and a marked decrease in discipline problems. The following is representative of principals' comments reported by Cowen et al. (1975):

> Primary Project creates an atmosphere of understanding in the school. Instead of griping, as teachers do from time to time about "naughty" kids, it's my impression that they are now much more willing to seek ways for helping them. They are initiating face-to-face contacts with project personnel. As a result of working more constructively, and therefore more effectively, with difficult children, the whole atmosphere of the classroom is calmer, quieter. (p. 288)

PMHP is thus illustrative of the way in which individual cases can be used to foster systems change. On the other hand, it is a good example of the need to consider issues concerning systemic structure and entree before beginning interventions on behalf of individual children.

Interpersonal Cognitive Problem-Solving Training

Although Cowen's work has involved early secondary prevention almost exclusively, another widely researched educationally based treatment program, Spivack and Shure's Interpersonal Cognitive Problem-Solving (ICPS) training (Shure & Spivack, 1978; Spivack & Shure, 1975; Spivack, Platt, & Shure, 1976), has variously involved primary, secondary, and even tertiary prevention. ICPS training is more "psychological" than the other programs reviewed in this chapter in the sense that it is intended to alter specific cognitive processes. The basic premise is that the way in which a child perceives and thinks through problems affects the quality of his or her responses. Although the power of specific ICPS skills varies across age groups (see Spivack et al., 1976, Chapters 2–5), Spivack et al. have identified five ICPS skills that mediate the quality of a youngster's social adjustment. The particular skills that Spivack et al. (1976) have studied include:

[a] an awareness of the variety of possible problems that beset human interactions and a sensitivity to the existence of an interpersonal problem or at least to the potential get together ... (p. 5)

[b] the capacity to generate alternative solutions to problems ... (p. 5)

[c] articulating the step-by-step means that may be necessary in order to carry out the solution to any interpersonal problem [means–end thinking] ... (p. 5)

[d] considering the consequences of one's social acts in terms of their impact on other people and on oneself [consequential thinking] ... (p. 6)

[e] the degree to which the individual understands and is ready to appreciate that how one feels and acts may have been influenced by (and, in turn, may have influenced) how others feel and act. (pp. 6–7)

Spivack and Shure have developed curricula that can be used to foster these interpersonal cognitive problem-solving skills. Of particular import for preventive efforts is the fact that these curricula do not require professional backgrounds for persons actually carrying out the program. Therefore, given evidence that ICPS mediate adjustment, it might be possible to use ICPS training programs as cost-efficient primary and secondary prevention measures.[5]

In Spivack and Shure's (1974) initial studies involving ICPS training, they had worked with a group of 4- and 5-year-old inner-city children who already were demonstrating behavioral problems. Well adjusted children in this age group already had been demonstrated to be differentiated from the

---

[5]See Urbain and Kendall (1980) for a comprehensive review of studies of the effectiveness of social-cognitive interventions with children.

target group in this secondary prevention effort on the basis of degree to which they could generate alternative solutions to interpersonal problems (e.g., a conflict with another child over a toy). After three months, children in the target group who received ICPS training showed substantial improvement. Inhibited children became more outgoing, more aware of their feelings, and better liked. Aggressive children became less impatient and less aggressive. Moreover, these gains persisted at least through first grade.[6]

In later work (Shure & Spivack, 1978), the feasibility of achieving these effects through parent training was successfully demonstrated. Mothers' own ICPS were found to predict their behavior with their children (i.e., the degree to which they explained to their children solutions and consequences when the children had interpersonal problems). Furthermore, the mothers' means–end thinking in adult interpersonal situations was found to be highly correlated with their facility for means–end thinking in childrearing situations. It was thus suggested that children's adjustment might be indirectly affected by training their mothers in ICPS. Such training did indeed result in improved ICPS of the mothers themselves, improved ICPS of their children, and improved school behavior by the children.

Still more indirectly, training of teachers in social problem-solving curricula has been found to be an effective means of primary prevention. In one such program (Allen, Chinsky, Larcen, Lochman, & Selinger, 1976), adoption of a problem-solving curriculum resulted in increased problem-solving skills, both in hypothetical situations and in Structured Real-Life Problems (behavioral samples). Children also developed more internal locus of control and greater expectation of success in making friends.

In earlier less sophisticated work concerning the *specific* social-cognitive skills that are involved in a child's social adaptation, Ojemann (1961) demonstrated similar effects of programs to train teachers in facilitating "casual thinking." Although conceptualized more broadly, causal thinking appears to subsume Spivack and Shure's means–end thinking and consequential thinking: "a 'causal individual' . . . is one who is sensitive to the probable future consequences of behavior, as well as to how behavior develops from the past" (p. 379).

In short, Spivack and Shure's work is an excellent example of the interweaving between personal and social factors in a child's adjustment. More-

[6]While there was a no-treatment control group for this research, there was not an attention-only group. The conclusion that the positive results achieved were directly the consequence of changes in ICPS is therefore somewhat equivocal.

over, it is an example of a program that can be implemented by teachers, parents, and paraprofessionals on a large-scale basis to prevent mental health problems through development of social competencies. ICPS training can be an effective blend of educational and community interventions.

Primary Prevention

There is ample evidence that increasing teachers' attention to children's emotional needs can facilitate their pupils' adjustment and achievement. For example, in another prong of Allen et al.'s (1976) "behaviorally oriented multi-level preventive approach" to community/school psychology, teachers of children with identified psychological problems were trained in behavioral analysis techniques. The program was conceptualized as "tertiary prevention" of the children's behavior disorders. In fact, the teacher training did result in the teachers' using verbal reinforcement of positive behavior more frequently and their observing children's behavior more accurately. Not surprisingly, the changes in teacher behavior translated into changes in the behavior of the target children; their "on-task" behavior increased significantly. Of most interest in the present context, however, is that the program had a spillover primary-preventive effect on children without identified behavioral disorders. Children in the classrooms of trained teachers generally showed improvement in on-task behavior. Thus, although the training was focused on positive responses to particular children, the teachers learned to use behavioral techniques in a more generalized way to support the growth and positive behavior of other children in the class as well.

From a somewhat different theoretical perspective and with a different focus, "affective education" programs have been demonstrated to have similar effects (see, e.g., Griggs & Bonney, 1970; Kilmann, Henry, Scarbro, & Laughlin, 1979; Long, 1971; Stilwell, 1978; Weinstein & Fantini, 1970). Such programs would be expected to facilitate children's mental health and psychological development—including cognitive development—for several reasons:

1. As implied earlier in this section, training teachers to teach children about feelings may have the side effect of making the teachers more responsive to the children's needs.
2. As represented by Spivack and Shure's work, social and emotional functioning in fact involves a number of concrete skills that must be learned.
3. Learning is facilitated by some degree of affective arousal and emotional investment in the subject matter.

The final point is worthy of more discussion. Perhaps the most articulate exponent of the theory that learning is tied to affective arousal has been Des Lauriers (1971). He has postulated a theory of personality growth that states that ego development is a function of learning process—a striving for autonomy—that requires some degree of affective arousal. Des Lauriers has argued specifically that the reinforcing nature of rewards is based not so much on the temporal relationship of stimuli and responses as on

> their capacity . . . to create an effective state of arousal in the child which permits the assimilation of new experiences and their consolidation into habitual, learned forms of responses. The learned process in the child is so closely related to the level of the child's affective arousal at any one time, that only those forms of behavior will be truly learned which can become part of the child's total effort at expressing his autonomy through the assertion of his mastery over his own body and over the objects of his environment. (p. 196)

In order for psychological growth in occur, a state of "optimal arousal" that alerts the child to novel stituations and reinforces his mastering them is required. From Des Lauriers's point of view, it is only in such an affective climate that "meaningful" learning (i.e., learning that contributes to ego development) can occur.

The relevant experimental psychology literature is in fact largely supportive of Des Lauriers's theory. There are numerous studies suggesting that learning that takes place during an arousal increment is more likely to be retained long-term.[7] In addition to their role in retention, affective variables seem to play an especially important part in the acquisitional phase of learning. Specifically, arousal seems to be directly related to both exploratory behavior and attentional phenomena (Berlyne, 1960, 1963, 1964; Levonian, 1966). Taken together, these findings suggest that the job of the teacher in some sense is quite literally to "turn on" the students. Moreover, it is not too much of a jump from the experimental data to the commonsense conclusion that students' learning is directly related to the general affective climate of the school.

This conclusion leads to antoher point. Most of the existing primary prevention work in schools has been directed toward building *individual* children's skills. As suggested in the discussion of the work of Spivack and Shure and of the Primary Mental Health Project, these programs are of considerable practical significance as relatively inexpensive means of enhancing children's development. Relatively little work has been devoted to primary prevention

[7]E.g., Deffenbacher, Platt, and Williams, 1974; Geen, 1973; Kleinsmith and Kaplan, 1963, 1964; Levonian, 1967, 1968, 1972; McLean, 1969; Walker and Tarte, 1963.

through efforts to change schools as *institutions* to be more conducive to children's mental health (cf. Sarason, 1971).

This lack of attention to primary prevention through basic institutional change should perhaps be unsurprising. As Novaco and Monahan (1980) clearly showed in their analysis of articles published in the *American Journal of Community Psychology,* the actual foci of work by community psychologists have seldom matched the rhetoric of commitment to systems change and primary prevention. For example, using a generous definition of "prevention" (i.e., a mention by the authors of an article that they were concerned with prevention), only about 13% of articles published in *AJCP* were concerned with prevention and few of them involved *primary* prevention (2.4%, primary prevention; 10.2%, secondary prevention). There are probably at least three reasons for this lack of productivity in the area of prevention.[8] First, as discussed in more detail in Chapter 5, psychologists (and other mental health professionals) may, by the nature of their training, be "stuck" at an individual level of analysis of problems. Second, changing institutions may require a technology that remains to be developed. Simply put, it is more difficult to implement change in large complex institutions than in individuals. Third, severely disturbed persons—particularly severely disturbed adults—are both bothersome and obviously in need of help. Given this fact (and children's generally low status),[9] primary prevention is likely to remain a low priority, even though the latter would ultimately be more cost-efficient in both human and fiscal terms. Funding patterns have in fact been biased toward research on, and treatment of, already existing conditions. This reality is likely to persist (and indeed become worse) in a political climate in which "social research" is perceived as undermining traditional social institutions and as outside government's legitmate domain.

In short, there are both professional and political constraints on mental health professionals' having significant effects in fostering social climates supportive of children's healthy development. Ultimately, primary prevention, particularly at institutional and societal levels, may involve "pure" child advocacy rather than clinical or even community psychology. Basic political and social changes are involved. At the same time, however, psychology may be able to inform as to the nature of factors enhancing, or adversely affecting,

---

[8]It should be noted, however, that there is now a *Journal of Prevention* solely devoted to this topic.

[9]It is recognized that primary prevention need not be limited to children. However, because childhood is obviously important as the "formative" period, primary prevention typically is discussed in terms of children's programs (cf. Rappaport, 1977, chapter 7).

children's development and consequently to assist in setting the agenda for child advocacy.

Renfrow: Some Prevention Issues. A recent federal case *(Doe v. Renfrow)*[10] concerning an Indiana school system is a good example. The facts of the case were as follows. Officials of Highland Town School District had become concerned about what they perceived as a significant drug problem in their junior and senior high schools. They had no reason to suspect any *particular* student (students caught with drugs already had been expelled) and, as Judge Swygert noted in a dissent on appeal to the Seventh Circuit, "conditions [with respect to drug use] at the Highland schools were at least average and could well have been better than at most other schools."[11] Nonetheless, Superintendent Renfrow and his colleagues concocted an elaborate and plainly outrageous plan to subject all of the junior and senior high students in the district to a canine search. Judge Swygert vividly described the events that ensued:

> The raids began at 8:45 A.M. on March 23, 1979. The searchers were divided into teams consisting of at least one dog, one dog handler, one school administrator or teacher, and one or two uniformed police officers. Fourteen dogs were on hand. For the duration of the raid, all schoolhouse doors were either locked or tightly guarded by police and school officals. All students were detained in their first period classrooms; any late arrivers or visitors were led to and detained in a room set aside for that purpose. No student was allowed to leave his or her classroom, and if any claimed to need to use the lavatory facilities, school or police authorities escorted and watched over them.
>
> Every student was instructed to place his belongings in view and his hands on his desk. Girls placed their purses on the floor between their feet. The teams of searchers moved from room to room, and from desk to desk. Every single student was sniffed, inspected, and examined at least once by a dog and a joint school–police team. The extraordinary atmosphere at the school was supplemented still further when representatives of the press and other news media, invited in by school authorities, entered the schoolhouses and classrooms during the raid and observed the searchers while in progress.
>
> The raid lasted about three hours. After the sniffing and examination of 2,780 students, the searchers found fifteen high school students—and no junior high students—in possession of illicit materials. School and police authorities removed five high school students—three girls and two boys—from their classrooms and subjected them to personal interrogations and thorough, but not nude, searches. None was found to be in possession of any contraband. Three or four junior high students

---

[10]475 F. Supp. 1012 (N.D. Ind. 1979); *remanded in part and aff'd in part,* 631 F.2d 91 (7th Cir.1980); *rehearing en banc denied,* 635 F.2d 582 (1980); *cert. denied,* 49 U.S.L.W. 3880 (5/26/81). *See* Melton (in preparation) for detailed discussion of the psycholegal issues in *Renfrow.*

[11]631 F.2d 91, 93.

were similarly treated and cleared. Four junior students—all girls—were removed from class, stripped nude, and interrogated. Not one of them was found to possess any illicit material.[12]

Diane Doe, age 13, was one of the girls humiliated by a strip search. In retrospect, the dog probably "alerted" to her because she had been playing that morning with her dog, which was in heat. (In fact, 33 of the 50 students to whom the police dogs alerted had no contraband.) Diane claimed a violation of her constitutional rights under the Fourth, Ninth, and Fourteenth Amendments and sued the school and police administrators.

Incredibly, the federal district judge, Allen Sharp, held that the canine search was not in fact a "search" under the Fourth Amendment, that pocket searches of students to whom the dogs alerted were a reasonable exercise of the school officials' authority in loco parentis, and that the strip search was an unreasonable invasion of privacy but one for which the school officals acting in good faith bore no liability for damages. On appeal, the Seventh Circuit reversed only on the issue of the school officials's immunity from suit for damages. Finally, with Justice Brennan in lone dissent, the Supreme Court denied certiorari (refused to hear the case).

The legal merits of Diane Doe's case, which I believe to be quite strong (see Melton, in preparation), are beyond our discussion here. Of considerable interest in the present context, however, are the psychological assumptions underlying Judge Sharp's opinion. His understanding of privacy in childhood and adolescence defies both common sense and psychological research (e.g., Wolfe, 1979) on the subject. A few quotes from the opinion are illustrative:

> No incidents of disruption occurred in the classrooms because of the presence of the dogs or the teams.[13]
>
> Students are exposed to various intrusions into their classroom environment. The presence of the canine team for several minutes was a minimal intrusion at best and not so serious as to invoke the protections of the Fourth Amendment.[14]
>
> Any expectation of privacy necessarily diminishes in light of a student's constant supervision while in school. Because of the constant interaction among students, faculty and school administrators, a public school student cannot be said to enjoy any absolute expectation of privacy while in the classroom setting.[15]
>
> Respect for individual dignity of the student was carefully maintained. A light relaxed atmosphere was created. The effect was anything but a gestapo-like effort run by gestapo-type people.[16]

---

[12]Id.
[13]475 F. Supp at 1017.
[14]Id. at 1019.
[15]Id. at 1022.
[16]Id. at 1026.

Presumably Judge Sharp's misconceptions about adolescents' need for and conceptions of privacy are shared by the Highland school administrators, assuming that they did act in "good faith." Doubtless the climate of the Highland schools even before the dragnet search was quite authoritarian and destructive, without basic respect for the personal dignity of the students. At a minimum, such an atmosphere retards development of a sense of tolerance for diversity and of understanding of democratic principles (Kohlberg & Turiel, 1971; Melton, 1982).[17] Moreover, there actually may be a cost in terms of classroom discipline. Although low in teacher control, alternative high schools not only show a high emphasis on personal relationships among teachers and students and on innovation in educational practices but also on order and organization and rule clarity (Trickett, 1978).

The situation in the Highland schools was extreme. Fortunately, dragnet searches are not an everyday occurrence in American public schools. Nonetheless, a lack of respect for privacy and individual rights of children is, if not ubiquitous, certainly not uncommon in American public schools (see Jackson, 1966). To the extent to which such a climate represents fundamental views of children and the proper role of school authority, it is unlikely to be amenable to change by usual preventive mental health intervention. Even if consultants obtained entree into the Highland schools, it is unlikely that their domain would have included these basic programmatic issues.

Ultimately such change in schools probably will require political action. Advocates can "blow the whistle" on settings disrespectful of children as persons and organize parents to express their concern. At the same time, however, psychologists can provide "expert" information about the effects on children of denying privacy, or more positively, of providing a supportive environment in which children are in fact recognized as having personal rights. Nonetheless, to the extent to which primary prevention entails basic changes in the climate of schools and other institutions, advocacy, rather than consultation

---

[17]Justice Brennan acknowledged this point in his dissent on denial of certiorari:

> We do not know what class petitioner was attending when the police and dogs burst in, but the lesson the school authorities taught her that day will undoubtedly make a greater impression than the one her teacher had hoped to convey. I would grant certiorari to teach petitioner another lesson: that the Fourth Amendment protects "the right of the people to be secure in their persons, houses, papers, and effects, against unreasonable searches and seizures," and that before police and local officers are permitted to conduct dog-assisted dragnet inspections of public school students, they must obtain a warrant based on sufficient particularized evidence to establish probable cause to believe a crime has been or is being committed. Schools cannot expect their students to learn the lessons of good citizenship when the school authorities themselves disregard the fundamental principles underpinning our constitutional freedoms. (49 U.S.L.W. at 3881).

or other techniques typically in the mental health professional's arsenal, is likely to be the means by which prevention is achieved.

PROBLEMS OF IMPLEMENTATION

The programs described earlier in this chapter may raise similar issues. They generally were resource-rich demonstration programs, which may bear little resemblance to the "real world" of service delivery. The problem of implementation of these innovations presents at least one issue bridging "pure" clinical/community intervention and child advocacy. No matter how effective an intervention may be demonstrated to be in a particular social context, such a program is empty in another context if it cannot be implemented there. Too frequently clinicians have naively begun an intervention without attention to the politics of entree or the system-specific implementation hurdles in "natural" settings. Whether more properly viewed as art or as science, the effectiveness of the clinical enterprise simply cannot be evaluated independent of the social setting.

This principle has been best demonstrated in terms of behavior modification programs. Skinner (1971), of course, has discussed behavior modification as a social technology that could profitably be applied to the resolution of broad social problems and, indeed, could serve as the basis of a utopian society (Skinner, 1948). However, in a series of articles, Reppucci and Saunders have noted that behavior modifiers generally have not demonstrated success in changing relatively confined settings, such as prisons and hospitals, much less society as a whole. The basic reason, they argue, is a lack of attention to problems of implementation. In a 1974 article in *American Psychologist,* Reppucci and Saunders identified eight such problems:

1. *Institutional constraints.* Large institutions typically have considerable "red tape" and general administrative structures in place which make consistent alterations of contingencies difficult and perhaps impossible.
2. *External pressure.* Flexibility in response to external political demands is a fact of life in administering a facility. Such flexibility may be inconsistent with a behavior modification program.
3. *Language.* "Behavior Modification" and related terms sound "unhumanistic." The aversive images associated with such terms may result

in resistance to implementation of any behavior modification programs (Saunders & Reppucci, 1978).

4. *Two populations.* The staff's behaviors must be altered before clients' can be. Given civil service and union rules, there may be little room for the former changes (Reppucci, 1977).

5. *Limited resources.*

6. *Labeling.* The labels used to describe organizational activities are often inexact and may lead to confusion.

7. *Perceived inflexibility.* Because of his or her programmatic need to maintain clear, consistent contingencies, the behavior modifier may be viewed as passive-aggressive and inflexible.

8. *Compromise.* Therefore, the behavior modifier will have to compromise on many of the procedures that in theory should work.

Saunders and Reppucci (1978) have argued further that insensitivity to these problems of implementation has resulted in a spiraling series of failures of "real-life" behavioral community interventions.

> [B]ehavior modifiers have yet to take seriously the possibility that there are settings into which transfer may be impossible in which failure is unavoidable, and where a clear decision not to intervene is the better part of valor and good sense. While the assumption of universal applicability for behavior modification may be valid *in theory,* it is not necessarily valid in the real world of limited resources, politics, finances, and so forth. Every decision to implement where inappropriate is a potential contributor to a growing list of program failures but also to a negative social identity for behavior modification. Therefore, it is essential that behavior modifiers assume the task of learning to identify the "fitness" of natural environments with regard to their adaptibility to behavior modification programs, giving equal weight to the possibility that they should not intervene. (p. 152)

Given the social reality that Reppucci and Saunders have described, it is hard in some sense to imagine successful clinical-community innovations *without* advocacy, especially where the interventions involve systemic change in relatively intractable, bureaucratized complex institutions. In such instances, there almost inevitably will be a need for external pressure and advocacy before the service program can be fully implemented. Viewed in such a light, direct-service providers—at least those who look beyond the 50-minute hour—*need* child advocates to help to "grease the skids" of program implementation.

Particularly in the contemporary context of declining resources for social programs and of a prevailing "fiscal conservatism" that favors "guns" over "butter," even the most well-conceived programs require the support and political manipulation of skillful advocates before they can begin to serve children and youth.[18] To the extent to which the prevailing political and economic ethos precipitates infighting for scarce resources among those seeking to serve children, problems of entree are likely to become increasingly intense and increasingly complex. Locally administered block grants as primary sources of funding almost assure that complex political maneuvering will be necessary to implement significant program innovation and reform. In the face of fights for small pots of money with ambiguous strings attached, bureaucratic "resistances" seem certain to intensify and to make "normal" implementation problems more difficult.[19] The "good guys" indeed are likely to become the competitors.

The problems described thus far are involved in "just" implementing relatively discrete interventions. When the locus of intervention rises to *fundamental* problems of "loot and clout," the need for advocacy becomes still more obvious, if indeed the technology is at all available for such basic socioeconomic changes. Implementing a "Great Society" for children and families requires more than good intentions. To the extent to which the social technology is available, the real arena is likely to be midst the clash of advocates rather than of service providers. If often insensitive to the implementation problems involving their own services, clinicans trained to identify and treat *individual* problems are likely to become lost when attempting to design large-scale social interventions and indeed may be resistant to such changes.

Warren's (1971) account of the role of mental health in planning for the Model Cities program is exemplary. In an attitudinal survey of helping professionals during planning for this program to provide aid to deteriorating urban neighborhoods, mental health services were perceived to be of low priority, particularly by mental health professionals themselves. Of particular interest here, however, was the low emphasis that mental health professionals, espe-

---

[18]The importance of advocacy in such a political climate was starkly demonstrated in the jockeying for funds in the first Reagan budget. Two groups that effectively mobilized their constituencies (i.e., veterans and old people) were able to prevent proposed cuts. In both cases, of course, there were vote-rich groups involved; it is quite the opposite with children.

[19]Although the focus in this discussion is on changes in relationships among agencies and individuals (i.e., "positions") created by the shrinking pie, there are other related problems. For example, Reppucci (1977) has discussed the difficulties that narrow civil-service rules and job descriptions can present. The developer of institutional programs may have little control over who is charged with actually running a program or how they do it. Given staffing cutbacks, this problem is likely to be exacerbated. The most senior employees are likely to be retained regardless of their level of training or motivation and of the nature of current staffing needs.

cially psychiatrists and mental health administrators, placed on basic systems change. The administrators also particularly devalued citizen participation in the planning process. Thus, where trained to think in terms of individual pathology or of service delivery as a management problem, professionals were uninclined to support programs designed to enhance low-income citizens' control over their environment. It is perhaps at this point that the interests of clinicians and advocates are most likely to part. Child advocacy, whether by clinicians themselves or by other groups, may be necessary before children's programs are to be implemented successfully, particularly where a substantial change of policy or a redistribution of resources is involved. On the other hand, where clinicians resist community control and attention to underlying systemic problems, they may find themselves—often properly—the targets rather than the beneficiaries of efforts of child advocates.

CHAPTER 5

The Nature of Advocacy

The interventions reviewed in Chapter 4 have in common the provision of direct clinical services aimed at enhancing a child's development. Furthermore, most of these interventions involve an attempt to meet this broad goal through direct alteration of the child's ecology, the fit between the child and his or her environment. That is, key adults in the environment are given skills in relating to the child on a supportive basis or, more commonly, attempts are made to increase the child's own adaptive skills. Advocacy, as conceptualized here, differs from these programs by the lack of emphasis on provision of direct services. Rather, advocacy involves active attempts to make institutions affecting children responsive to their needs. The primary function is one of *enabling* children to make use of societal resources. For example, public schools often systematically have excluded children from their services because of handicap or language barrier. One model advocacy program, the Massachusetts Advocacy Center, grew from an effort to make the schools responsive to and inclusive of all children regardless of handicap or primary language (Task Force on Children Out of School, 1970). Thus, the emphasis was not on provision of direct educational services to children but rather on advocacy on behalf of excluded children for changes in the policies and practices of those charged with providing services.

As discussed in Chapter 1, "rights" by definition involve entitlements, "just claims." Nonetheless, as has been vividly and painfully demonstrated by the history of minorities in this country, guarantees even of legal rights are often hollow ones for groups whose political and economic powers are limited. "Natural rights" or "human rights" that depend exclusively on ethical rather than legal claims are even less likely to be fulfilled for groups at the bottom of the social hierarchy. Given an assumption that large institutions often do not bend even for relatively privileged, well educated citizens, it seems imperative for those without power or savvy in "bucking the system" to have an advocate to help to ensure that rights are fulfilled. Such thinking underlay efforts for "consumer advocates" to oversee the work of large corporations and "blow the whistle" when necessary so that at the smallest possible harm was done by powerful institutions at public expense (Nader, Petkas, & Glackwell, 1972).

There is a long-standing assumption in common law that society owes protection to children (parens patriae doctrine). Child advocacy takes this assumption one step further. It is based on an assumption that, given children's basically powerless, dependent position, they require not just legal protection from gross harm. Rather, given their lack of control over their fate, they need advocates to work *actively* for fulfillment of children's rights and attainment of the resources necessary to meet their developmental needs. Children need advocates to take positive steps to cut red tape and increase the accountability of institutions affecting children and families. Advocates are needed to enable children to achieve access to societal resources.

Child advocacy is not unique in American history. It has roots in the child-saving movement of the late nineteenth century (Platt, 1977; Takaniski, 1978). The current impetus for "child advocacy" per se, however, came from the report of the Joint Commission on the Mental Health of Children (1970). Its primary recommendation was for a national system of child advocacy councils and centers.

The primary fault of the report—and of many of the "advocacy" programs that developed in response—was political naivete (Knitzer, 1971, 1976). The underlying assumption was that establishment of agencies with a purported constituency of children and youth would result in significant social change in their best interest. Little attention was given to what these agencies actually would *do* to achieve their goals. The technology of advocacy was left undefined. Furthermore, there was a lack of recognition of the "political realities." As one commentator has tersely put it, social change ultimately requires a redistribution of "loot and clout" (Ryan, 1971), a change that almost always will meet resistance. In a political system that is based upon a clash of relative power of interest groups, it is naive to think that a new agency without a powerful constituency can alter policies simply by announcing it is "advocating."

The fanfare surrounding the "International Year of the Child" in 1979 was a good example of this fallacy. Considerable attention was given to the IYC by both the popular press and professional publications (for example, a special issue of *American Psychologist,* edited by Scarr, 1979). In the end, however, little of practical significance was accomplished despite the hoopla.

No new major legislation affecting children was enacted and we still do not have a national family policy (see Keniston, 1977; National Academy of Sciences, 1976). Indeed, it is arguable that most of the IYC events would have occurred anyway. Professional conferences and children's festivals that would have been conducted anyway became observances of the IYC. In one analysis of the balance sheet after the IYC, Brown (1979) made the point of the political complexities involved. In addition to the basic problem of the nation's lack of commitment to children, the IYC ran into trouble because of its affiliation with the United Nations, a common target of the extreme right wing, and peripheral issues that aroused conservative ire. In particular, antiabortion groups and the coalition opposing the Equal Rights Amendment seized upon the IYC as a forum for airing their views about family life. In retrospect, the IYC became primarily a "PR" endeavor that had little chance of making a real impact on the lives of children.

If child advocacy is to be effective, it needs to be conceptualized better, with particular attention to selection of strategies for making bureaucracies, courts, corporations, etc. responsive to children's needs (Davidson & Rapp, 1976). Without such careful planning and evaluation, "child advocacy" is likely to be "consciousness-raising" without much clout or, as with many extant "advocacy" programs, simply relabeled old approaches to service delivery (Kahn, Kamerman, & McGowan, 1972).

FORMS OF ADVOCACY

Knitzer (1976) has postulated six principles of advocacy that may be considered underlying assumptions of advocacy programs and which summarize the discussion thus far:

1. Advocacy assumes people have, or ought to have, basic rights.
2. Advocacy assumes rights are enforceable by statutory, administrative, or judicial procedures.
3. Advocacy efforts are focused on insititutional failures that produce or aggravate individual problems.
4. Advocacy is inherently political.
5. Advocacy is most effective when it is focused on specific issues.
6. Advocacy is different from the provision of direct services.

Even among programs adhering to these general principles, however, there is considerable diversity along a variety of dimensions. There are at least five parameters determining the form that an advocacy program takes: constituency, geographic jurisdiction, basic processes and strategies, target systems, and auspices (Knitzer, 1976). Several of these variables are descriptive ones that require little further explanation. In terms of constituency, some programs purport to serve general constituencies, such as all children living within a state, whereas others advocate on behalf of specific constituencies, such as children with a particular disability. Geographic jurisdiction varies similarly, from neighborhoods to the entire country.

In terms of target systems, some programs limit their efforts to a particular system, such as the schools or the juvenile justice system. In so doing, a project can become expert in the workings of a particular system. "Watchdog" functions are manageable in this context. Others take a multiple-systems approach, which has the advantage of having fewer limitations in dealing with problems that involve multiple institutions. The focus of advocacy is determined by the problem rather than a predetermined interest in a particular system.

Inside or Outside

The freedom to tackle particular problems or institutions is in large part a function of a project's auspices: "how it is paid for, who authorizes it, and who runs the program" (Knitzer, 1976, p. 213). The basic issue here is obvious. One can hardly imagine Ralph Nader launching a crusade on the Corvair while employed by General Motors. Even the most competent and well-intentioned advocates will find it difficult to bite the hand that feeds them. On the other hand, those advocates who work within the system are more likely to have credibility with decisionmakers and to have an insider's view of policy formation and implementation.

The most common variant of the auspices issue in child advocacy is the advocate's position inside or outside of government. The most obvious institutions dealing with children are governmental agencies or at least closely linked to government by financial support: public schools, juvenile justice, welfare departments, mental health centers, etc. A concern is that an advocate's function is severely compromised if he or she is accountable to the administrators of these very programs. The problem is particularly acute when one is employed by the particular setting about which one is advocating, as in many "patient advocacy" and "ombudsman" programs. This puts the advocate in the bind of being accountable to a supervisor while having the job of "blowing the whistle" on that same supervisor when such action is needed. Furthermore, if the advocate also has direct-service responsibilities, there are opportunities for personal conflicts of interest.

Massachusetts Advocacy Programs. Whether a project is under government auspices undoubtedly has some effect on its choice of issues and strategies. A good example is Massachusetts, where there are two well-established statewide child advocacy agencies. One of these agencies, the Massachusetts Advocacy Center, is a private agency with funding coming primarily from foundations. The other, the Office for Children, is a state agency with a commissioner-level director, who is responsible to the Secretary of Human Services. Although directly independent of state bureaucracies that serve the children, such as the Department of Public Welfare, OFC is still ultimately accountable to the secretary with administrative authority over these agencies.

There are apparent stylistic differences between the two agencies that probably result primarily from their different auspices. Developing from the Task Force on Children Out of School (1970), the Massachusetts Advocacy Center has tended to center on particular "class" issues affecting large numbers of children, publicize abuses, and push for change. It tends to use an adversarial approach. For example, it supported a class action suit against the Boston School Committee for failure to implement fully Chapter 766, Massachusette's innovative special-education law.

The Office for Children's focus is more on increasing administrative accountability and responsiveness of service providers than on organizing communities around basic policy issues. Central to OFC's work is Help for Children, a case-advocacy branch of the agency that provides information and referral services and advocates on behalf of individual children whose cases are "stuck" for one reason or another. If the individual advocate is unable to resolve the problem successfully, the case is referred to a regional interdepartmental team composed of representatives of regional directors of state agencies dealing with children. If resolution does not happen there, it is moved "upstairs" to a state-level team and ultimately to the Secretary of Human Services or the governor's office. Essentially, the focus in on cutting bureaucratic red tape and enhancing agency coordination of service so that children will not fall between the cracks. There is much less of a policy focus than at the Massachusetts Advocacy Center and much more of a tendency to work quietly through established administrative procedures on behalf of children. OFC's involvement does extend to particular issues around implementation of legislation, such as lack of adherence to Chapter 766 (special education) procedures, but the emphasis is on untangling administrative problems that adversely affect particular children. OFC also is involved in sensitizing government officials to children's issues, especially through the preparation of a Children's Budget earmarking items of the state budget involving children for the information of state legislators.

In short, the Massachusetts Advocacy Center and the Office for Children are exemplary of the differences between private and governmental advocacy projects. Government programs are more prone to use administrative, conciliatory strategies, but they also are more likely to be in a position to untangle administrative bottlenecks and to be involved with problems of individual children as they arise. They are not, however, likely to challenge the policies of a particular administration of which they are, after all, a part.

Some Broader Problems. In order to allow freedom to challenge governmental policies and actions, many advocacy programs have attempted to maintain independence from government financing. For example, the Mental Health Law Project, an organization that has been active in class litigation on behalf of persons labeled mentally ill and mentally retarded, until recently had not sought government grants. Although there are particular problems in government-based child advocacy, the issue really is broader. If a project receives foundation funds it must remain sensitive to the foundation's priorities. Problems may arise if a confrontation is established with an agency whose director is on the foundation board of directors.

Less dramatically, if professionals within an agency serving children decide that they are going to assume advocates' roles on behalf of their clients, they may find that they are spending much of their time in ways that are not fee generating. Agency survival may dictate that clinicians limit their involvement to the treatment relationship itself, a service for which the agency can receive payment. Similar constraints obviously fall upon private practitioners.

The significance of the auspices issue then is not simply one of whether an advocate is a government employee. Although that variable certainly has an effect, every advocate, regardless of the basis of his or her support, ultimately will come to a point where there is a risk in pursuing a particular cause. There is an empirical question of the effects of various bases for advocacy, but ultimately the issue becomes an ethical one. How much risk is an individual advocate or an agency willing to bear for child-clients?

Lamenting what Polier (1975) has termed the "professional abuse of children," Knitzer (1978) has phrased the issue starkly:

> There is no easy way to work out the relationships between professionals and case and class advocacy activities. Consider case advocacy first. What is the ethical obligation of a professional to be an advocate for an individual child, not in the sense

of providing high-quality service, which is an obvious professional obligation, but in the sense of manipulating systems on behalf of that child? What is the obligation to challenge a decision made by another professional or by bureaucrats that will hinder a child's progress or actively harm the child? On the other hand, the risks are often not as great as we perceive them to be. It is also true that some professionals, who may be excellent at providing direct service, may simply not be good advocates. The balance of professional activities between traditional roles and advocacy is, in part, an individual decision. But if the professional chooses not to take an advocacy stance, there is nevertheless a clear ethical obligation to see that *someone* does fulfill that role on behalf of the child. It is simply irresponsible to ignore the impact of structural forces on the child while purporting to help. It is also unethical. (pp. 85–86)

Despite this ethical imperative, the reality is that demands of superiors and funding sources exert a powerful influence on workers' willingness to assume an advocacy role. A survey of workers in two private child welfare agencies (Billingsley, 1964) is exemplary. Ninety-seven percent of the workers surveyed stated a belief that agency policy should be followed "even if this requires violating community expectations." Only 25% agreed that "a caseworker should meet the needs of his clients, even if this requires violating explicit agency policy."

There are two important implications here. First, even highly "professional" workers in children's services require outside advocates to ensure that they are responsive to their clients. Second, advocacy programs cannot divorce themselves from political and fiscal realitites. Nonetheless, careful planning needs to be performed in structuring child advocacy projects in such a way that potential conflicts of interest are minimized.

Class or Case

The terms *class advocacy* and *case advocacy* already have been used several times. The distinction is an important one in characterizing child-advocacy strategies. Simply put, case advocacy involves an attempt to manipulate a system on behalf of a particular child. Class advocacy involves efforts on behalf of a group of children with similar grievances or needs.

The case/class distinction is derived from law, and it is useful to examine the legal criteria of a class.[1] For purposes of litigation, a class is defined by Rule 23 of the *Federal Rules of Civil Procedure*. According to Rule 23(a),

one or more members of a class may sue or be sued as representative parties on behalf of all only if (1) the class is so numerous that joinder of all members is

---

[1]The use of class actions in litigation is explored in some detail in Chapter 8.

impracticable, (2) there are questions of law or fact common to the class, (3) the claims or defenses of the representative parties are typical of the claims or defenses of the class, and (4) the representative parties will fairly and adequately protect the interests of the class.

Rule 23(a) suggests a key concept that forms the basis of class advocacy. There are instances in which a group of children bear similar claims and in which the resolution of each of these claims on an individual basis would be impractical or at least inefficient. For example, pushing a state on a case-by-case basis to provide treatment services to all of the institutionalized children in its care would be costly, frustrating, and time-consuming. For that reason, many advocacy projects seek class issues as the most effective way of changing the system on behalf of children.

It is important to note, however, that in the law a class is represented by individuals. That is, class actions grow from individual cases. Similarly, class advocacy is likely to grow from concerns that arise in work with individual children, and particular cases may dramatize systemic problems. Frequently, advocacy groups use work with individual cases as a means of monitoring a system and gathering data (Kahn, Kamerman, & McGowan, 1972). Even when an issue has ostensibly been resolved at a class level, there often still is a need for case advocacy. For example, a right to treatment may be recognized at a class level, but an individual child still may require an advocate to ensure that the right is implemented for him or her.

In short, there is often a logical progression from case to class and back to case. Effective advocacy efforts require a willingness both to deal with problems of children on an individual, human level and to confront broader social issues. The strategy issue should not be whether to engage in both levels of advocacy but when and how to move from one level to the other.

TOWARD CLINICAL ADVOCACY

Despite the distinction drawn between advocacy and direct service, I have argued elsewhere (Melton, 1977a) that advocacy may itself have therapeutic benefits and that clinicians may have expert knowledge to contribute to the advocacy process. Particularly in view of ethical obligations of the clinician to safeguard clients' interests,[2] advocacy well may be a necessary com-

[2]In addition to a general injunction to protect the welfare of consumers (Principle 6), the American Psychological Association's (1981) *Ethical Principles* require special attention to children's interests: "When working with minors or other persons who are unable to give voluntary, informed consent, psychologists take special care to protect the minors' best interests" (Principle 5d).

ponent of clinical services to children. Indeed, as discussed in Chapter 4, clinical services are unlikely to be successful in work with children unless someone advocates for the child to receive appropriate educational services and, in general, to have supports available for the child and his or her family. Thus, in child clinical work advocacy on at least a case-by-case basis seems required on both ethical and pragmatic grounds. From this point of view, advocacy essentially is the means by which the environment can be made conducive to the development of ego strength and to therapeutic change:

> The most obvious benefit of child advocacy as an aid to the therapeutic process is the enhancement of a supportive social network. As child-clinicians, we are all aware of the therapeutic significance which a well-designed educational program can have (as well as the ill effects of a "bad" school or teacher). Similarly, the acquisition of adequate housing on the resolution or a squabble with the welfare system may make life considerably more liveable for a child and his family already under great stress. It is in the context of doing such systemic reorganization that advocacy will inevitably play an important role. (Melton, 1977a, p. 27)

Although advocacy sometimes is downplayed by clinicians as cutting into "real" service-delivery time, it may actually be a cost-efficient intervention for two reasons. First, in instances in which several agencies are involved with a "multi-problem" family, thousands of dollars in professional time often can be wasted while agencies avoid responsibility for the family. Advocates who place client welfare foremost can reduce costs by attempting to delineate responsibilities for serving the family. Second, advocacy involvement on behalf of particular child-clients often can have a pay-off for other children. For example, intervening to loosen an agency's overly restrictive admission policies would have a positive effect for other children in need of a particular serivce. Case advocacy can in fact have class-wide benefits.

The latter point is significant in that it suggests a means of bridging clinical and community psychology. As the community psychology movement has grown, a clear dilemma has arisen in the delivery of services. For most problems, there are two broad needs. One, derived from a public health model, is for prevention and change of the systemic factors that foster maladaptation. The other general need is for treatment and rehabilitation of the "casualties" who already exist. Given scarce resources, a service provider generally has to make a choice (often largely based on ideology) as to which need will be addressed. Roughly speaking, the approach involves community interventions, and the latter is descriptive of clinical interventions.[3] The result is that in the

---

[3]It is recognized that this dichotomy is somewhat oversimplified. In particular, community psychologists and psychiatrists have engaged in tertiary prevention programs in which they have trained natural helpers and non-mental health professionals (e.g., clergymen, teachers, etc.) to help persons with identified problems.

first instance efforts are made for broad social change without attention to people already in distress. On the other hand, a purely clinical approach seems to risk shoveling sand against the tide: providing bandaids to those who are hurting while the root social causes are unchanged and the number of "cases" is not significantly affected. There is another risk within a purely clincal approach. Some have argued that mental health interventions have a subtle social-control function of "cooling out" the anger of societal casualties that might be channeled into social change (Keniston, 1968).[4]

Clinical advocacy would appear to be one way out of this dilemma. If clinical services are delivered with an accompanying emphasis on altering ecological mismatches that are underlying the maladaptive behavior, both general needs can be addressed. That is, through an advocacy stance while working with individual clients, help can be given to "identified patients," and at least small positive changes can be made in the social system. Therapeutic gains can be solidified through social supports, while the environment is also made more ego-enhancing for the "class" to which the child belongs.

Direct Psychological Benefits

If careful efforts are made to keep the child and his or her parents involved in the advocacy process, the advocacy work can become part of the therapy per se. Clients can learn skills (through modeling or direct involvement) in confronting institutions on their own behalf. An example of this approach is a family advocacy program (Morse, Hyde, Newberger, & Reed, 1977) developed at Children's Hospital in Boston for families in which child abuse or neglect was suspected. Starting from a premise that child abuse is highly related to social isolation (see Chapter 3), the general thrust of this project has been described by Hyde (1979):

> By working with parents around specific environmental and social problems, advocates help them to develop a renewed sense of personal efficacy and control. Parents begin to see themselves, not as passive victims, but as active agents, better able to control their children.
>
> Of critical importance in understanding the conceptual notion underlying fam-

---

[4]An alternative hypothesis is that the poor cool themselves out. O'Neill (1981) has suggested that poor people may apply the just-world hypothesis (i.e., the belief that people get what they deserve) to themselves. If so, there are difficult intervention issues raised:

> Any strategy to bring about changes in the allocation of power in a community, to give the powerless more clout, will have to confront the just-world bias as people apply it to their own situations. But paradoxically, convincing people that they are not responsible for their own problems may reinforce another obstacle to action—the belief in external control. (p. 466)

ily advocacy is the fact that it is process oriented. Advocacy is not merely concerned with what kinds of problem solving behavior people learn in the process of address- ing a specific goal. The process once learned may be applied to seeking solutions to other problems. In the long run, what an individual learns about his/her ability to effect change in his/her own life is of far greater importance. (pp. 3, 5)

Operation Exodus. There is considerable anecdotal evidence to sup- port the premise that learning advocacy and organizing skills has positive effects itself. One of the programs in which positive effects of community con- trol on parents have been documented was Operation Exodus. Described by Teele (1973), Exodus was a voluntary busing program developed in Boston's black community in the mid-sixties as a response to the Boston School Com- mittee's apparent neglect of Roxbury schools and resistance to ending de facto segregation. Parents in the Roxbury community organized to transport their children to uncrowded, predominantly white schools in other Boston neigh- borhoods. This self-help organization performed the enormous tasks of raising $150,000 or more per year, obtaining buses and drivers, developing and mon- itoring bus schedules, providing tutorial services, etc. These tasks were accomplished by a group composed almost entirely of nonprofessionals. Among 25 members of the board of directors of Exodus, only two could claim occu- pational status as professionals: the chairperson, who was a professional writer, and his wife, who was a schoolteacher. Among the Exodus staff, only one person had any college education and she had completed only one year.

Teele's evaluation of Exodus was centered on educational gains. Sub- stantial improvements in reading achievement, as compared to controls, were noted among children who had been in Exodus for one year. Of more concern to us here, though, are Teele's anecdotal reports of effects of the program on the parents who administered it. While it cannot, of course, be *proven* from such reports that the changes observed were a direct result of Exodus, it does appear that the parents in Exodus learned much during their experience. Per- haps the most obvious example was Ellen Jackson, the president of Exodus. A high school graduate, Ms. Jackson became widely recognized as a Boston com- munity leader and was appointed a fellow in the Institute of Politics at Har- vard. She has since earned a graduate degree at the Harvard Graduate School of Education.

Another participant, a high school dropout, was in charge of the Exodus recreational program. On the basis of that experience, he left his job as a fac- tory worker to become a YMCA recreation director. Still another participant, who had coordinated tutorial services, was appointed to a faculty position at a local teachers college.

Teele cited numerous success stories not described here. The point is that many of the Exodus parents used their experiences in organizing services for their children for their own development. A side effect of the community involvement and control by the parents was their own growth. It is possible that the educational advancement of the children in Exodus can be attributed as much to their parents' enthusiasm and investment of energy as to the change of schools itself.

Increased Control by Children. The effects of participation in Exodus on the parents could have been predicted by application of an extensive literature on personality effects of increased control (see reviews in Perlmuter & Monty, 1979). In general, to the extent to which people perceive themselves as having increased control over their lives, they are healthier and more satisfied with their lives. They also are more likely to be achievement-oriented (because they perceive their actions as in fact having systematic effects) and actively involved in shaping their lives.

Interestingly, the research available thus far indicates that similar effects can be observed in children when they are given increased control and autonomy (Melton, 1983). Choice itself has been demonstrated to be a reinforcer for children; the opportunity for choice increases performance on academic tasks, for example (Brigham, 1979). Direct participation in choices about education (Rosen, 1978) and health care (Lewis, 1983) also results in increased internal locus of control and increased treatment efficacy. Experience with assertion of rights is also likely to enhance legal socialization and eventual participation in the democratic process (Melton, 1983). In short, the available evidence suggests that there may be direct benefits from children's involvement on advocacy on their own behalf.

Clinical Skills for Advocates. The clear thrust of this chapter thus far is that there are both needs for and benefits from blending clinical and advocacy roles. Nonetheless, even if professionals assume the clinician-advocate's role proposed here, there is still a need for full-time child advocates. There are several reasons why people with such an occupational specialty are needed. First, as already discussed in this chapter, helping professionals themselves may require prods from outsiders to ensure that clinets' interest are given primary focus. Second, clinicians may lack training or motivation in the "politics" required for systemic change and successful advocacy. Full-time advocates are more likely to know available resources and means of obtaining them. Third, "watchdog" agencies may serve a deterrent effect on conduct that is not in clients' interests. Even if their regulatory power is in reality quite circumspect, agencies with a "whistle-blowing" authority often can achieve more child-centered practices simply through monitoring. When I was working both at a community mental health center and the Massachusetts Office for Children, I learned to identify myself as affiliated with OFC when I contacted schools and other agencies on behalf of my mental-health clients. Somehow, as an "official" regulatory agency, OFC brought more attention than an affiliation with the average agency, even though its "objective" enforcement power was actually quite limited. Similarly, Massachusetts has a law that is intended to treat "CHINS kids" ("children in need of services" or status offenders) as nondeliquent. Despite the intent of the law, CHINS kids often were being placed in detention centers for periods of weeks. OFC workers simply calling the centers weekly to obtain counts of CHINS kids in detention had the effect of reducing the number of children held.

Assuming then the need for persons who are child advocates by profession, there is a question of the contributions that clinicians can make to their work. The most obvious is simply giving them "ammunition": i.e., bringing stuck cases and issues to their attention. Beyond that collaboration, however, advocacy-minded clinicians can be helpful to advocates through consultation and training. Two areas of clinical skill useful to advocates already have been discussed: (a) assessment of a child's particular situation and (b) an ability to apply a knowledge of individual and group dynamics to the advocacy process. In particular, clinicians may be useful to advocates in developing strategies for forming strong working relationships with potential allies. As will be discussed in the following chapters, organizational psychologists also may be helpful to advocates through their knowledge of systemic processes and strategies of "organization development."

A third area of clinical skill in which clinicians can assist advocates is in providing a perspective on advocacy work on behalf of disturbed clients and, where necessary, strategies of management of these cases.

An example was Mrs. P., a middle-aged woman who called a child-advocacy agency about her 18-year-old son, Sean. The referral problem was a need for additional housing. Mrs. P. said that her apartment in public housing had been overrun by Sean's barbells and that she had no place to live. She described her whole life as regulated by Kevin's demands: a specific amount of fresh fish every three hours and other "health" requirements. She found herself continually needing to borrow money to pay for his rather extravagant diet. Mrs. P. also said that Sean had dropped out of school to avoid the air pollution from daytime traffic and now spent all of his time in weightlifting. As she told her story, Mrs. P. became more and more distraught and rather incoherent. Everyone in the agency who spoke with Mrs. P. felt that she was crazy and that the tale she was relating was incredible. At the very least, the advocates felt at a loss in communicating with her.

A home visit revealed that the story Mrs. P. had related was accurate. It becamse obvious that Sean was a paranoid schizophrenic and that Mrs. P. felt helpless in dealing with him. The tasks became different from those that Mrs. P. had posed initially. Clinical consultants were useful in helping the advocates to help Mrs. P. to move into other living space and to refrain from meeting Sean's irrational demands. Interviewing techniques for focusing her concerns were suggested. Given Sean's own refusal of treatment, ways in which provisions of supports for Mrs. P. and assistance in her limit-setting would force the issue with Sean were pointed out. Ways of managing him when Mrs. P. refused to continue meeting his demands were suggested.

In general, clinicians may be helpful in building advocates' interviewing skills and in providing strategies for determining if clients' complaints are real.

In addition to teaching clinical skills, there are other, more personal ways in which clinical consultants may be useful to child advocates. Most notably, consultants may be useful as a support system for the advocate himself or herself. In Chapter 3, the significance of a support system for families and children was emphasized; such supports also are important to those advocating on their behalf. In recent years there have been numerous workships of "burnout" phenomena among various "line" professions (nurses, teachers, police, social workers, etc.) and the need for assistance in stress managment. Although no research exists on such phenomena among professional child advocates, it is probable that full-time advocacy is accompanied by a high risk of burn-out. Bureaucracies are often well entreached and well supported. The result is that changing them often requires tremendous investment of energy and repeated risk-taking in terms of the advocate's own professional position.

In addition, the advocate may find that, as needs increase, the resources at the disposal of the advocate may decrease. During periods of recession, the need for services to children is likely to increase, but the tax base shrinks or at least does not expand accordingly. The advocate may find himself or herself simply overwhelmed by the enormity of the task. For example, when state government in Massachusetts was on the brink of fiscal disaster during the mid-seventies, a hiring freeze was imposed that left many services grossly understaffed. The OFC office with which I was affiliated had only one full-time case advocate and one part-time advocate to serve Boston and four of its suburbs. Under such conditions I heard line staff several times describe a wish to be fired, presumably to relieve themselves of the burden they were experiencing. Given such demands, simple affirmation of the advocate's efforts by an outsider (such as a consultant) and help in setting realistic goals can be of great help in building morale.

In the context of discussing the potential benefits of clinical consultation to advocates, the role of the mental health clinician as "expert" has been implicit. It is important for clinicians to be aware of the limits of this expertise and to exercise restraint in consultative work with professional advocates. In my own work at the Massachusetts Office for Children, disdain for the Department of Mental Health by workers in other human services was obvious. The general perceptions were (with some accuracy) that mental health professionals are unwilling to deal with the really tough cases and that they often are unwilling to move beyond the 50-minute hour in helping their clients. Consequently, the OFC advocates frequently perceived mental health professionals as their major adversaries. Although the advocates wanted help and support in dealing with their difficult cases, they were understandably "resistant" to clinical consultation and doubted that clinicians had much to offer them. This initial ambivalence can most effectively be reduced if the clinician refrains from "psychoanalyzing" his colleagues and demonstrates a willingness to follow cases beyond the weekly hour in the office in his or her own work. The clinician's recognition of the advocate's particular skills and knowledge in work on behalf of children is also useful in cementing the consultative relationship.

Problems of Clinical Advocacy. There are several potential difficulties in the merger of the roles of the clinician and the advocate (Melton, 1977a). The first has been implicit in much of the discussion within this book thus far. That is, mental health professionals often have a tendency to be "too clinical" and to fail to perceive systemic factors in their approach to problems. Most clinicians prefer to deal with individual problems and dynamics and find involvement with bureaucracies at best a necessary evil interfering with their *real* work in helping individuals. In short, engaging in "politics" is distasteful to many professionals.

Furthermore, even if they have the inclination to become involved in advocacy, many health professionals' applied training is limited to the individual or, at most, to a small-group therapy setting, and they accurately perceive themselves as lacking the skills to tackle bureaucracies. In such instances, the professional would appear ethically obligated to seek assistance or consultation from such as staff of child-advocacy agencies, with the time and training to advocate for child-clients. It well may be that clinicians' time often can be spent most effectively on behalf of children in doing what they do best: delivering direct clinical services and supervision, *provided* that the clinician realizes that the responsibility to the child-client does not end at the 50th minute of the therapy hour. As Knitzer (1978) has pointed out, a strict dichotomy between advocates and service providers ignores the fact that one goal of child advocacy is the provision of direct services.

Another factor that may detract from clinicians' effectiveness is an over-emphasis on "professional" decorum and undue caution in criticizing other professionals' work. My experience at the Office for Children was that the more highly educated and credentialed an advocate was the more conciliatory he or she tended to be. This style is likely to be facilitative of long-term working relationships, but it may delay resolution of a problem and provision of services to a particular child.

Directly relevant is the usual ethical injunction against open disagreement with other professionals. The Ethical Principles of the American Psychological Association (1981) offer little specific guidance for "correct" behavior when there is a dispute among professionals (or professional agencies) about services for a particular child. The principles provide generally that "psychologists act with due regard for the needs, special competencies and obligations of their colleagues in psychology and other professions. Psychologists respect the prerogatives and obligations of the insitutions or organizations with which they are associated" (Principle 7). Obviously, professionals, like everyone else, deserve respect. Few would question that it is unethical to engage in public criticism without verification of damaging facts and that private efforts to correct a problem generally should be attempted initially.

At some level, the avoidance of criticism of other professionals is often predicated on an implicit belief that professionals should be immune from criticism, especially by nonprofessionals. Beyond guild self-protection, however, the avoidance of criticism of other professionals ultimately is ethically based on protection of the consumer. In general, such criticism is unlikely to be in a client's interest because of the potential undermining of existing services to a client (APA, 1981, Principle 7b). At some point, however, professional practices may be so shoddy or serivces so poorly coordinated that a more adversarial strategy may be the only way of achieving adequate services for a child. Practically, the question essentially is one of what style of professional relationship is most likely to achieve service goals for a particular client or group of clients in a particular context. Professional cautiousness in relationships with other professionals sometimes can become perceived as a goal in and of itself. It is important, however, to recognize that it is actually a means to a higher goal of enhancing client welfare.

Another problem of clinical advocacy is a conceptual issue that has been minimally addressed thus far in the literature on child advocacy. That is, there may be circumstances in which a clinician's taking an advocate's role would disrupt a therapeutic relationship, at least within particular modalities and orientations of treatment. Specifically, there may be instances in which the clinician's adoption of an active advocate's stance on behalf of his client would distort the transference relationship and impair the process of psychodynamic treatment. For example, a child's fantasies of the omnipotence of his or her therapist may in a sense be confirmed if the therapist is in fact manipulating the environment. Although this objection is of some significance to therapists in "pure" psychoanalytic forms of treatment, the difficulty can be minimized if the child is actively involved in his or her treatment planning so that the advocacy by the therapist is more likely to be experienced as working *with* the child. Furthermore, modeling of successful advocacy efforts may increase the internalization of the child's locus of control. That is, the child's vicarious sense of mastery of a troublesome situation in the environment might enhance his or her belief in the possibility of affecting one's own fate. Also, as has been discussed previously, enhancement of the environmental supports through advocacy may reduce the external stresses that are likely to affect adversely the child's ability to work through intrapsychic conflicts in therapy. It must be admitted, though, that the effects hypothesized here of a child's therapist's involvement in advocacy are essentially speculative. Outcome reserach on "clinical advocacy" is needed (see Davidson & Rapp, 1976).

A final problem of clinical advocacy is a pragmatic one. Making phone calls, attending meetings, and offering consultation are consuming of time as well as often draining of energy. For clinicians in private practice or in agencies dependent on fees for the service, the cliché that "time is money" is a practical reality. Such clinicians also often cannot afford to antagonize agencies which may provide referrals of clients. Clinicians in such situations may find it advisable to make use of full-time child advocates and other resources, such as self-help groups, to assist them.

Summary: The Case of George R.

It may be useful in conclusion briefly to describe a case that illustrates concretely the model of clinical advocacy that has been described in this chapter. Specifically, it is a case in which both case and class advocacy were integrated with clinical work with George and the R. family.

At the time of referral by his school to the community mental health center, George R. was 13 years old. Presenting problems were aggressive behavior in school and underachievement. As the clinicians came to know George, they were struck more by his *passive*-aggressiveness than by direct physical aggres-siveness. Indeed, in the first sessions of psychotherapy, George never sponta-neously said anything, and his responses to questions were staccato, brief answers. Similarly, at this time George had been placed in a private therapeutic day school by the public schools, which felt unable to deal with his misbehavior and academic deficits. The private school, however, was also impressed with George's striking passivity. He was constantly tight-lipped and seemingly unable to show feelings or to express himself.

George was one of 10 children born to Mr. and Mrs. R., a black middle-class couple in a large Northeastern city. Mr. R. is a policeman who has patrolled the same neighborhood for almost 20 years. He is a very well-defended man who has considerable concern about aggression; he has an "attack or be attacked" philosophy which he has tried to impart to his children. At the same, he is quite concerned about maintaining strict middle-class morality. Mrs. R. is a rather quiet but controlling woman who seems to call the shots in the family but in a rather "discreet way." She frequently spoke through clenched teeth, however, and there was clear evidence for considerable anger seething beneath the surface.

Seven of the 10 children in the R. family, including the five oldest siblings, are girls. The oldest son, Neal, Jr., had clearly been expected to be special; Mr. R. indeed was preoccupied with having a son. However, Neal, Jr., is moderately mentally retarded with some motor involvement and severe behavior distur-bance, bordering at times on psychosis. After Neal was born there was another daughter, followed by George, who has a twin sister Georgia. Georgia has always been more successful in school than George, a clear source of conster-nation. The youngest child was also a son, Carl, who has been more successful than George in meeting his father's expectations but who also has presented some behavior problems.

Treatment included individual psychotherapy, with an initial focus on activities, monthly "triad" therapy with George and his partents, and weekly phone consultation with the counselor at George's school, supplemented by peri-odic meetings with his teachers. A "breakthrough" of sorts occurred in the fifth session when George broke his silence long enough to volunteer to set up the first triad meeting. He also had helped to set up the school consultations. It became clear that George was using these sessions as an initial effort to com-municate things on his mind; others could say the things that he felt unable to say himself. At the first session, the topic surfaced that was to persist throughout the two years of treatment. Neal, Jr., had been belligerent and things had esca-lated to the point that there was an "explosion" with his father. As was the family custom in such instances, Mr. R. called his police colleagues, and Neal, Jr., was picked up and taken to the state hospital for a few days.

With the combination of psychotherapy and a supportive school environ-ment in which his feelings could be clarified and his skills enhanced, George made dramatic progress. Free to be more verbal, he made gains of at least two grade-levels in most subjects within a year. Moreover, he loosened up to the extent that he would smile *and speak* to passersby in the clinic waiting room.

He also was active in the school's athletic and group programs. Nonetheless, George occasionally would retreat into sullen silence with rare physical aggressiveness. These episodes were almost perfectly correlated with family crises concerning Neal, Jr.'s, behavior.

There were important clinical issues presented: (a) George's inability to express his feelings about his having to do much of the care for Neal and (b) the family's inability to separate generally and with Neal specifically. All of the adult children lived close to Mr. and Mrs. R. and visited daily; Christmas and Thanksgiving were described as being like any other day. One attempt to place Neal in a group home for adult retardates was sabotaged because the R.s refused to set limits on his coming home whenever he wanted.

As progress was made on these issues, however, "reality" issues arose that predisposed recurrences of the family crises. First, the adult outpatient clinic of the mental health center initially refused to provide services to Neal because of his retardation. He was essentially written off without any effort to understand the nature of his outbursts. After several phone calls and meetings, however, the clinic agreed to provide counseling and day-hospital services for Neal, Jr., and weekly counseling for Mr. and Mrs. R. aimed at supporting his separation and semi-independence in a group home. This plan was stymied by a policy that the Department of Mental Health had adopted to allot only one of every eight group-home slots to maturing retardates from the community; the remainder were to go to deinstitutionalized individuals. The results were that the new group homes were becoming mini-institutions and that there were not placements available for moderately retarded adolescents and young adults who had been reared at home.

Thus, in addition to direct clinical services and to advocacy within the mental health center itself, the advocacy efforts went in two directions. First, the local Association for Retarded Citizens was enlisted to assist in finding suitable group-home and workshop placements for Neal, tasks that were in fact met. Second, through the efforts of the Office for Children, the Department of Mental Health was forced to re-evaluate its policies and services for adolescent and adult retardates.

As noted early in this chapter, the label of *advocacy* applied to direct services is a misnomer. Furthermore, advocacy without the ultimate provision of services is simply empty verbiage, "politics" for its own sake. However, as the case of George R. illustrates, clinicians may add to the effectiveness of their interventions by assuming a role of advocate for their clients. Without such efforts to cut red tape in this case, the conditions that maintained George's discomfort would have persisted. On a "class" level, unfair de facto exclusion of retarded young adults from DMH programs would have continued if the therapist had not deviated from a "pure" clinical role. Such an argument is not intended to underemphasize the importance of the clinical work itself, which enabled the R.s to participate in the advocacy and to make use of the services that did develop. Indeed, in this particular case, George came back into therapy at age 17, much more verbal and competent, but still troubled, in part because of the family's continuing difficulty in supporting Neal's separation. Rather, the point is that a model of "clinical advocacy" can enhance therapeutic work in individual cases as well as facilitate the empowerment and growth of "classes" of children and families in particular areas. Child advocacy is a useful, often necessary complement to clinical service delivery, which may in fact ensure that clinicians themselves are held accountable for the treatment that their child-clients do or do not receive.

CHAPTER 6

Administrative Advocacy

CHANGING BUREAUCRACIES

Research on techniques and efficacy of techniques of lobbying—of efforts to affect legislation—are reviewed in Chapter 7. Governmental policymaking is of course not limited to those elected to enact laws. Administrative agencies share much of this responsibility. Bureaucratic decision making is in fact important at three points. First, legislatures depend to a large extent on the executive branch to generate legislative proposals. The professional staffs needed to examine the multiplicity of issues with which lawmakers must deal are in fact concentrated in the executive bureaucracy. (Congress and some state legislatures have of course attempted to counteract this imbalance of expertise and authority by creating their own factfinding agencies; e.g., the General Accounting Office, the Office of Technology Assessment, the Congressional Budget Office, state legislative research services.) Second, in interpreting statutory provisions, administrative agencies in fact generate policies. For example, most of the specifics of implementation of the Education for All Handicapped Children Act (Public Law 94-142), discussed in Chapter 3, are present in the regulations of the Department of Education, not the authorizing statute. Thus, the important provisions dealing, on an individual level, with the development of Individualized Educational Plans are the product of regulatory (administrative) law. Moreover, to the extent to which an agency has broad regulatory authority, it may more or less independently generate legal rules with broad policy import. The Federal Trade Commission's movement toward specific rules governing televised children's advertising is illustrative. Third, in implementing laws, agencies make decisions concerning individual cases, which, while less public and dramatic than the aforementioned forms of bureaucratic decision making, may have major consequences for particular children and families. The examples are seemingly infinite. Agencies decide the eligibility of individual children for educational programs, Supplemental Security Income (SSI), Aid to Families of Dependent Children (AFDC), subsidized day care programs, and so forth. Whether a child goes to a particular foster home and how long he or she remains there is, to a large extent, a decision of a single bureaucrat.

Given, then, the significance of bureaucracies in shaping the lives of children, it is important to review issues related to increasing their responsiveness to children's needs. Our discussion will pursue three main topics: (a) the general character of bureaucracies; (b) the use of administrative remedies for redress of wrongs inflicted upon both individual children and classes of children; (c) means of monitoring and changing bureaucracies. As will be noted in the first section of this discussion, the term *bureaucracy*, as used by sociologists, applies to a form of social organization, which is of course not limited to governmental agencies. Indeed, much of our discussion could be analogized, for example, to private child welfare agencies or, for that matter, to businesses that affect children and families. In view, however, of the special role of government in shaping the lives of children, through its parens patriae duty and authority, the discussion will be concentrated on governmental agencies.

THE NATURE OF BUREAUCRACY

There can be little doubt that the term *bureaucracy* is associated with negative images. The word evokes images of mindless individuals sourly sending the client on to the next office, and back again, in an endless morass of "red tape," procedures designed at best for their own sake and at worst to frustrate the client's efforts to obtain services or to seek redress. Almost no one will admit to being a "bureaucrat"; if someone does, the admission is likely to be part of a self-deprecating confession.

Most people probably can recall anecdotes that seem to confirm these negative stereotypes. Exemplary was a pair of presidential columns in the American Psychological Association's Division of Community Psychology Newsletter by Murray Levine (1978a, 1978b). The first of these, doubtlessly reflecting the feelings of many, was entitled "Should the Surgeon General Require that Some Government Agencies Carry a Label Warning that Dealing with Them May Be Dangerous to Your Mental Health?" A follow-up column was entitled, with some chagrin, "Even When You Win, You Don't Win." These columns were a poignant, angry description of Levine's efforts to contest Blue Cross/Medicare's denial of nursing home benefits to his 85-year-old father-in-law, who recently had undergone a mid-thigh amputation as a result of peripheral vascular disease, who was learning to use an artifical leg, and who had just suffered a heart attack. Levine learned that Blue Cross routinely rejected nursing-home claims. No one seemed to know who was responsible, how the decision was made, or to whom appeals might be made. Even after an administrative law judge ultimately ruled in their favor, there was a long, confusing delay in implementation, and Blue Cross attempted to argue that the nursing home should be responsible for the costs by reason of the "mistake" they made in predicting Medicare's initial denial of benefits. Blue Cross claimed that the nursing home should be responsible because they had misinformed the client:

1. The nursing home told us that my father-in-law's claim might not be honored by Medicare.
2. Medicare did refuse to pay.
3. We filed an appeal and won, with the Judge stating the claim had been justified.
4. Therefore, the nursing home told us something later proven to be incorrect.
5. Therefore, the nursing home is responsible for covering the costs of care on the disputed days. (Levine, 1978b, p. 2)

Given such bureaucratic gobbledygook, Levine's (1978b) cynical conclusion hardly can be criticized:

[A moral] is the paradox that the very solution of a problem of individual helplessness, the public provision of care, may itself become part of the problem by exacerbating feelings of helplessness and producing alienation. I don't believe we are describing either a mere nuisance or an aberration in procedures. I think our experiences reflect serious, patterned problems in the bureaucratic form of service organization. (p. 2)

At another point, Levine's (1978a) conclusion is even more stark:

Not only have we had an object lesson in the ways of bureaucracy, but we have also learned that some agencies of government seem to define their mission, ignore individuals and respond to questions by treating questioners as adversaries. Moreover, bureaucratic processes stack the deck in such a way that dealing with the agency leaves the individual feeling frustrated, helpless and cynical. (p. 1)

The kind of experience that Levine described is of course not limited to governmental bureaucracies. Efforts to correct a billing error by a large department store chain may result in the same kind of frustration. Indeed, it is arguable that corporate bureacucracies are more likely to engage in secret procedures, which are then harder to understand and to deal with. On the other hand, the very controls to which government workers are subject may make their decisions particularly unresponsive to individuals circumstances. Moreover, strict civil service rules may both limit individual responsibility (it is within the job description for another position) and deter efforts to replace incompetent or uncaring administrators (cf. Fried, 1976). Also, although managerial processes obviously are compatible with corporate tasks, it is arguable that they are basically incompatible with democratic government, even if a bureaucratic structure is realistically necessary for delivery of government services. Dumont (1972) has described this dilemma as "the paradox of contemporary American civilization": "To the extent that we are bureaucratized we are not democratic; to the extent that we remain democratic our bureaucracies are not functional" (p. 21). Moreover, Dumont argues that attempts to compromise between democratic and managerial goals are inevitably unsuccessful:

> Unhappily, the resultant forces between a continued fealty to the pluralism, populism, and libertarianism of democratic principles, and the efficiency of bureaucratic mechanisms are not a wholesome compromise. Dysfunctional bureaucracies do not serve the interests of democracy and artificial limitations of individual freedom do not augment the competence of bureaucracy. We have, in short, the worst possible arrangement for doing business in this country. The trains do not run on time *and* the people are not free. (p. 21)

Weberian Theory

In the face of such cynical impressions of the nature of bureaucracy, particularly in the public sector, it is important to note that classical sociological theory has tended to treat bureaucracy as a positive modern development, as a functional means of meeting the demands on large organizations without the inequities endemic to more personalized social structures. An overview of such theory and the empirical literature concerning it may clarify the ways in which child advocates can minimize adverse effects of bureaucratic processes and facilitate their responsiveness to the needs of children and families. In particular, it will be suggested that the stability of a given bureaucracy, rather than the fact of its being a bureaucracy, will affect an agency's level of responsiveness.

The eminent German social theorist Max Weber (1947) was particularly influential in fostering a positive view of bureaucratic organization. Describing bureaucracy as "rational legal authority," Weber understood bureaucracy to be a rule-based structure with clear, specialized division of labor. Administrators were perceived to be appointed on the basis of technical knowledge and subject to a career ladder with strict hierarchical discipline.

Staff accordingly are isolated from the means of production or administration and exercise authority based on rules rather than self-interest. In short, in Weber's view bureaucracies are typified by technological efficiency and dispassionate, fair exercise of authority. As Katz and Danet (1973a) have summarized, bureaucratic norms are believed by sociologists to be typified by specificity (specialization of function), universalism, and affective neutrality.

Weber's theory has not been without its critics. For example, Friedrich (1952) argued that Weber had elevated hypotheses to statements of fact without testing these hypotheses. Moreover, Friedrich noted that, in the guise of a value-free description, Weber postulated a theory that glorified one-dimensional, technocratic life and implicitly denigrated humanistic values. In short, efficiency is not, in Friedrich's view, the sine qua non of the good society. Rather, he would prefer a society that valued openness over formality of administrative governance. Less fundamentally, Gouldner (1952) has questioned the empirical accuracy of Weber's theory. In particular, he has noted that the level of responsiveness to clients, including particular classes of clients, may vary across levels of the bureaucracy. In short, Gouldner argues that the idea of an efficient, highly ordered structure may be mythic rather than real.

Bureaucratic Personality

Regardless of the level of verisimilitude of Weberian theory of bureaucracy, it has been an important stimulus to the examination of the effects of formal organization on both clients and bureaucrats themselves. Much of this work has involved analyses of the "bureaucratic personality." Starting from Weber's contention that bureaucracies are typified by attention to rules rather than personal factors, social theorists frequently have lamented the presence of the "organization man" (cf. Whyte, 1956) who isolates himself from the community and overattends to rules and precedent. The result, it is argued, is dehumanization of the bureaucrat himself or herself and inaccessibility of services to the client. Stating the problem more dispassionately, Merton (1952), for example, has asserted that bureaucratic structure induces "trained incapacity" or inflexibility which leads to procedures becoming valued for their own sake. To the extent to which such argument is accurate, it is of course important in the present context; to increase services for children it would be necessary to loosen the organizational forces leading to bureaucratic intransigence. At a minimum, such inflexibility would be likely to discourage potential clients from seeking services to which they were in fact entitled.

Unfortunately, much of the discussion of bureaucratic personality has consisted of speculation derived from Weberian theory rather than from empirical tests of the theory and its progeny. The empirical literature that is available is, to a large extent, actually unsupportive of the hypotheses derived from Weber's conceptualization of "ideal" bureaucracy. In a frequently cited study, Miller and Swanson (1958) compared the child-rearing practices of parents of entreprenurial versus bureaucratic middle classes. Bureaucratic parents were found to reward independence, but with less emphasis on risk-taking and competitiveness and more on interpersonal skills, such as cooperation. Although it might be concluded that the conformity presumably fostered by such a child-rearing style ultimately stimulates the development of the organization man, it also is possible, as Miller and Swanson in fact speculated, that bureaucracy results in less presured, more sociable, psychologically healthier individuals.

Perhaps more compelling findings toward this conclusion come from a more recent study by Kohn (1977). Kohn studied a national sample of employed men; level of bureaucratization of their workplace was defined by the nubmer of supervisory levels present and the size of the organization. Bureaucratic background was then correlated with a variety of personality variables: values, orientation, and intellectual functioning. Without exception, correlations were small (less than .20), but consistently in the opposite direction from predictions derived from Weberian theory. Bureaucrats tended actually to be mildly nonconformist. These relationships persisted across settings (government versus private) and occupations (white-collar versus blue-collar).

It seems clear from the studies that are available that the bureaucratic/nonbureaucratic typology is, at best, oversimplified. For example, particularism (responding to the client on the basis of "who" he is) and a high level of diffuseness (the number of areas of life included in the relationship) have persisted in non-Western bureacuracies (Katz & Danet, 1973b). Societies, such as Israel, that have a Western/non-Western mix, also tend to have a mix of "ideal," impersonal bureaucracy and personalized, diffuse bureaucracy (Danet & Gurevitch, 1972; Danet & Hartman, 1972). It is thus suggested on a global scale that bureaucracies tend to adapt to cultural demands for a particular style of interaction with clients.

On a more discrete level, there is evidence that an individual's level of security within the bureaucracy determines the degree to which he or she feels obligated to assume a bureaucratic "personality." For example, in one study of a private welfare agency (Blau, 1960), it was found that compulsive attention to rules was negatively correlated with length of tenure in the agency. Presumably, junior staff felt obligated to "cover their backside with paper" so as not to risk deviating from rewarded behavior. Similarly, Blau found that the level of peer-group solidarity among staff was correlated with their level of orientation to service to clients. When a staff member feels support from colleagues, he or she may direct attention away from "toeing the line" to providing services. Thus, there is some suggestion that, contrary to traditional sociological theory, the more integrated a worker becomes within the bureaucracy, the less impersonal and inflexible his or her behavior will be. There are parallel findings at the agency level. Level of internal integration of staff is positively related to agencies' collaboration with other agencies (Aiken & Hage, 1968). Although the causal link is of course not clear from such a finding, it seems reasonable to assume that agencies will be more likely to venture into the "turf" of other agencies when their own mission and identity are clear.

Taken in sum, the existing literature, while admittedly sparse, indicates that "bureaucratic personality" is far from an inevitable consequence of working in bureaucratic organizations. Rather, such rigidity seems to be a function of the level of threat to (a) individual workers and (b) the organization as a whole. Under conditions of threat, a retreat to fulfillment of clearly defined roles and to protection of turf might be expected. Assuming the general validity of such a principle, there are several corollary principles, or hypotheses, of importance to child advocates facing the bureaucracy.

The first is that workers in children's agencies may be especially vulnerable to threat. As already has been noted at several points throughout this volume, services to children are rarely a top priority. Consequently, in periods of "belt-tightening" it would be unsurprising to find bureaucrats in agencies charged with serving children reverting to ritual and fulfillment of rules as an end in itself. Moreover, work with children often follows ambiguous rules. For example, standards for child placement are largely indeterminate (Mnookin, 1975). In the face of such ambiguity, it would be unsurprising to find junior and lower-status workers cautiously "passing the buck" to supervisors or other offices and avoiding decision making.

A second point is that advocates seeking changes in bureaucratic practices or rules must be sensitive to the level and sources of threat to which the agency or individual worker is subject. For agencies or workers in shaky positions, a highly confrontational style actually may trigger more intransigence and clinging to the existing order. In such a situation, the advocate seeking change would be advised to find a "quid pro quo" that would result in solidifying the position of the worker or agency whose behavior one is attempting to shape. On the other hand, where the problem is more one of bureaucratic complacency than of bureaucratic insecurity, confrontation might stimulate increasing attention to the job being neglected. Essentially, in the former instance, the goal is a "freeing up" from a constricted bureaucratic role. In the latter case, however, the objective is administrative responsiveness to the roles already assigned. The advocate should regulate the level of threat that he or she generates accordingly.

The Client's Perspective

Although much of the attention has been focused on the effects of bureaucracy on workers within the organization, presumably the bottom line is the effect on clients, at least insofar as human service organizations are concerned. Classical theory of bureaucracy would lead us to expect two major negative effects on clients (Katz & Danet, 1973b). First, given the concentration of power in a central administration over which the client is likely to have little or no control or even contact, a sense of helplessness might result. Second, with the emphases on written, rather than face-to-face, communication and on impersonal response, a sense of depersonalization and anomie might result. On the other hand, the bureaucractic structure would be expected to result in more efficient delivery of services.

As might be expected from the preceding discussion of research on bureaucratic personality, the available evidence suggests that the effects on clients are in fact more complicated. The lack of simple direct effects should be unsurprising. First, impersonality of *procedures* need not imply impersonality of worker–client interaction. Rather, attention to rules should, at least in the ideal, relate to the fair distribution of resources rather than the nature of the services themselves. (The law's emphasis on due process as a predicate of fairness is analogous.) Second, even if the process of bureaucratic service delivery is unpleasant or cold, clients still may be pleased if the result of the process is an effective service.

Most of the research that is available has used client satisfaction as the primary outcome variable. There are, of course, some problems with conceptualizing "success" in such a manner. Besides the usual problems with obtaining valid self-reports (e.g., social desirability, memory distortion), satisfaction obviously is colored by level of expectation. If the consumer learns not to expect high quality services, then he or she may achieve satisfaction with services that in fact were brusquely administered or ineffective or both. For example, although rural residents are aware of the constricted range of social and medical services available to them, they also tend to be satisfied with the level of service that is available (Korte, 1982).

Nonetheless, client satisfaction measures probably are the best indicators of the subjective experiences of users and therefore are worthy of some attention. The most important study of they type is a national survey of adults conducted by the Institute for Social Research at the University of Michigan (Kahn, Katz, & Gutek, 1976; Katz, Gutek, Kahn, & Barton, 1975). The ISR study examined citizens' experiences with government agencies as they provided seven types of services (i.e., finding a job, job training, workmen's compensation, unemployment compensation, public assistance, hospital/medical care, reirement benefits). Problems with public "constraint agencies" (i.e., driver's license, traffic violation, income tax, police interference) also were examined.

Probably the most important general finding was that client satisfaction was, for the most part, quite high, with notable exceptions in the areas of welfare and medical services, where fewer than 60% of respondents who had encounters with these agencies reported satisfaction. Moreover, only 15% of the sample reported having has problems with one or more of the constraint agencies. Of significance in the present context, however, was the fact that age was the best predictor of problems with constraint agencies. It is unclear, of course, from this correlation finding why young people would be more susceptible to problems with these agencies. Possibly adolescents and young adults simply do more things that get them into trouble, or they may have higher expectations than older adults and consequently may be more troubled when they perceive themselves as having been treated badly. The alternative hypothesis, that young people are in fact more often treated badly, would not be discarded prematurely, however. Also, the interpretation place on the ISR results depends upon whether the observer takes a "half-full" or "half-empty" analysis. Although the fact that 75% of users of government services are quite pleased with the responsiveness of the bureaucracy in these individual "episodes" is heartening, the dissatisfaction of 25% of clients may represent a major social problem in absolute terms.

Still, the major finding that clients do not perceive bureaucrats as treating them in a stereotypic bureaucratic manner should not be ignored:

> In addition to the finding that most people were relatively satisfied with public services, the data were also not supportive of certain negative stereotypes about bureaucracy. Respondents did not perceive the service bureaucracies as inefficient, unfair, and error-ridden in their own encounters with them. Nor did they find the

personnel in these offices elusive, irresponsible, or authoritarian. Overall, three out of five clients stated that their problem had been resolved. Only one in five thought the agency personnel had not exerted enough effort to be helpful. Only one in ten felt that the appropriate bureaucrat had been hard to find, and only one in five thought that the agency had been inefficient. A particularly significant finding was that most respondents (three out of four) felt that they had been treated fairly. Furthermore, 47 percent said they had the right to appeal decisions which were not to their liking. But only 14 percent of those who were aware of the appellate process actually exercised that privilege. (Katz et al., 1975, p. 184)

There are no large-scale data to indicate the reverse side of the equation. That is, based on agency records, how many citizen contacts are made? How many problems are resolved? Perhaps the most extensive study in that regard was performed in only one city and did not include analysis of records of human services agencies. Nonetheless, Mladenka's (1977) study of municipal agency records in Houston is important because it indicates the possibility of citizen complaints being easily "lost" in the bureaucracy. Mladenka found that most citizen-initiated contacts concern very narrow, "particularized" benefits (e.g., the need for repair of a pothole in front of one's house). Furthermore, some agencies customarily ignored these complaints. For example, while the Public Works Department in Houston received 45% of recorded citizen-initiated contacts, it provided only 14 of the substantive responses. The rationale of that department was that it was more efficient and fair to follow master plans for construction or repairs than to respond to individual complaints or suggestions. On the other hand, some departments, such as the Water and Rabies Control Departments, depended upon citizens to alert them to problems. Presumably in human services, where agencies' mandates are, to a large extent, concerned with *individuals'* problems, there also would be greater responsiveness to what Mladenka calls "direct dialing democracy."

However, the fact that Public Works and other agencies could find it politically feasible to ignore citizen complaints suggests that, when resources are scarce, human service programs also might resort to a disregard for individual complaints in order to meet needs that are perceived to be of broader concern. When problems are particularized, their lack of resolution is unlikely to arouse sufficient indignation to result in policical response. In such a context, concern arises about the widespread ignorance of appeal procedures and the even more widespread inability or unwillingness to take the time to lauch appeals, when procedures are known. This concern may be particularly profound in the case of minors, who are not likely to be able to launch appeals on their own anyway. In their case, there is a more basic concern about the possibility of essentially anonymous decision making without substantial review. The need to generate clear, statutorily protected provisions for review of decisions in such areas as foster care planning is obvious in a situation in which there is potential for "losing" individual cases without political uproar (cf. Bush & Gordon, 1978).

ADMINISTRATIVE REMEDIES

It should be clear by now that simple descriptions of bureaucratic organizations do not match reality. Bureaucracies qua bureaucracies are not paragons of efficiency; nor are they usually unresponsive and cold. Citizens generally are satisfied with services they have received as individuals from government. On the other hand, there is evidence for the possibility of unresponsiveness to individual citizens, at least when clear procedures for external review of decision making are absent. Although speculative, there is some reason to believe that children's services may be vulnerable to the more sterotypic aspects of bureaucracy, but descriptions of service bureaucracies more generally (and the absence of empirical studies directly on point) render this conclusion uncertain.

Given this mixed picture, advocates should consider *using* the bureaucracy both to regulate itself internally and to develop favorable policies. One definitional characteristic of bureaucracy is that it is hierarchical; there are clear channels of authority. Although, as already has been noted, the hierarchy may be used to frustrate consumers and critics through buck-passing, there also is the benefit that there will almost always be an avenue of appeal. At a minimum, there is the possibility of informal appeal to a worker's supervisor. More typically, Congress and the state legislatures have recognized the possibility of administrative abuse of discretion and have institutionalized clear procedures for challenging administrative decisions, at both case and rulemaking levels. Federal agencies, for example, must follow the procedures established by the Administrative Procedure Act and the Freedom of Information Act (see Fuchs, 1977, for discussion); many states have similar general procedural rules of administrative law. Such statutes have the effects of making policy decisions public and of giving affected parties the opportunity to contest these decisions. In the case of some regulatory agencies, these procedures are so formalized that actions taken under them are "quasi-judicial" with written opinions and the possibility of actual judicial review on appeal.

Moreover, in some instances regulatory agencies have authority to engage in punitive or correcting actions (e.g., revoking the license of a day care operator not in complicance with safety regulations) with substantially greated speed and sometimes greater efficacy than traditional civil remedies in the judicial system. Hence, in individual cases, administrative remedies are, as a practical matter, often preferable to judicial action.

It should be noted, however, that as agencies assume "quasi-legislative" (i.e., rule-making) and "quasi-judicial" (e.g., formal review of the legality of a licensee's behavior) roles, there is an inevitable tension. For example, when the Federal Trade Commission (FTC) considers the alleged unfairness of a business practice, it does so essentially as a judicial panel after structured proceedings. In the course of the action, however, the commission's staff act as "prosecutors" and investigate the potential cause of action. Alternatively, the commission staff may proceed in a quasi-legislative, rule-making manner with respect to all members of a particular industry, rather than on a case-by-case basis. (In the present political climate, however, rule making may be a disfavored option.)

Meanwhile, the commission must be sensitive to political considerations demanding attention toward or away from particular courses of regulatory action. Besides raising claims of prejudiced decision making, this mix of executive, legislative, prosecutorial, and judicial roles may lead to procedures that do not fit a particular role demand. For example, the necessity of maintaining an appearance of judicial neutrality in an advisory process may deter the agency from actively seeking scientific evidence on its own, once a complaint is formally lodged against a party. Thus, the "quasi-judicial" and "executive" roles conflict. Furthermore, an active prosecutorial or quasi-legislative role may raise political hackles and jeopardize the agency's stability and credibility.

Regulating Children's Advertising

A detailed look at a highly publicized case, the efforts of the FTC and the FCC (Federal Communications Commission) to regulate televised children's advertising, may illustrate some of the various forces that come to play when attempts are made to use administrative processes to generate policies affecting children. The children's advertising issue is exemplary of the principle that administrative processes are hardly apolitical, in contrast to the claims of Weberian theory. Indeed, the ultimate result of efforts to regulate children's advertising was a statutory prohibition against the FTC's promulgating such rules.[1] Moreover, the children's advertising issue was probably the primary catalyst for the addition of a requirement for congressional review of new FTC rules, with the possibility of a congressional veto.[2] Thus, regulation of children's advertising is an example of an attempt to undertake a major reform through administrative means, an effort that not only was unsuccessful but ultimately was partially responsible for a curtailment of the authority of the regulatory agency most involved. A review of the regulatory efforts in this instance may suggest some of the potential pitfalls in reliance on the administrative process to achieve significant policy change.

History of Regulation of Children's Advertising

Case-by-Case Regulation. Although the FTC's efforts to promulgate broad rules on children's advertising occurred primarily during the late 1970s, FTC attention to cases of unfair[3] practices in advertising directed toward children began as early as the 1930s. In one such early case (*FTC v. Keppell & Bro.*),[4] the Supreme Court reviewd the FTC's cease-and-desist order to a candy manufacturer to refrain from "break-and-take" packaging. This form of packaging involved the use of chance as a marketing ploy. Under one arrangement, the package sold to retailers contained 60 pieces of candy, each with the price (varying from 1 cent to 3 cents) hidden inside the wrapper and known only after the purchaser had selected the candy. The Court unanimously held that, although the break-and-take practice was not fraudulent or deceptive,[5] it was an unfair competitive practice:

> [H]ere the competitive method is shown to exploit consumers, children, who are unable to protect themselves. It employs a device whereby the amount of money is made to depend upon chance. Such devices have met with condemnation throughout the community.... For these reasons a large share of the industry holds out against the device, despite ensuing losss in trade, or bows reluctantly to what it brands unscrupulous. It would seem a gross perversion of the normal meaning of the word, which is the first criterion of statutory construction, to hold that the method is not "unfair."[6]

---

[1] 15 U.S.C.A. § 57a(i) (Supp. 1981)
[2] *Id.* § 57a-1.
[3] FTC authority extends to regulation of "unfair methods of competition in or affecting commerce, and unfair or deceptive acts or practices in or affecting commerce." *Id.* §§ 45(a)-45(b).
[4] 291 U.S. 304 (1933).
[5] *Id.* at 309.
[6] *Id.* at 313.

In short, given the vulnerabiltiy of children,[7] questionably ethical advertising directed toward them places moral businessmen at an unfair disadvantage. Accordingly, regulation of such practices, it was held, is well within the authority of the FTC under the unfairness doctrine.[8]

Some of the more recent cases involving children's advertising have centered on the deceptive potential of the television medium. In what has become known as the "Wonder Bread" case,[9] the FTC attacked ITT Continential Baking Company's use of commercials suggesting, through a "fantasy growth sequence," that Wonder Bread had special nutritional properties. The commission apparently relied in part on testimony by two psychiatrists and a pediatrician that young children tend to accept such fantasy as a literal representation of reality.[10] After finding the Wonder Bread commercial to be potentially deceptive, the FTC issued a cease-and-desist order, later upheld by the Second Circuit Court of Appeals.[11] In a case involving similar issues,

---

[7]"[T]he method of competition adopted by respondent induces children too young to be capable of exercising an intelligent judgment of the transaction, to purchase an article less desirable in point of quality or quantity than that offered at a comparable price in the straight goods package." *Id.* at 309.

[8]In *Keppell,* The Supreme Court expressly declined to establish a standard defining the limits of "unfairness" under the FTC Act. *Id.* at 314.

The prevailing standard at present is the "Cigarette Rule," a statement by the commission of its authority to attack business practices that are unfair even if no competitor is harmed. Trade Regulation Rule for the Prevention of Unfair or Deceptive Advertising and Labeling of Cigarettes in Relation to the Health Hazards of Smoking, 29 Fed. Reg. 8324 (1964) (Statement of Basis and Purpose). The Cigarette Rule established the factors to be considered in determining whether a practice is unfair:

(1) Whether the practice, without necessarily having been previously considered unlawful, offends public policy as it has been established by statutes, the common law, or otherwise—whether, in other words, it is within at least the penumbra of some common law, statutory, or other established concept of unfairness; (2) whether it is immoral, unethical, oppressive, or unscrupulous; (3) whether it causes substantial injury to consumers or competitors or other businessmen. (*Id.* at 8355)

The Supreme Court has affirmed that "unfair(ness)" under the FTC Act extends to practices that are unfair to consumers in the absence of a finding of a harm to competitors or of deception of consumers. FTC v. Sperry & Hutchinson Co., 405 U.S. 233 (1972).

[9]ITT Continental Baking Co., Inc. v. FTC, 532 F 2d 207 (2nd Cir. 1976).

[10]*Id.* at 213–214. Given the substantially greater involvement of psychologists in studying children's cognitive development generally and comprehension of television specifically, the complaint counsel's choice of *medical* experts to present this material is questionable. The experts did in fact reach well beyond the available data in their opinions. For example, one expert testified that "a young child might feel that something was wrong with him upon discovering that, unlike those in the fantasy growth sequence, he did not suddenly grow larger and taller after eating Wonder Bread." *Id.* at 214.

[11]*Id.*

the commission obtained a consent decree from Mattel, Inc., in which the toy manufacturer agreed to discontinue commercials showing toy racing cars at a camera angle that might lead the unsophisticated or immature viewer to misperceive their size and speed.[12]

In other investigations that resulted in consent decrees based on unfairness, the FTC achieved case-by-case bans of commercials that were believed to pose specific harms for children. In one such case, General Foods agreed to desist from further showings of Ewell Gibbons commercials,[13] which some experts believed might lead children to eat wild plants indiscriminately.[14] Similarly, Hudson Pharmaceuticals agreed to a decree prohibiting its showing commercials for Spiderman vitamins before 9:05 P.M.[15] In this case, the rationale was to avoid children's consumption of medicines as candy, particularly given the confusion stimulated by the association of the product with a superhero.[16] It is noteworthy that the *Hudson Pharmaceuticals* decree was consistent with the FTC's abandonment of a plan for a rule prohibiting televised advertising of children's vitamins directed at children themselves (Thain, 1976, pp. 662–664). As will be noted as a common pattern among regulatory efforts of the FCC as well, a rule ultimately was eschewed in favor of "voluntary" industry self-regualtion.

Rule Making. There are some potential advantages to a rule, as suggested elsewhere in this chapter. Rule making allows an agency to be "proactive" and to establish clear general policies in considered fashion without being tied to particular fact situations or to the time-consuming necessity of a series of cases to resolve closely related issues. The adversary situation that develops when actions are brought against individual parties alleged to have engaged in unfair or deceptive practices may not be conducive to resolution of technical policy questions.[17] Given these advantages, it is unsurprising that

---

[12]79 F.T.C. 667 (1971).

[13]86 F.T.C. 831 (1975).

[14]E.g., *The Problems Associated with Broadcast Advertising Toward Children, the Amount of Such Advertising and Its Content and the Regulatory Functions of the Federal Communications Commission and the Federal Trade Commission: Hearings before the Subcommittee on Communication of the House Comm. on Interstate and Foreign Commerce,* 94th Cong., 1st Sess. 321, 325–326 and 335–338 (1975) (statement of Robert M. Liebert).

[15]*See* Thain (1976) for discussion of this case.

[16]Modeling effects (in this case, taking medicines in imitation of a model) would be expected to be especially strong, given the preception of the model as powerful.

[17]Thibaut and Walker (1978) have argued persuasively that adversary procedures are well suited to disputes in which the goal is *justice* rather than *truth*. On the other hand, such procedures do not work well for the resolution of disputes concerning scientific facts.

advocates of broad reforms in children's television turned to petitions for rule making.

Proposed rule making on children's advertising by both the FCC and the FTC[18] was stimulated by petitions filed by Action for Children's Television (ACT). ACT is a remarkable parents organization founded and headed by Peggy Charren, a house from Newton, Massachusetts. It was founded originally to advocate changes in Boston commercial television, but soon became the catalyst in national efforts to improve children's television.

FCC Rule Making. In the first such effort, ACT filed a petition with the FCC in 1970 to adopt three broad rules: (a) a prohibition of advertising on children's television; (b) a prohibition of "host selling" on children's television, including performers simply using or mentioning products by brand names; and (c) a public service requirement for stations to devote at least 14 hours per week to children's television. About a year later, the FCC published notice of proposed rule making to incorporate the ACT proposals.[19] At the same time, the FCC invited comments and data on the amount and kinds of children's programming available at the time. The result of that inquiry can only be described as overwhelming. More than 100,000 comments filling 63 docket volumes were filed.[20]

On the bases of data presented, the commission acknowledged that children were especially vulnerable to exploitation by televised commercials:

> On the basis of information gathered in the course of the Commission's inquiry, it has become apparent that children, especially young children, have considerable difficulty distinguishing commercial matter from program matter. Many of the participants knowledgeable in the areas of child development and child psychology maintained that young children lack the necessary sophistication to appreciate the nature and purpose of advertising. Also, a study sponsored by the government[21] concluded that children did not begin to understand that commercials were designed to sell products until starting grade school. Kindergartners, for example, did not understand the purpose of commercials: the only way they could distinguish programs from commercials was on the basis that commercials were shorter than

---

[18]The FTC and the FCC have divided authority in regulating the televised advertising. Although the FCC is generally charged with ensuring that the airways are used with attention to the public interest (e.g., the amount of time allotted to commercials), regulation of *specific* advertising content and practices has been considered to be within the jurisdiction of the FTC. *See* Thain (1976, pp. 654–666).

[19]Petition of Action for Children's Television, 28 F.C.C.2d 368 (1971).

[20]Children's Television Report and Policy Statement, 50 F.C.C.2d 1, ¶ 4 (1974).

[21]There may be some tendency of both regulatory agencies and the judiciary to regard government reports of research as more reliable than reports in the general professional literature. In view of the bureaucratic constraints on in-house experts, such an assumption is highly questionable.

programs. The Commission recognizes that, as many broadcasters noted, these findings are not conclusive; psychological and behavioral questions can seldom be
resolved to the point of mathematical certainty. The evidence confirms, however,
what our accumulated knowledge, experience, and common sense tell us: that many
children do not have the sophistication or experience needed to understand that
advertising is not just another form of informational programming.[22] (citations
omitted)

In addition to the psychological evidence presented, the commission had
available its own economic studies suggesting that the demand for children's
advertising is price-inelastic.[23] Thus, the time available for such commercials
apparently could be reduced substantially without adversely affecting TV
revenues.

The FCC finally reached a policy decision in October 1974,[24] more than
4½ years after ACT filed its petition. Despite the outpouring of public senti-
ment and the apparent consistency and strength of the empirical evidence generated,[25] the commission decided not to promulgate the proposed rules, but
instead to issue a general statement of its concerns about children's programming and advertising. These concerns would be considered in future case-by-
case determinations of whether licensees were operating in the public interest.
Sensitive both to First Amendment issues[26] and, presumably, to potential political charges of regulatory overreaching, the FCC relied on moral suasion and
the threat of broad regulation to secure "voluntary" alterations of the Code
of the National Association of Broadcasters (NAB) to reduce children's
advertising time and to provide for separation of commercials and program
time. These self-regulatory measures were worked out in negotiations by the
FCC chairman and staff with the NAB and the Association of Independent
Television Stations (INTV).[27] Moreover, on appeal by ACT, the District of
Columbia Circuit Court of Appeals subsequently held both that the ex parte[28]
contact did not violate administrative due process and that the decision not
to promulgate rules was well within the FCC's discretion.[29]

[22]Children's Television Report, *supra* note 20, ¶47.
[23]*Id.* ¶ 40. *See also* Melody (1973).
[24]*Id.*
[25]*See* Rossiter (1979) for review. Perhaps the most compelling study of young children's lack of
understanding of commercials was conducted by Robertson and Rossiter (1974), who found that
the attribution of persuasive intent and the awareness of a distinction between commercials and
program were highly age-related. That study compared first-, third-, and fifth-grade boys.
[26]Children's Television Report, *supra* note 20, ¶ 19.
[27]*Id.* ¶ 41.
[28]Involving only one party; hence, "closed-doors" negotiations.
[29]Action for Children's Television v. FCC, 546 F.2d 458 (1977).

FTC Rule Making. While the FCC action was pending, the FTC also began consideration of several attempts to make rules regarding children's advertising (see generally Thain, 1976). These proposals for FTC rule making were generated both by public-interest groups such as ACT and by FTC staff themselves, an activism that stimulated considerable anti-FTC lobbying by business interests.

As already noted, one plan for rule making on a specific type of children's advertising (vitamin advertising) was aborted in favor of voluntary cessation of such advertising by the pharmaceutical companies. A second proposal on a specific form of advertising concerned rules on premium advertising. This rule would have prohibited televised ads that were directed toward children[30] and involved promotion of products by referring to premium offers unrelated to the products' merits.[31]

The proposed ban on children's premium advertisements rested on the unfairness doctrine as developed in the Cigarette Rule,[32] specifically, that "such a tactic transgresses the public policy of special protection for children, especially against commercial exploitation."[33] The assumption of harm to children rested on three psychological assumptions: (a) the premium distracts the child from the merits of the product; (b) the premium multiples the elements of the purchasing choice and, therefore, increases the difficulty of the choice and the probability of confusion; and (c) because it channels attention away from product attributes, premium advertising does not enhance consumer socialization.[34]

A study conducted shortly after publication of the proposed guide (Shimp, Dyer, & Divita, 1976) tested the first hypothesis (the distraction effect) and found that, while there was a striking age effect on recall of product information, introduction of premium information into a hypothetical commercial did not interfere with recall. In fact, inclusion of a small amount of premium information (10 seconds in a 30-second commercial) actually *enhanced* recall.

In a questionably efficacious technique of introducing more expertise into the rule making, the FTC formally invited public comment on the Shimp et

---

[30]For purposes of this rule, "children" is defined as an audience, the majority of whom reasonably may be expected to be children under the age of 12. Advertising of Children's Premiums on Television: Proposed Guide, 39 Fed. Reg. 25505 (1974).
[31]*Id.*
[32]*See* note 8.
[33]39 Fed. Reg. at 25509.
[34]*Id.* at 25509–25510.

al. study with regard to its sample and method.[35] Use of public comment procedures would seem to be a much less focused means of evaluating the scientific value of Shimp et al.'s work (and of other research on TV advertising) than use of peer-review panels or of in-house experts. (It is indeed interesting that the FTC never employed a developmental psychologist during its protracted attempts at policymaking on children's advertising,[36] especially given the FTC's—and FCC's—longtime reliance on house economists for stimulation and evaluation of policy-relevant empirical data.)

Ultimately the FTC concluded that, while Shimp et al.'s study was "hardly definitive,"[37] there was not sufficient evidence of unfairness to support a per se rule against all child-directed televised premium advertising.[38] While promising to continue "close monitoring" of children's advertising generally,[39] the commission rejected rule making on premium advertising in favor of case-by-case regulation:

> There are distinct advantages in preceeding on a case-by-case basis where, as in this instance, the evidence is less than clearcut. Particular commercials can present more concrete facts for the Commission's consideration. As a reuslt, more specific guidelines may emerge. Furthermore, the case approach is especially well-suited to developing information about the effects of certain types of advertising claims and techniques. Given our limited resources, such data will enhance the Commission's efforts to establish better enforcement priorities.[40]

In fact, however, the FTC soon began an even more far-reaching attempt to make rules limiting televised children's advertising.[41] It sought comment on a three-pronged rule proposed by its staff: (a) prohibit all televised advertising directed to or seen by children "who are too young to understand the selling purpose of or otherwise comprehend or evaluate the advertising"; (b) ban commercials directed to or seen by older children for the most highly cariogenic sugared foods; (c) require nutritional messages to balance sugared-food commercials directed to or seen by older children and not included under the

[35]Advertising of Children's Premium on Television: Request for Additional Comment on Proposed Guide, 40 Fed. Reg. 28489 (1975). The Commission also sought comment on an alternative proposal by the Cracker Jack Division of Borden Foods.

[36]See Hearings, supra note 14, at 343.

[37]Advertising of Children's Premiums on Television: Rejection of Proposed Guide, 42 Fed. Reg. 15069, 15072 (1977).

[38]Id.

[39]Id. at 15072.

[40]Id. at 15072.

[41]Children's Advertising: Proposed Trade Regulation Rulemaking and Public Hearing, 43 Fed. Reg. 17967 (1978).

second prong.[42] Again using the public-comment mechanism for gathering data, the commission requested comment on "any questions of fact, law or policy which they feel may have bearing on the proposed rule."[43] The commission also posed 16 specific questions covering medical, psychological, legal, and economic topics that seemed particuarly relevant to development of rules for children's advertising.[44]

The responses were rendered moot, however, because, as already noted, Congress subsequently statutorily forbade the proposed rule making.[45] With the growing conservative mood of the country, the FTC's involvement in children's advertising had become symbolic to many of Big Government's "hamstringing" private business and of administrative overreaching, in part as a result of a lobbying campaign by the Chamber of Commerce and other business groups. Indeed, the inclusion of a specific section on children's advertising in the revision of the FTC act was a remarkable indicator of the meaning that had been attached to the children's-advertising issue.

Conclusions

Perhaps the clearest conclusion to be drawn from this history of regulation of children's advertising is that the administrative process is inherently *political,* particularly when agencies turn their attention directly to policymaking. As a general rule, the bureaucracy is not as openly subject to public opinion and the clash of interest groups as the legislature. However, the choice of issues, the breadth of regulation, and the techniques for achieving change are, to a large extent, all within administrative discretion and subject to political influences. With all but the highest level positions allocated by civil service rules rather than political spoils, this politicization may be minimized. Nonetheless, politics is still there, given that policy directions are most likely to be established at high levels where there are political appointees and where decisions are relatively unlikely to be anonymous. Even at lower levels, bureaucrats must be sensitive to potential sources of "backlash," including potential threats to agency funding, if a particular decision becomes publicized. The Weberian ideal of the apolitical, "scientific" bureaucracy simply does not exist.

[42]*Id.* at 17969.
[43]*Id.* at 17969.
[44]*Id.* at 17969–17970.
[45]*Supra* note 1.

The bureaucracy is most vulnerable to adverse political influences when an agency clearly begins to move away from case-by-case administration to policymaking. Whereas an individual may be slightly harmed by an unfair business practice, the consumer is unlikely to feel it worthwhile to pursue his or her individual claim. On the other hand, the potential collective loss to an industry as a result of regulation of the practice may be huge. Accordingly, the business is likely to invest substantial money and staff resources in defending itself and in lobbying for a more favorable "climate" in which it can prosper. Thus, even if consumers do press their claims, they may be overwhelmed by the political and economic resources of the offending industry. In terms of regulatory agencies themselves, two kinds of threats to survival may result from industry lobbying. On the one hand, the agency may be co-opted and become dominated by those whom it is supposed to regulate. On the other hand, if the agency vigorously assumes an investigative, policymaking stance, it may leave itself open to a marked diminution of authority.

In a sense, the latter result occurred at the FTC. Even though there was considerable organized public involvement in the children's-advertising issue, groups such as ACT simply lacked the resources of the cereal, toy, and advertising industries, especially in coalition with business interests generally, who were offended and threatened by the FTC's activism in pursuing consumer interests.

There are, of course, some possibilities of minimizing the risks of cooptation and agency self-destruction. One is to rely on "jawboning" and voluntary measures so as not to antagonize potential political enemies through threats to their freedom. The obvious weakness here is that there is limited clout available then to curb the abuses that remain. Children's advertising is a case in point. Although the FCC diplomatically relied on the NAB to achieve its goals, many stations in fact do not subscribe to the NAB Code, and the NAB rarely has engaged in any disciplinary actions toward subscriber stations that violate the code.

A second alternative is to institutionalize means of citizen involvement to counteract private-interest groups' influence within the bureaucracy. Not only should there be *procedures* for such involvement, there should be resources available so that public interest groups can present their case reasonably effectively. In the case of the FTC, the provision of "public participation" funds to such groups under the Moss-Magnusom Act[46] is a positive

---

[46]15 U.S.C.A. § 57a(h) (Suppl. 1981). The Moss-Magnuson funds, while limited to $75,000 per party in a rule-making action, also may provide funds for generating research relevant to the proceeding. ACT in fact used such funds in that manner.

albeit controversial step toward balancing the influence of private interests and bringing additional evidence to the attention of the commission.

It should be noted that the room for politics and for potential threat to the agency is probably greatest when policy is made amid ambiguity (a point already made about case decisions of individual bureaucrats). Thus, when an agency is given broad, largely undefined authority (i.e., the FTC's mandate to regulate "unfair" business practices), virtually every foray into a new focus of regulation may (a) raise more questions about the proper reach of the agency and the legitimacy of its actions and (b) create new potential critics of the agency at budget time. On the other hand, when an agency has relatively clear jurisdiction and the legislature leaves specific procedures or standards of a program undefined, establishment of clear rules is likely, over the long term, to reduce the disputes (and threats to the agency authority) that would arise. In a sense, rule making operates in the latter instance to *limit* discretion so that there will be fewer chances of individual bureaucrats acting arbitrarily or capriciously, a point to be explored further in the next section.

Nonetheless, it must be admitted that in the present administration rule making of *any* sort may arouse political consternation. Rule making by agencies regulating business practices may be particularly suspect. Rule making is practically a "dead letter" at the FTC and other consumer-oriented agencies (e.g., the Consumer Product Safety Commission). Accordingly, advocates should be aware of the levels of potential responsiveness and of the political vulnerability of the agencies whose help they seek and thereby avoid highly publicized and practically inevitable defeats.

MAKING BUREAUCRACY RESPONSIVE

A theme throughout this chapter has been that bureaucracy is neither inherently evil nor inherently "rational." The central issue is that, absent provisions for reviw and accountability, there is the possibility of lack of responsiveness to public needs, particularly given the anonymity that is normally endemic to bureaucratic decision making. The risks are particularly great for children without competent adults to watch out for them. For example, in one study of children in foster care (Bush & Gordon, 1978), only 60% of the children in the sample knew who their caseworker was. About 25% of these children had not seen the worker in more than six months. The task then for child advocates is to increase the accountability of agencies charged with serving children and families.

It already has been noted that one way of fostering such accountability is to make use of the procedures for review that already are available. Two corollaries follow here. The first is that advocates need to educate themselves and their clients with regard to the appeal structure and administrative remedies available to them. The second is that, when advocating legislative reform, advocates must attend to the development of procedures to ensure that the new programs are fully implemented with due attention to individual clients' needs. As discussed in more detail in Chapter 8, considerable attention has been given to legal action to improve the quality of care in institutional settings, but much less has been given to the day-to-day implementation of the resulting judicial decrees (Haney, 1980). There is the potential for a similar lapse in advocacy for legislative reform. Advocates need to attend to the details of implementation and evaluation of new legislation.

Ombudsmen

One way of increasing accountability is to create agencies or positions for government-employed child advocates whose sole function is to monitor the efforts of bureaucrats in serving children. The most frequently cited model for constructing such a watchdog agency is the ombudsman of the Scandinavian countries. The effectiveness of this means of governmental self-regulation has been the focus of considerable commentary in recent years (e.g., Gellhorn, 1966; Rowat, 1968; Stacey, 1978; Weeks, 1978). Rowat (1968) noted the essential features of the ombudsman concept, as it has developed in a number of countries:

1. The Ombudsman is an independent and non-partisan officer of the legislature, usually provided for in the constitution, who supervises the administration;
2. he deals with specific complaints from the public against administrative injustice and mal-administration; and
3. he has the power to investigate, criticize and publicize, but not to reverse, administrative action. (p. xxiv)

It is not clear that the ombudsman model actually is applicable to problems of American bureaucracy (for a thoughtful critique, see Nader, 1968). Most notably, the ombudsman seems particularly suited to *parliamentary* governments; the ombudsman acts as an agent of parliament to ensure that the ministries carry out the legislative will. Also, the success of the ombudsmen in Scandinavia appears to have been dependent upon the strong personalities of the individuals who have held these positions in Sweden and Denmark. It is unlikely that the specific model of an individual watchdog is transferable to a country the size of the United States or even to individual states of the size of many American jurisdictions.

Although the specific model of the ombudsman may be inapplicable, the general concept of an intragovernmental watchdog still may be useful. In particular, there may be some utility to agencies charged specifically with monitoring the quality of services to children. As discussed in Chapter 5, there are some problems with placement of such agencies inside the government itself. Child advocacy agencies are responsible to the same administration as the particular agencies that may not be delivering services effectively to children. Nonetheless, state child advocacy agencies, such as the Massachusetts Office for Children, may help to ensure both that attention is given to children's needs in policy formulation and that attempts are made to meet the needs of individual children who have "fallen through the cracks." Given children's general lack of power in advocacy for themselves, there may be reason to have extraordinary review of administrative actions involving children.

Rule Making

Despite the current political climate in which regulations almost inevitably are seen as stifling the efficient delivery of services, there is reason to support increased attention to rule making as a means of fostering accountability. One pre-Reagan commentator (Fuchs, 1977) noted the advantages of this process:

> With respect to rule making, the current tendency toward increased use of binding regulations to resolve policy issues seems clearly desirable because of two main factors. One is that, in rule-making proceedings, attention is focused on a critical issue or set of issues that will arise later in specific instances, which can by this process be thoroughly explored in an atmosphere not charged by the immediacy of a specific case. The other is that the resulting determinations can be applied, when later need arises, with little added utilization of procedures. (p. 116)

Essentially, absent clear statutory guidelines, administrative rules are most likely to limit discretion in such a way that individual cases are not lost in indecision or bureaucratic conflict.

Although not of the level of authority of statues, it is possible that change can come faster and more effectively in many instances through the administrative process, particularly when there are technical matters involved. Arguably, many governmental decisions concerning children, at both case and policy levels, require the application of expertise that, at least in theory, is most available within the executive branch.

Two caveats should be added, however. One is that attention to established procedures of agency rule making hardly guarantees that the public interest—specifically, the interest of children—will be protected:

> The quality of the policies developed by government agencies, as by other institutions, turns largely in the end on the competence and character of the individuals who make decisions and on the climate of opinion that surrounds them than on the processes they employ. These aspects of public administration turn on other factors than those here considered—on methods of personnel selection and management, especially the qualifications and training to be sought and cultivated, on the character of the nation's official and unofficial leadership, and on the changing aspirations of society. Unless these matters are well attended to, the better structuring of processes cannot produce great improvement of results. It can, nevertheless, contribute significantly to successful government if the other elements of statesmanship are present. (Fuchs, 1977, p. 110)

Second, insofar as the rules to be drawn are *federal* strings on money allocated to the states, the rules may need to be based on very clear statutory authority to pass judicial (and, in the present administration, executive) scrutiny. The Supreme Court's construction of the Bill of Rights in the Developmental Disabilities Act as not binding on the states may be analogous.[47]

The Need for Evaluation

Given attention to procedure and the delineation of clear rules, perhaps the most effective means of ensuring bureaucratic accountability is an emphasis on evaluation research. In the case of many child welfare programs, even the most elemental information—how many children are being served—is lacking (Kirst, Garms, & Opperman, 1980). Although this lack of data-based program review and policy planning is certainly not limited to services for children, the problem seems particularly acute there, for at least a couple of reasons. First, services for children have tended to be decentralized to the local level with notoriously poor coordination. For example, California has more than 160 children's programs administered thorough 7 state cabinet departments and an additional 30 state agencies, departments, offices, or commissions (Kirst et al., 1980). The lack of standard federal requirements for reporting the nature and quantity of services delivered is likely to continue and indeed to become more severe, given the current trend toward disbursement of federal funds in block grants. Second, until recently there has been no real questioning of the proper directions for children's services (even if these services were never actually adequately funded). As noted elsewhere in

[47] *See* Pennhurst State School v. Halderman, 451 U.S. 1 (1981).

this volume (see especially Chapters 1 and 9), children's services have tended to follow the prevailing social ethos. In most of the twentieth century, the worth of a "therapeutic" clinical approach to problems of youth generally has gone unchallenged. With the post-*Gault* skepticism about therapeutic efficacy and about unbridled paternalism, this attitude is now substantially less stable, however.

Moreover, in an age in which there are demands to eliminate "waste" by government agencies, there may be a measure of sympathy for attempts to examine systematically what programs work and under what conditions. There is, of course, the risk of sloppy evaluation (e.g., pre–post designs with no controls) or of "playing with numbers" (e.g., "creaming" to eliminate difficult clients from the caseload) to ensure the desired results without any addition of accountability. This risk may be minimized, however, through the review of projects (particularly the evaluation component) by independent experts. In that sense, the FTC's use of public comments to review research on children's advertising was probably worthwhile, even if it could have been accomplished more efficiently through contracts with a few highly qualified experts.

Some of the benefits of increased accountability through emphasis on program evaluation may come from assignment of experts to conduct internal reviews. There are obviously some specific advantages of in-house experts. They can be counted upon to respond to particular policy questions as they arise and to provide some means of evaluating external proposals. In fact "policy analysts" have sprung up throughout the bureaucracy in the past two decades. Although the accumulation of such brainpower in the bureaucracy may add to the rationality of policymaking, analysts are unlikely to consider new alternatives very much because of internal political constraints (see Meltsner, 1976, esp. pp. 132–139). For the same reason, they may "censor" unfavorable findings from dissemination to the public or even to superiors in the bureaucracy. Accordingly, although use of internal experts may increase the thoughtfulness of bureaucratic decision making, it is unlikely to add much in the way of accountability. For that purpose, external evaluation (or, at least, external review of evaluations conducted internally) is probably necessary.

The Problem of Expertise

Although the increase in expertise available to policymakers by consultants both inside and outside the bureaucracy is largely a positive development, it must be noted that there is a danger in overreliance on expertise. Not only must the usual injunctions against confusing normative and empirical judgments and against overextending the data be considered, but it must be admitted that in many instances lay interventions may be as effective or more effective than "scientific management" (see generally Rappaport, 1977, Chapter 11). As Lenrow and Cowden (1980) noted in a provocative recent essay, reliance on professionals and on bureaucracy to solve problems has had a common history associated with a cultural belief in the power of science. That both professional training and bureaucratic organization have been viewed as "scientific" may account for their dominance in human services. Indeed, the bureaucratic/professional destinction is frequently blurred (cf. Billingsley, 1964). Even independent practitioners may become subject to quasi-bureaucratic controls through licensure, which may have the effect of excluding unorganized, nonprofessional services (Danish & Smyer, 1981). In the end, the question may be less one of minimizing the undesirable psychological effects ("dehumanization") alleged to accompany bureaucratic organization than of ensuring that formal organizations do not undermine democratic control and informal sources of help. Based on the research reviewed in this chapter, the emphasis on bureaucratic *style* (e.g., bureaucratic personality) is misplaced; the more telling question is one of *substance,* assurance that the bureaucracy remains dedicated to the public interest.

Although the need for expert checks on bureaucratic action has been emphasized here, there also is a need for citizen involvement in administrative policymaking. Not only do we need accountability to experts; there also is the need for meaningful citizen representation, whether through statutorily authorized boards or other means. In that context, the need for involvement by youth themselves in ensuring responsiveness to their concerns should be a prime consideration in fashioning the form and content of citizen involvement in children's services. Indeed, children helping children (Gartner, Kohler, & Riessman, 1971) may be one of the most effective forms of delivery of services to children. We must not allow services to become so professionalized and bureaucratized that such self-help becomes illegitimate or unfeasible.

CHAPTER 7

Legislative Advocacy

LOBBYING ON BEHALF OF CHILDREN

A recent comparison of policies regarding children and families in 14 countries (Kamerman & Kahn, 1978) indicated the striking lack of systematic economic and political supports for young American families relative to other developed nations. As in Nixon's fabled veto of the Brademus-Mondale Child Development Bill in 1971 (see Steiner, 1976, Chap. 5), lack of such supports has been justified on grounds of noninterference in family life. This "American myth of personal self-sufficiency" (Keniston, 1977) has reached its most grotesque form recently in the new fundamentalist Right's attack on research and service programs for battered women and their children as "antifamily."

THE NEED FOR LOBBYING

The reality nonetheless is that "normal" American families are under stress. Two blue-ribbon panels sponsored by the National Academy of Sciences (1976) and the Carnegie Foundation (Keniston, 1977) have chronicled the changes taking place within the American family (see also National Education Association, 1979). In an invited address before the American Psychological Association, Edelman (1981) incisively put to rest the myth that "families are self-sufficient; they should take care of their own children":

Many of us picture the typical American family as two parents—a working father and mother who stays at home—and two normal children. This nuclear family, we believe, should be able to take care of all of its children's needs. But in this day and age, no family is totally self-sufficient. All families need help from time to time in raising their children, whether it is the services of doctors, teachers, housekeepers, or baby-sitters, or temporary aid such as unemployment compensation or student

137

loans. Only 1 out of every 17 families today is the "typical American family." The other 16, or 94% of all American families, may need some form of day care (while one or both parents are working), special help for handicapped children, job training, or temporary homemaker services. To deny this reality is to deny necessary services for children and to undermine the very concept of family we profess to want to protect. In 1979, approximately 10.8 million children in the United States were part of single-parent families. This was 18.4% of all children in the country, or almost one in every five. Between 1970 and 1978, the number of families headed by unmarried women increased by 48%. Between 1970 and 1978, the number of families headed by unmarried men increased by 19%. (p. 112)

Given such changes in the supports available to children, it seems clear that attention needs to be given to development of policies that will strengthen the supports that *are* available. Such action inevitably carries one into the development of a statutory framework for such policies, i.e., into the legislative process. Within this chapter, we will examine how lobbying for children and the "public interest" generally now proceeds and consider ways in which individuals might attempt to lobby for legislation on behalf of children.

WHO LOBBIES ON BEHALF OF CHILDREN?

There is little question that the label *lobbyist* carries a pejorative loading. Even registered lobbyists frequently deny that they are *real* lobbyists, and many of those who admit to their job description prefer euphemisms such as "legislative representative" (Deakins, 1966). Clearly the prevalent image of lobbyists, sustained by political cartoons and campaign rhetoric about "special interests," is of cigar-chomping, rotund, abrasive men waving cash and favors in front of public officials in return for subverting the public interest.

Although there doubtlessly have been episodes of lobbyists' distortion of facts and attempts to undermine the public welfare for their own or their employers' gain (see Deakins, 1966, Chapter 3), the available studies of lobbyists (e.g., Deakins, 1966; Milbrath, 1963) suggest that their negative image is a rather gross distortion of reality. Most lobbyists are in fact highly educated professionals who did not actively choose a career in lobbying. Rather, their lobbying activities began as a natural progression from earlier professional activities within or on behalf of particular groups. The modal lobbyist is an attorney; for him or her, presenting the client's case before a legislative committee may not seem very different from presenting it before an administrative agency or in negotiation with another private party. To a large extent, the lobbyist is simply a provider of information on the effects of a particular piece of legislation, from the vantage point of the interest group that he or she represents:

> The main service that lobbyists provide for legislators is the collection, transmission, and dissemination of information: technical information on the ramifications of proposed legislation, as well as political information on the impact of the bill on a company and/or the legislator's district or within Congress itself. Lobbyists can generate grassroots support for legislators' positions, compile background information for speeches and draft legislation, prepare witnesses' schedules for hearings in order to highlight particular viewpoints. (Greenwald, 1977, p. 203)

To a large extent, lobbying is a necessary corollary of representative government. It is a means of interest groups' making their views known to their elected representatives. Perhaps as a reflection of its necessity, the Bill of Rights (First Amendment) explicitly protects the right of petition. Indeed, lobbying has been a part of American government since its earliest days (Deakins, 1966). What is a new phenomenon, however, is the development of organized lobby groups to assert the public interest.

Public Interest Lobbies

It is interesting that Milbrath's (1963) seminal study of Washington, D.C., registered lobbyists included only six representatives of "citizens' organizations," despite a 90% response rate. The situation today is quite different. Perhaps as a reflection of post-sixties desire to work "within the system" for social change, there are numerous public interest lobby groups. Some such groups, most notably John Gardner's Common Cause and Ralph Nader's Public Citizen (see *Congressional Quarterly,* 1979, for a discussion of the lobbying efforts of these groups), have undertaken broad missions as public watchdogs. Some equally well known groups have sought to guard the public interest in specific areas, such as the Sierra Club's active involvement in lobbying for environmental protection.

There have been analogous, but less visible, developments in the last 15 years or so on behalf of children. Some attempts, mostly unsuccessful, have been made to forge broad lobbies on behalf of children and families. The best known and most successful children's lobby at the national level has been the Children's Defense Fund (CDF), headed by a charismatic attorney, Marian Wright Edelman. There are also, of course, smaller lobbies devoted to advocacy on behalf of specific groups of children or in specific areas of children's policy. For example, the North American Council on Adoptable Children

(NACAC), a group composed largely of adoptive parents, has been concerned primarily with legislation aimed at increasing permanency for children whose biological parents are unable or unwilling to provide them with adequate care. NACAC was, for example, a prime mover behind the passage of the 1980 adoption subsidy bill.[1] Similarly, the Children's Foundation is focused solely on nutrition issues and thus has been concerned with legislation relating to school breakfast and lunch programs; the Women, Infants, and Children (WIC) program; Food Stamps; and so forth.

Although there has not been research on the characteristics of children's lobbyists per se, there have been recent studies of public interest lobbyists generally (Berry, 1977; Greenwald, 1977). These studies suggest that although public interest lobbyists share the upper-middle-class backgrounds of their corporate and trade-association peers, they also typically differ from the "special interest" lobbyists in important ways. In a 1972–1973 survey of lobbyists for Washington-based public interest groups, Berry (1977) found that the modal public interest lobbyist was a young liberal activist lawyer. More than 60% were less then 40 years old, and 65% had graduate degrees; they were both younger and more highly educated on the average than private interest lobbyists. Thirty-five percent were trained as lawyers, but there was a wide variety of other kinds of job experience represented in the sample. Three-fourths of the lobbyists surveyed identified themselves as liberal to radical and many had been highly active in the McCarthy and McGovern presidential campaigns.

It is indeed their activism that distinguishes public interest lobbyists. In previous research on private interest lobbyists, Milbrath (1963) had noted that many of them had weak commitments to the causes they represented. The lawyers in that sample tended to view their task as analogous to that of the rest of their practice: presenting their client's case dispassionately and in the best possible light.

In contrast, the public interest lobbyists in Berry's (1977) sample tended to be strongly or even fanatically committed to their cause:

> Indicative of the commitment to organizational policy is the personal sacrifice that many public interest activists make to work for their groups. Low salaries [one-fourth were earning less than $10,000 per year], long hours, and uncertainty over the future existence of the organization are job conditions often associated with public interest work. For some, the sacrifice has been extraordinary. (p. 100)

---

[1]Adoption Assistance and Child Welfare Amendments of 1980, Pub. L. 96–272. *See especially* provisions dealing with adoption assistance. 42 U.S.C. §§ 670–676.

Professional Interests

Presumably many lobbyists for children in organizations such as CDF and NACAC share the social activism and dedication of public interest lobbyists generally. It should be noted, however, that the children's lobby groups with the most resources and potential clout are probably those that represent professional interests. Although these interests are certainly not entirely separable from children's interests or, even more broadly, the public interest, "guild interests" sometimes may color the professional groups' responses to children's policy issues and make formation of broad, sustained coalitions for children difficult. Largely for this reason, some of the most important congressional battles on children's issues in the last decade have involved conflicts among child advocacy groups. Two examples have been struggles over federal assistance for day care and establishment of a cabinet-level Department of Education (DOE).

Day Care. Within-group fighting on day care has focused on issues related to professional jobs and prerogatives: credentialing of child-care workers and support for day care centers versus family day care. The result has been what one commentator (Steiner, 1976) described as "wasteful and overblown" disputes (p. 149). These conflicts have persisted, at least in terms of style and emphases. For example, in an interview for this volume, the director of one small child advocacy group referred to the well established voluntary association of child welfare agencies, Child Welfare League of America, as the "child development elitists." Another children's lobbyist long active in efforts to coordinate child advocacy efforts predicted that the issue ultimately will come to a fight between day-care proprietors and professional educators, as public school enrollments continue to decline and the education establishment looks for new "markets."

Education squabbles over DOE erupted in 1978 and 1979, as a classical conflict among special interest groups (*Congressional Quarterly,* 1979). The National Education Association (NEA) with its one and one-half million members had wielded considerable political muscle in pushing for a cabinet-level department devoted entirely to education. In return for President Carter's strong (and ultimately successful) support for the DOE, the NEA produced a large proportion of Carter delegates at the 1980 Democratic convention. *Congressional Quarterly* (1979) noted, however, the panoply of groups that began attacking the DOE legislation:

> Countering the well-organized tactics of department supporters was an
> unusual assortment of conservative members of Congress who feared the new

department would interfere with the traditionally local nature of public schools and a variety of more liberal organizations who feared their influence would be reduced in a department run by professional educators.

The most active opponent may have been the American Federation of Teachers (AFT), an AFL-CIO affiliate and arch rival of the NEA for the allegiance of the nation's teachers. It was widely thought that AFT opposition to the department stemmed from fears that NEA would dominate it.

The AFL-CIO itself opposed the department, in part because of concern that it would lead to a sundering of labor's coalition with education interests in dealing with Congress.

Civil rights groups opposing the department worried that its leadership would not be so responsive to civil rights efforts as was the existing leadership in HEW. They also complained that the Office for Civil Rights within the new department would not have enough institutional support.

With AFT help, labor and civil rights opponents in April announced formation of a Committee Against a Separate Department of Education. This coalition was joined by the presidents of more than 50 colleges and universities. (p. 209)

Other groups, such as the Children's Defense Fund, opposed the bill because, in part, of a string of amendments conservatives in the House attached concerning busing, school prayer, and abortions. (These amendments eventually were dropped or modified in conference committee.) More fundamentally, CDF and some other liberal groups feared the loss of community input and parental involvement and of "whole-child" approaches in broad child development programs such as Head Start. (Intense lobbying specifically on Head Start resulted in its retention in the reconstituted Department of Health and Human Services.)

Problems of Coalition Building

These squabbles among groups involved with lobbying for children's programs have destroyed attempts to forge united coalitions for children. Both the Coalition for Children and Youth (CCY) and the Children's Lobby (organized by Jule Sugarman, a former director of Head Start) were short-lived. In an interview, some former participants in CCY noted that the Coalition could not even manage a statement on the proposed Child Health Assessment Program (CHAP) legislation without its being significantly watered down.

These difficulties are likely to worsen as competition for government and foundation funds increases. Akerley (1979) provided an excellent example in her discussion of jockeying among groups of parents of handicapped children for inclusion of particular handicaps within the definition of "developmental disabilities." With the new emphasis on "block grants," not only will the pie be smaller, but it will be divided among larger numbers of programs and interests.

This within-group competition and accompanying tenuousness of coalitions is not limited to child advocates (see Hall, 1969, for a general account of "cooperative lobbying"). For example, although organized labor has a reputation for effective lobbying, splits within the labor movement are common (*Congressional Quarterly*, 1979; Deakins, 1966; Ziegler & Baer, 1969). Similarly, various business groups often have conflicting interests. For example, despite a strong stand by the automobile manufacturers and "Big Business" generally (e.g., the Chamber of Commerce and the National Association of Manufacturers) in opposition to strict auto emission standards under consideration by Congress in 1977, business was far from united on the issue:

> Rogers, floor manager for the bill, issued a list of 58 business associations, corporations, and public interest groups supporting the committee version. On that list were the American Retail Federation, the Building Owners and Managers Association, the Independent Gasoline Marketers, the Independent Council of Shopping Centers, J. C. Penney, Montgomery Ward, and Sears, Roebuck and Company. The diversity of that list reflected the complexity of the bill. Congressional aides explained that the retailers, shopping center interests and realtors were concerned that relaxation of the emissions limits would shift the burden of cleaning the nation's air to local developers and would curb local growth. Other groups, such as auto parts people, were concerned over comparatively obscure, but to them vital, provisions such as those on the warranties on clear air equipment and who would be allowed to do warranty repair work. (*Congressional Quarterly*, 1979, p. 186)

Although the experience of fragmentation within business or labor interests is common, it is important to note that there are a number of factors making formation of stable coalitions for children especially difficult. Perhaps the most important is that neither the constituency nor the target for such a coalition is clear.

Greenwald (1977) noted the problem of diffuse constituency in discussing public interest groups' difficulty in effectively using the mass media to mobilize concerned citizens:

> Business and good government/citizen/environmental groups seek to use the media—television, radio, newspapers, magazines—to enhance their status, but it is easier for business to use media effectively.... [B]usiness interests are generally concerned about narrow issues directly affecting a specific constituency that can be targeted in public relations campaigns. Public interest issues, by definition, affect all the people and, as such, are often harder to pinpoint and identify with any one person's specific interest. Consequently, these issues are harder to advertise and sloganize. (p. 91)

The battle of the Federal Trade Commission over children's advertising (see Chapter 6) is a good example. The extra parent–child conflict that such advertising induces is not of sufficient consequence to arouse individual parents' ire or professionals' concern to the degree to which they would lobby for regulation of children's advertising. On the other hand, the stakes for broadcasters, cereal manufacturers, and toy manufacturers are high. Indeed, the pressure that these groups exerted was largely responsible for the eventual curtailment of the FTC's authority (*Congressional Quarterly,* 1979).

Furthermore, as discussed earlier in this volume, "children's issues" are sufficiently disparate that there is unlikely to be any consensus on their definition. Even if some consensus can be reached, the key beneficiaries, children, are of course unlikely to be directly involved in any lobbying. To the extent to which the basic problem is conceptualized as opportunities available for poor children, even their parents are unlikely to be an available constituency. Historically, the poor have been uninvolved in—some would say excluded from—the political process (Milbrath & Goel, 1977). They are relatively unlikely to vote, much less to become actively involved in lobbying. Moreover, it is arguable that the gulf between the typically upper-middle-class lobbyist and his or her impoverished constituency is too broad to be bridged successfully. It is noteworthy that the poor themselves were even minimally involved in planning and lobbying for the Great Society programs.

Not only is the constituency of child advocates ill defined, so too is the target of lobbying for children. Until recently there was no committee on Capitol Hill devoted specifically to children's concerns. In the fall of 1982, however, under the principal sponsorship of California Congressman George Miller, the House passed a bill creating the Select Committee on Children, Youth, and Families. This committee now provides child advocates with a place in Congress to which they can bring general concerns about child and family policy. Yet the authority of the new committee is purely investigative, so child advocates must still cultivate support among such diverse Senate committees as Agriculture, Nutrition, and Forestry (nutrition programs); Judiciary (juvenile justice); Finance (Supplemental Security Income; Aid to Families with Dependent Children); and Communications (children's television). There is similar diversity in committees considering "children's legislation" on the House side: Interstate and Foreign Commerce (health programs); Agriculture (food stamps); Government Operations (Appalachian Regional Commission Child Development Program); and so forth. Thus, except for child advocacy groups specialized in particular problems (e.g., nutrition), there is a need to watch and court numerous congressional committees and subcommittees. For that reason, children's lobbying is likely to be diffuse in part because of highly varied targets.

NEEDED: "RATIONALITY AND COMMITMENT

Some of the difficulty in forging a broad alliance on behalf of children is likely to be persistent, if for no other reason than the widely disparate views among child advocates of the nature of children's rights. Nonetheless, there seem to be two keys to whatever success does occur.

The first is emphasis on coalitions around single issues rather than organizational themes. To cite a cliché, "politics makes strange bedfellows." Two groups may support the same legislation for very different reasons. The alliances that formed on the auto emissions bill mentioned earlier are good examples. The United Auto Workers sided with their usual rivals, the automobile manufacturers. On the other hand, various retail and auto parts businesses were allied with the environmentalists.

The second key factor in building a lobby for children seems to be uniting professional groups with activists for children and with community groups. The professional groups, most notably of teachers and social workers, have both large memberships and the aura of expertise. To the extent to which the primary task of lobbying is to inform, the professional groups may be in a particularly good position to state the case for programs for children. As suggested in the general discussion of public interest lobbyists, the child advocacy groups (distinguished in this instance from the related professional associations) add a sense of missionary fervor and a commitment to improving children's lives. Finally, the community groups can show, in human terms, the impact of various programs.

Although it must be admitted that some groups (e.g., physicians) have substantial clout on their own, something is missed if any of these three groups, or types of groups, is omitted from a coalition for children. Facts without a sense of personal commitment are unlikely to be persuasive, particularly if there is a question of taint by professional self-interest. On the other hand, pure emotion, particularly if accompanied by an air of self-righteousness, also is unlikely to be effective. Finally, besides diminishing the impression that it is really the public interest at stake, omission of the community groups is likely to result in a less stark picture for legislators of how a program is really affecting, or might potentially affect, the folks back home who will decide their re-election. In short, as one advocate stated succinctly, the successful lobbyist combines "rationality and commitment."

The need for "rationality" may deserve more discussion. Public interest lobbyists use organized protests as a tactic much more frequently than representatives of trade associations, corporate groups, and so forth (Berry, 1977).

Such action sometimes may serve to dramatize a situation and to mobilize public opinion, at least in the short term. At the same time, however, it does not take training as a psychologist to realize that adversary confrontations with legislative opponents or with "swing votes" are unlikely to lead to positive feelings and a more favorable vote down the line. Rather, such a stance is likely to result in avoidance and association of hostile feelings with the cause.

One experienced child advocate stated this point starkly:

> The child advocates rely on pure emotional appeal. Then they *brow-beat* the politicians! It's like the evangelist preachers. The politicians duck when they see child advocates coming. Then they [the politicians] assign the worst staff people.

When an advocate perceives his or her mission as making the world a better place for children, there is a danger in perceiving one's political opponents as "anti-child." When that message is communicated directly, particularly without the *facts,* it is no wonder that there is little success.

As discussed in Chapter 3, advocates need to assess points of potential alliance with real or potential opponents. For example, one staunchly conservative senator came around on adoption subsidy legislation after the lobbyist admired the pictures of his family in his office. That opened the door for the lobbyist's showing pictures of *her* large family, several of them adopted, and discussing the problems of supporting them without assistance. Other senators were reached through their special concerns about handicapped children (given special problems in placing such children for adoption) and even abortion (given the need to provide homes for unwanted children, if abortion is not an option).

Some indications of legislators' pet concerns can be obtained by reading their biographies in legislative directories. Newsletters to constituents also give an indication of the accomplishments of which a legislator is proud or that he or she believes respond particularly to constituents' concerns. Where possible, it also is useful to gather statistics concerning the impact or potential impact of a given legislative proposal on a legislator's home district.

The bottom line is that the behavior of legislators, as with everyone else, is most effectively shaped by positive reinforcement. A legislative guide published by the National Mental Health Association (Brandt, 1980) states the "Do's" on this point well:

> [A]lways write and thank your legislator when he does something for you or mental health. Thank him for granting you an interview. Thank him for speaking on behalf of your cause. Thank him for the way he voted. This is not only a matter of common courtesy but also of common sense. Most letters your legislator receives

are either criticisms or complaints or they are asking some personal favor. A letter of appreciation is a rarity. It does wonders for your legislator—and for you too. (p. 5)

TACTICS

Direct Contact

There is general agreement among lobbyists and legislators in both Congress and the state legislatures that the most effective lobbying technique is direct contact with legislators or their staff (Berry, 1977; Deakins, 1966; Milbrath, 1963; Ziegler & Baer, 1969), a point perhaps implicit in the discussion thus far. Testimony, although glamorous, is unlikely to sway legislators; as one advocate put it, it is "the show you put on at the end" after the real work has been done on the telephone or behind closed doors. Grassroots campaigns are much more expensive and not likely to be as timely as lobbyists' direct involvement. Essentially, direct contact gives the opportunity for focused discussion of the action that the lobbyist supports and of the relevant facts without the possibility of distortion by a third party.

Given the multitude of demands on a legislator's time, succinct presentation of the case is appreciated. A written outline of the points that the lobbyist thinks important can be a valuable supplement. One aide to a Senate committee made these points in an interview by Milbrath (1963):

> If he wishes to be successful with me or the Senator, he had to be informed. I often know more about the subject than the lobbyist, so I can tell whether he's informed or not. If he isn't well informed, he just isn't effective at all. The most important thing is being able to present the case in a succinct fashion. He's got to be able to handle ideas in an orderly way. If he just runs off at the mouth, you just want to shut him off. The first thing you do is to try and figure ways to get out of it. A good lobbyist should be able to cover the subject in 20 minutes or less, and probably in 10 minutes. If he is really good he sends some of the material ahead of time and this can be read before you talk to him orally; at the very least, he ought to have something written that he can leave with you. It is comparable to filing a brief before a court and then having oral arguments. Other than that, of course, the lobbyist should possess the obvious things like good manners and a pleasant appearance. (p. 222)

Largely because of the time press that congressmen themselves are under, Washington lobbyists often prefer to work directly with legislative aides. Milbrath (1963) noted several reasons for this preference:

1. Aides usually can in fact give more time.
2. Given that the aides will probably be involved in gathering informa-

tion on the topic for the Congressman anyway, it makes sense to communicate with them directly.

3. Because they may regularly be assigned to doing background work in a particular subject area, the aides may be more expert than their bosses and better able to evaluate the information which the lobbyist presents.

4. The process is two-way. Lobbyists want information (i.e., "leaks") from decision-makers, and aides are more likely to have time to engage in these discussions.

5. "[D]ecision-makers and assistants are so interdependent that talking to staff is almost equivalent to talking to an official." (p. 269)

It should be noted, however, that these advantages are likely to be negated in the state legislatures. Unlike their Washington counterparts, state legislators are likely to have only one or two aides, if any. Moreover, the aides' task is more likely to be simply responding to constituent requests or complaints (i.e., rendering services to constituents) than the kind of specialized background work that congressional aides often perform. Indeed, to the extent to which such research services are available, they often are provided by a "pool" research service. Nonetheless, it is important not to antagonize legislative aides, even in the state legislatures, and sometimes they can be helpful.

Regardless, however, of whether contact is made with the legislator or his or her aide, a decision has to be made concerning which legislators to target. A lobby group rarely has the resources to make a concentrated effort to sway each individual legislator. As a result, lobbyists usually work hardest with legislators known to be friendly or to be "sitting on the fence" (Milbrath, 1963; Ziegler & Baer, 1969). Although there is some risk in giving up too soon on legislative opponents (the anecdote in the previous section about a conservative senator who turned adoption advocate is a case in point), there also is little reason to spend inordinate time trying to sway a particular legislator whose position is well known and consistently held. Indeed, legislators may try to avoid lobbyists from the "wrong" side. A legislator who frequently engages in polemics about "Big Labor" or, conversely, "Big Business," is likely to turn off messages from these groups. Lobbyists often can spend their time most effectively working directly with friendly legislators, almost as adjuncts to their staffs, providing information and acting as liaison with other groups as needed on particular legislation (Milbrath, 1963).

It is important to note that the choice of targets for lobbying in Congress has been complicated by the relatively new budget process. The Congressional Budget and Impoundment Control Act of 1974[2] was intended to give Congress more control over the budget, independent of the executive branch. The Budget Act set new timetables for legislation and effectively changed the legislative process. To become implemented, not only must enabling legislation (i.e., the legislation setting up a program) and an appropriation be passed, but the appropriation now also must be reconciled with the budget bills passed in each house and then worked out in conference committee. The important point in the present context is that child advocates need to cultivate allies not only on the committees (e.g., House Education and Labor Committee and Senate Labor and Human Resources Committee) and subcommittees substantively concerned with children's issues but also on the Appropriations *and* Budget Committees.

Use of Intermediaries

Sometimes rather than directly contacting a key legislator, lobbyists will use a third party to communicate the message. The goal in such an instance is essentially to gain access. Consider, for example, the hypothetical case mentioned earlier of a senator who wants nothing to do with "Big Labor." In such a case, an intermediary would be more likely than a labor lobbyist to be able to bring to the senator's attention a matter of importance to labor. In other instances, a legislator may be unreachable simply because of the press of time. In such cases, someone with special access to the legislator is needed to get through.

In either instance, the lobbyist may seek access through a constituent or, less likely, a friend of the legislator. Presentation of the arguments by a constituent also helps to frame the case as a constituent/district problem rather than the wishes of a "special interest" and to indicate that *votes* back home are contingent on the legislator's stance on the issue.

It is important to note, however, that this tactic has its drawbacks. In Berry's (1977) sample of public-interest lobbyists, about one-third of those surveyed thought the tactic to be effective, but 38% of the sample did not use the tactic at all. The primary drawback is that the lobbyist loses some control over the process. There is a possibility that the intermediary will err in presentation of the facts or of the specific actions needed. Moreover, constituents and, to an even greater extent, legislators' friends are often difficult to locate.

---

[2]31 U.S.C. § 1301.

When they are available, it is usually not possible to "go to the well" with them too often. In short, intermediaries may be useful in particular instances as a means of access, but their use rarely will be effective as the primary tactic.

Testimony

Regardless of whether testimony is presented by the lobbyist himself or herself or by an organizational representative "from the field," testifying at hearings is the "glamour" tactic that is most likely to receive public attention. Nonetheless, there is a consensus among both congressmen and lobbyists that such testimony is rarely as effective as direct contact (Berry, 1977; Milbrath, 1963). Hearings often are poorly attended by congressmen and they may be involved with other matters during them even if they do attend. In addition, the message presented in testimony cannot be as effectively tailored to individual legislators' concerns in testimony as in direct individual contact.

Nonetheless, lobbyists feel defensively compelled to present testimony in order to make certain that their position goes on the record. They also may be able to use the hearings to speak through the media to mobilize public opinion. Legislators themselves also may use hearings for this purpose. A well publicized recent example was Senator John East's parade of "experts" before a subcommittee to recite "scientific evidence" that life beings at conception.

It is important to note that the ineffectiveness of testimony described thus far may not apply in the state legislaturues. Based on lobbyists' and legislators' reports in state capitals (Ziegler & Baer, 1969), hearings take on more significance there than in Washington. Given their lack of staff, state legislators are more likely to rely on formal hearings as sources of information. Because of geographic proximity, state legislative hearings are also more likely than congressional hearings to provide an opportunity for participants in programs to give first-hand reports of their experiences and needs. Such testimony can be particularly effective.

Grassroots Campaigns and Protests

Next to testimony, perhaps the most visible lobbying tactic is encouraging people at the "grassroots" to write their congressmen to seek their support for a particular position. Forty-seven percent of Berry's (1977) sample of public interest lobbyists perceived letter-writing campaigns as an effective tactic, but about one-third of the total sample never used it. Part of the division stems from the fact that it is unclear what effect such campaigns in fact have, although there seems to be general agreement that clearly "manufactured" letters (e.g., identical postcards) have little impact on decision makers. Perhaps sheer numbers of letters, especially if they are *thoughtful* letters, do on occasion result in swaying an undecided legislator or alerting him or her to specific aspects of an issue. It is noteworthy that lobbyists for large-membership organizations, such as labor unions, are particularly likely to perceive grassroots techniques as effective (Ziegler & Baer, 1969). The clearest effect may be simply raising the political awareness and involvement of the letter writers themselves and perhaps ultimately enhancing the group's political savvy and power.

Even more indirect tactics are those that explicitly purport to "create a climate" for eventual adoption of a particular position. A good example would be utility companies' self-congratulatory advertisements; Mobil Oil's political commentaries also are well known. A large proportion (62%) of public interest lobbyists do not use public relations techniques, however. Besides lacking immediacy and focus, such techniques are expensive. Furthermore, tax-exempt groups obviously do not enjoy tax deductions for public relations advertising which may make it appear cost-effective.

Organized protests may be an effective, inexpensive way of focusing public attention on an issue. Such tactics are most likely to be necessary if groups do not have access to decision makers (as was the case in the early days of the civil rights movement) or if the significance of an issue has not fully reached public consciousness (as was the case in the movement against the Vietnam war). As noted previously, however, there is a cost of such tactics in terms of polarizing the opposition.

LEGAL PROBLEMS CONNECTED WITH LOBBYING

Regardless of the tactics planned by a group seeking to affect the course of legislation, it must take into account legal constraints on lobbying. There are two principal streams of law regulating the practice of lobbying at the federal level: (a) requirements for registration of lobbyists[3] and (b) requirements for maintenance of tax-exempt status as "public charities" under § 501(c)(3) of the Internal Revenue Code,[4] as amended by the Tax Reform

[3]Federal Regulation of Lobbying Act, 2 U.S.C. §§ 261–270.
[4]26 U.S.C. § 501 (c)(3).

Act of 1976.[5] In addition, many of the states have requirements for registration of lobbyists before their legislatures and for reporting of expenditures by lobbyists.

Federal Regulation of Lobbying Act

It should be noted, first of all, that the statutory definitions of "lobbying" are substantially narrower than the colloquial use of the term. Congress and the courts have endeavored to ensure that such laws do not result in a chilling effect on the public's First Amendment right to petition the government. For example, registration is not required of anyone who merely testifies before Congress in support of or opposition to legislation or of publications (including organizational newsletters) that urge particular legislative action.[6] As construed by the Supreme Court, the Lobbying Act applies only if three criteria are met:

(a) the "person" must have solicited, collected, or received contributions;
(b) one of the main purposes of such "person" must have been to influence the passage or defeat of legislation by Congress;
(c) the intended method of accomplishing this purpose must have been through direct communication with members of Congress.[7]

Under this definition, "grassroots" tactics are exempted, as are volunteer lobbying efforts. Perhaps of most consequence, there is an exemption for activities that do not have the "principal purpose" of influencing the defeat or passage of legislation by Congress.[8] Accordingly, many groups claim to be exempted from the registration requirement because their primary purpose is providing information rather than persuading members of Congress. They claim to be only "incidentally" involved in lobbying (Berry, 1977). Moreover, no agency has authority to monitor enforcement of the Act, and charges of failure to register have been brought rarely. In short, the Lobbying Act, which after all only requires registration of lobbyists, is of relatively minor consequence, particularly given the narrow definition of who is subject to its provisions.

[5]Pub. L. 94–455, § 1307.
[6]Lobbying Act, § 308.
[7]United States v. Harriss, 347 U.S. 612, 623 (1953).
[8]Lobbying Act, § 307.

Tax Reform Act of 1976

Of much more importance in limiting public-interest and professional groups' lobbying activities is the possibility of losing tax-exempt status. This possibility became stark after the Internal Revenue Service in the Nixon Administration revoked the tax-exempt status of the Sierra Club for taking full-page ads in major newspapers to express its views on a particular bill. The tax-exempt status of several other groups, such as the Maryland division of the National Mental Health Association, also was threatened as a result of their dealings with state legislatures. The problems of the Maryland Mental Health Association were the result of particularly strict interpretation of "substantial" lobbying by the Baltimore Internal Revenue Service office, a reflection of the wide discretion available at that time to district directors.

In order to prevent capricious revocation of public-interest groups' tax-exempt status, in 1976 Congress clarified the requirement that no group could maintain tax-exempt status if a "substantial part of the activities" of the organization was "attempting to influence legislation." These terms were clearly defined for the first time in the Tax Reform Act of 1976;[9] moreover, it added intermediate penalties short of loss of tax-exempt status.[10] Although a detailed discussion is beyond our purposes here (see Brandt, 1976, for such a discussion), a description of a few key provisions will show the considerations that a tax-exempt group must take into account in planning lobbying activities.

Under the 1976 tax reforms, lobbying is broadly defined as any expenditures aimed at influencing legislation through an attempt to affect the opinions of "the general public or segment thereof" or through direct communication with legislators, legislative aides, or government officials involved in drafting legislation.[11] Thus, both grassroots and direct lobbying are covered. Purely informational efforts are not included, however, provided that they consist merely of "making available the results of nonpartisan analysis, study, or research"[12] or of providing "technical advice or assistance" on written request of a legislative committee.[13] Moreover, an organization is free to inform its members concerning pending legislation provided that it does not

---

[9]26 U.S.C. §§ 501(h) and 4911.
[10]26 U.S.C. §4911.
[11]26 U.S.C. §4911(d).
[12]26 U.S.C. § 4911(d)(2)(A).
[13]26 U.S.C. § 4911(d)(2)(B).

in so doing directly encourage members to attempt to influence that legislation.[14]

Even those lobbying activities not included within the exceptions described in the preceding paragraph are permissible if the expenditures for them do not exceed the organization's "lobbying nontaxable amount."[15] This figure is based on a proportion of the organization's total annual expenditures (e.g., 20% if the annual budget does not exceed $500,000). There is an additional constraint: no more than 25% of the lobbying nontaxable amount may be spent on grassroots lobbying.[16] If these limits are exceeded, a tax is assessed of 25% of the overrun.[17] Only organizations that "normally" exceed their limits are vulnerable to loss of their tax-exempt status under the 1976 law.

In short, the Tax Reform Act of 1976 makes clear the limits of permissible lobbying by tax-exempt organizations. These limits are sufficiently broad that public-interest groups should have ample opportunity to make their views and expertise known to legislators. The principal limitation on lobbying is a disincentive against expensive public relations campaigns, a tactic that in any case is of dubious cost-effectiveness.

TRAINING AND RESEARCH NEEDS

Given the range of tactics available to lobbyists, what sorts of characteristics are useful in a lobbyist for children? Three general themes concerning what makes a good lobbyist are found consistently both through the literature and our interviews with lobbyists for children:

1. the ability to "articulate one's emotions"
2. consistent accuracy and honesty
3. a good fund of knowledge about the issues

The first point already has been discussed in this chapter. In order to maintain access to decision makers, advocates need to avoid personalizing issues and to keep cool even when the opponents are recalcitrant "to hear negative information and use it well." Patience is a prerequisite for a career in lobbying. When Berry's (1977) sample of public-interest lobbyists was

---

[14]26 U.S.C. §§ 4911(d)(2)(D) and 4911(d)(3).
[15]26 U.S.C. § 4911 (c)(2).
[16]26 U.S.C. § 4911 (c)(4).
[17]26 U.S.C. § 4911 (a)(1).

asked to identify the issue on which they had been the most successful and the issue on which they had been the least successful, 43% named the same issue. Legislative change typically happens in small increments and amid numerous compromises and lobbyists must be able to accept this fact and work persistently for the aspects of their program that can be adopted.

The second point may be less obvious. The popular image of lobbyists is that they distort the truth so as to achieve policies slanted in their favor. However, when lobbyists are caught in lies or even simple factual errors, their credibility is diminished. To the extent to which legislators and their aides look to lobbyists for information, lobbyists' usefulness is minimized if they cannot be depended upon to provide accurate data.

The final point is related. A lobbyist is most likely to be successful if he or she in fact has information to offer legislators to assist in their decision making. As one lobbyist put it, the real sign of success is when legislators begin *asking* one for information. Not surprisingly, this phenomenon is related to an organization's ability to supply information. Frequency of solicitation of information and advice by legislators is highly correlated with the resources that a lobby group puts into collection and analysis of data (Berry, 1977).

It is in this vein that child psychologists may be of most usefulness to legislative policymakers. The classic example is the formulation of the Head Start program (Steiner, 1976, Chap. 2), which relied heavily on the work of Hunt (1961) and Bloom (1964), which suggested the importance of early experience and the plasticity of intelligence. It should be noted, however, that the kinds of research that may be most persuasive on a particular piece of legislation may not be the sort that will bring reinforcement for social scientists. Legislators are likely to be interested in cost-effectiveness data, purely "applied" research that may go unrewarded in academe. Nonetheless, psychologists and sociologists can be of great help in the lobbying process by providing sound evaluation research. It should be noted, however, that some of the research that is needed may be simple descriptive statistics that may be beyond the resources of individual social scientists. How many children and families are in fact served by a particular program? Where are they? Such data often are hard to obtain, in part because of inconsistent or inadequate reporting requirements. This situation is likely to worsen if the trend away from categorical programs and toward local discretion in expenditure of federal funds continues.

Finally, useful research not only must be performed; the results must be disseminated. Lobbying requires not only knowledge, but also the ability to communicate that knowledge. Representatives of one specialized children's lobby group noted that virtually their whole staff had teaching experience. This kind of experience in summarizing a body of knowledge may be useful to a lobbyist. Analogously, experience as an attorney may be helpful in presenting the case for a particular piece of legislation for children. In terms of child development professionals specifically, however, the bottom line would appear to be expertise combined with a knowledge of how to communicate that knowledge.

Given the ultimate importance to the society of dissemination of such knowledge to policymakers, there is a need for more programs to provide such training in application of developmental research to legislation. The Society for Research in Child Development's Congressional Science Fellowship program may have some impact in this regard. It may well be, however, that there is not substantial transfer of this training from one setting to another. One lobbyist we interviewed who has impressive experience on Capitol Hill noted that knowledge of state legislatures seldom has much transfer in terms of effectiveness as a lobbyist in Congress. The idiosyncracies of the process, such as the congressional budget process, make such specific knowledge important in gaining access and using it effectively. As training programs for research/lobbyists develop, it is important to conduct evaluation research of these programs themselves in order to try to identify the kinds of experiences that will assist researchers in helping to translate their findings into policy and action on behalf of children and families.

CHAPTER 8

Legal Advocacy

SOCIAL CHANGE AND THE LAW

Since the early days of the Warren Court, the courts have been identified by friends and foes alike as instruments of social change. They have become actively involved in running schools,[1] jails and prisons,[2] and facilities for the mentally ill and the mentally retarded.[3] Although the more conservative Burger Court has shown some distaste for some of the standards established in law by the Supreme Court in the fifties and sixties, it has shown little inclination to undercut altogether the work of the Warren Court in such areas as criminal procedure[4] and desegregation[5] (Saltzburg, 1980). In short, the courts, especially the federal courts, remain an avenue for redress of grievances of disadvantaged groups, including children. This chapter will examine

---

[1] *See, e.g.,* Morgan v. Kerrigan, 401 F.Supp. 216 (D.Mass. 1975), *stay denied,* 523 F.2d 917 (1st Cir. 1975), *aff'd,* 530 F.2d 401 (1st Cir. 1976), *cert. denied,* 426 U.S. 935 (1976).

[2] *See, e.g.,* James v. Wallace, 406 F.Supp. 318 (M.D. Ala. 1976); Inmates of Suffolk County Jail v. Eisenstadt, 360 F.Supp. 676 (D. Mass. 1973), *aff'd,* 494 F.2d 1196 (1st Cir. 1974), *cert. denied,* 419 U.S. 977 (1974).

[3] *See, e.g.,* N.Y.S. Ass'n for Retarded Children, Inc. v. Rockefeller, 357 F.Supp. 752 (E.D.N.Y. 1973), *enforced sub nom.* N.Y.S. Ass'n for Retarded Children, Inc. v. Carey, 393 F.Supp. 715 (E.D.N.Y. 1975), *enforced,* 409 F.Supp. 606 (E.D.N.Y. 1976) (review panel may monitor institutional policies before they are fully developed and implemented), *aff'd,* 596 F.2d 27 (2d Cir. 1979), *enforced,* 492 F. Supp. 1099 (E.D.N.Y. 1980); Wyatt v. Stickney, 324 F. Supp. 781 (M.D. Ala. 1971), *enforced,* 344 F. Supp. 373 (M.D. Ala. 1972) *and* 344 F. Supp. 387 (M.D. Ala. 1972), *modified sub nom.* Wyatt v. Aderholt, 503 F.2d 1305 (5th Cir. 1974).

[4] "The meaning of *Miranda* has become reasonably clear and law enforcement practices have adjusted to its strictures; I would neither overrule *Miranda,* disparage it, nor extend it at this late date." Rhode Island v. Innis, 446 U.S. 291, 304 (1980) (Burger, C. J., concurring in the judgment).

[5] *See, e.g.,* Swann v. Board of Education, 402 U.S. 1 (1971).

problems attached to such use of the legal system and provide a review of changes in the status of minors achieved through the courts.

Before embarking on this discussion, it should be noted that "the law" encompasses much more than processes of litigation. Indeed, the previous two chapters dealt with law-related topics: administrative law (Chapter 6) and the making of statutory law (Chapter 7). Law can be seen even more broadly to encompass the standards and procedures of dispute resolution within a society, even if those rules are not always formalized (Nader & Todd, 1978; Weyrauch, 1977). Even within a stricter definition of law as formal authority, many "everyday" transactions that never are identified as legal in fact are governed by law (e.g., a dispute over a grade between a student and a teacher, acting under color of state law; the expectations attached to a purchase agreement, as an example of a contract). Moreover, many disputes that most people would recognize as "legal" (e.g., child custody disputes) rarely reach a trial (cf. Mnookin & Kornhauser, 1978).

This brief exposition on the nature of the law is made simply as a caveat of sorts. There is some danger in jumping to litigation without consideration of other means of achieving resolution of a dispute that may be less costly, less time-consuming, and ultimately more effective. Moreover, overemphasis on courtroom drama and even the "black-letter" law itself may obscure efforts to socialize children to be law-creators rather than simply law-obeyers or law-maintainers (Tapp & Levine, 1974; Tapp & Melton, 1983). Nonetheless, the importance of the legal system as ultimate arbiter demands attention to the use of litigation on behalf of children.

BRINGING CHILD PSYCHOLOGY TO THE COURTROOM

There are several avenues by which psychological evidence can reach the fact finder in a case. Certainly the best known of these is expert testimony. The use of experts at trial has the advantage of subjecting the opinions presented to cross-examination and accordingly has more legal "legitimacy" (at least in the eyes of some jurists) than other means to be discussed here. In addition, experts have in fact been important in presenting evidence about psychological phenomena or "social facts," especially with regard to institutional care,[6] as well as the more common "case facts" discussed in cases where

---

[6]Most right to treatment cases as well as cases challenging prison conditions as "cruel and unusual" have involved the presentation of such testimony.

clinical expertise is sought. Indeed, it is arguable that experts typically have presented more probative evidence in public-interest cases (where the evidence offered is typically a presentation of relevant research) than in criminal, juvenile, and family law cases (where the experts' opinions may be within the province of laypersons and based upon unreliable diagnoses; see Morse, 1978).

There are two major problems in application of psychology through expert testimony at the trial level. The first is a practical one. Unless a case is explicitly brought as a "test case" on a particular issue (e.g., the adequacy of procedures for commitment of adolescents in a particular jurisdiction), the issues with substantial social import may not arise until trial or even until after the judge has made his or her findings. Obviously, then, key evidence on an important issue (e.g., standards to be used in determining a child's "best interests" in a custody dispute) often must await presentation on appeal (through appellate briefs), simply because the issue was not framed as such when the case was brought to trial.

The second problem is a more substantive one. That is, the adversary procedures of a trial *may* be ill suited for presentation of scientific evidence. The limitation essentially is that the expert of necessity must discuss the relevant facts in response to the questions posed to him or her; a "balanced," complete presentation of the facts may not be possible. As Thibaut and Walker (1978) have argued, adversary procedures are not the most effective for resolution of disputes concerning the *truth* of a proposition. In cases where the social consequences of a policy are the key factual issues, the public interest is at stake and the proceeding may in practice become an exercise in ascertaining the current state of scientific knowledge. On the other hand, the emphasis placed on "may" in the first sentence of this paragraph is well taken. In many—indeed, most—legal disputes, the goal is not truth but *justice* (Thibaut & Walker, 1978). As a matter of policy, we want to ensure that the parties have the opportunity to put forth the evidence most favorable to their cases even if the distribution of facts presented does not match the distribution in reality. Although it has become fashionable to attack the adversary model, it is clear that many kinds of cases in which such procedures are allegedly evil (e.g., family-law cases) are in fact conflicts in interest—not scientific disputes—for which the parties deservedly want the opportunity to present their side of the conflict, to have their day in court (Melton & Lind, 1982).

Regardless of whether psychological evidence is presented at trial, such evidence may be brought before appellate courts in briefs and arguments. (Appellate courts do not take testimony.) Such briefs can be proffered by the parties or by amici curiae (friends of the court). In the former instance, one or both of the parties may contract with consulting psychologists to aid in the preparation of their briefs with regard to the social facts in dispute. As in the case of expert testimony, the party usually will present only that portion of the evidence that is favorable to its case. On appeal, there is the additional problem that the expert obviously is not subject to cross-examination, although the opposing party is free to present counter-arguments. Where the psychologist (or, more commonly, a group of psychologists or other experts) enters the case as amicus, the goal explicitly is to aid the court in resolution of policy questions about which the psychologist has specialized knowledge. Although amici have the disadvantage of lacking the standing[7] to frame the issues to be decided, they have the advantage of being able to discuss the issues (and the relevant psychological knowledge) in a relatively balanced, "scientific" fashion, although it should be added that organizations often enter cases as amici to advance their particular professional and political interests.[8]

Finally, psychological knowledge may enter the legal process through the judge himself or herself. The obvious problem posed by this technique of taking "judicial notice" of a social fact is that the judge may be relying on "fireside inductions" that, while "common knowledge," are wrong (cf. Meehl, 1977). Nonetheless, educational efforts through judicial "colleges" at least may make judges more discerning examiners of the probative level of psychological evidence and may make them aware of specific relevant substantive knowledge.

Some Paradigm Problems[9]

Regardless of the means by which psychological evidence enters the legal process, there are a number of philosophical problems that arise in its application. Simply put, the law and the social sciences operate according to different philosophical worldviews or paradigms. For example, although only the purest Rogerians in psychology base their work on an assumption of free will,

---

[7]"Standing" refers to a party's having sufficient interest in a dispute to have a "justiciable" claim. For example, a party wishing to join a suit to contest the decision of a government agency would have to show that he or she was adversely affected by the decision.

[8]See, e.g., Jenkins v. United States, 307 F.2d 637 (D.C. Cir. 1962). In Jenkins, both the American Psychiatric Association and the American Psychological Association submitted amicus briefs on the question of a psychologist's qualifications to give an expert opinion on a defendant's sanity. Not surprisingly, the two APAs reached different conclusions on this question.

[9]Portions of the remainder of this chapter have previously appeared in somewhat different form in the introduction to Melton, Koocher, and Saks (1983).

that belief is clearly a cornerstone of the law. Thus, attempts to study the "voluntariness" of consent by children are difficult when the concept is foreign to the paradigm within which psychologists work. Indeed, the clash of paradigms may lead to some paradoxical conclusions. For example, some physicians (e.g., Grodin & Alpert, 1983; Lewis, 1983) argue that children should have the opportunity to exercise greater power of consent to medical treatment, particularly when the proposed regimen is complex or long-term, in order to heighten compliance. The psychological expectation is that when children make an affirmative choice they will be more likely to follow through on that choice in order to avoid dissonance (cf. Melton, 1983; Saks, 1983). In a sense the stated purpose is to increase compliance through the exercise of liberty!

In addition to assumptive differences, there are differences in style of analysis of problems between the social sciences and the law that may make application of research difficult. On a practical level, perhaps the most consequential of these differences is the law's reliance on moral or logical analysis versus the reliance of scientists on empirical analysis. Some jurists perceive attempts to inform the law with "hard data" as undermining legal analysis through logic and commonsense. Chief Justice Burger appears to be much more comfortable in making inferences from the "pages of human experience"[10] than from systematic empirical research. A classic example of this bias came in *Ballew v. Georgia*,[11] the most extensive use of social science data by the Supreme Court thus far. In *Ballew*, the Court held that juries of fewer than six persons unconstitutionally deprived criminal defendants of their right to a trial by jury. In the opinion for the Court, Justice Blackmun relied heavily on small-group research, particularly the work of Saks (1977), to substantiate his arguments concerning the effects of jury size. Nonetheless, in a brief concurring opinion, Justice Powell, joined by Burger and Rehnquist, contended that small juries were unconstitutional essentially because the line has to be drawn somewhere (presumably by intuition). Powell went on to attack the use of empirical evidence:

> I have reservations as to the wisdom—as well as the necessity—of Mr. Justice Blackmun's heavy reliance on numerology derived from statistical studies. Moreover, neither the validity nor the methodology employed by the study was subjected to the traditional testing mechanisms of the adversary process. The studies relied on merely represent unexamined findings of persons interested in the jury system.[12]

---

[10] *See* Parham v. J. R., 442 U.S. 584, 602 (1979).

[11] 435 U.S. 223 (1978).

[12] *Id.* at 246.

As Haney (1980) has noted, the conservative intellectual tradition embodied in the *stare decisis* principle in the law may make "untested" social science evidence appear unreliable: "[D]ata are not always enough: in law, data plus authority are preferable to 'merely' authoritative data" (p. 171). Thus, although social scientists may rely on systematic collection of empirical data to inform their views as to social facts, many jurists believe such data are "untested" and untrustworthy unless there has been formal evidence taken and adjudication of these issues. Indeed, for some jurists intuitive common-sense judgments are less suspect than "numerology."

To take an optimistic (perhaps overly optimistic) stance, it may be that judicial prejudice against empirical data ultimately will be of relatively little consequence in the courts' examination of developmental phenomena. Historically, the law has been most open to the behavioral sciences in resolution of questions of juvenile and family law. Indeed, mental health services and social services for children grew up to a large extent with the juvenile court (Levine & Levine, 1970). Moreover, the massive attention given to Goldstein, Freud, and Solnit's (1973) controversial volume on custody standards (cf. Crouch, 1979) suggests that the courts may be particularly open to social science research and theory concerning children. However, it should be noted that clinical input into judicial decisions (and, for the most part, Goldstein et al.'s work does not stray from such a model) tends to serve the law as the law currently is framed and generally does not challenge the assumptions under which the law operates. Furthermore, clinical opinion is compatible with the law's idiographic approach and does not raise the conceptual problems imposed by researchers' nomothetic approach or by advocates' attention to group problems (cf. Davidson & Saul, 1982). Indeed, part of the receptivity of many judges and clinicians to Goldstein et al.'s work—and the scientific criticism it has evoked (e.g., Katkin, Bullington, & Levine, 1974; Melton, 1978b)—may have resulted from their sense of *certainty* about *individual* functioning. They were essentially unconcerned with problems related to the application of probability data to the law (which views "facts" quite differently than do scientists) or of application of findings regarding group differences to individual cases.

Finally, although perhaps obvious, the caveat that social science findings cannot be translated directly into legal policy bears emphasis. For example, the question of whether competence should be the determinant of whether children have a right to self-determination in particular situations is an ethical or a legal judgment, not a scientific one. Similarly, the standards for competence are legal, not psychological issues, although psychologists might inform legal decisionmakers about the particular results associated with various standards. Perhaps a particularly politically charged example would illustrate this point best. Lewis (1983) reported that there were some clear differences based on the socioeconomic status of the children in the effects of a system to allow children to make routine health decisions in school. The rate of removal of children's privileges to use the system at will was similar (about 3%) in both a university school in which children were from upper-middle-class families and two schools in which children were largely from disadvantaged families and the majority were black or Hispanic. However, rates of use were much higher in the low-SES schools and the children tended to perceive physicians and medicine as the primary means of health maintenance. Moreover, although there was a definite shift from nurse to self in perceptions of "who decided" what to do when they made use of the system among white children, this shift did not occur for minority-group children. Lewis suggests that the latter finding may result from a generalization of the overall lack of opportunities for minority groups, such that an actual shift in decision-making power may not seem real. This finding parallels Melton's (1980a) observation that development of concepts of rights as entitlements applicable to oneself occurs much later on the average among children from disadvantaged backgrounds than among children from high-SES families (see Chapter 2).

The implications of the findings of class differences for policy vary widely, depending on one's value preferences. One might, for example, value personal liberty and privacy as a primary purpose of the law, even for children. In that instance, the finding that there is marked variability in the rate in which children come to understand that a right means that they really *can* make a personal decision would imply the need for case-by-case determinations of competency to consent so that youngsters achieving such competence relatively early would in fact have their privacy protected. On the other hand, one might assert equality of opportunity as a primary value. In that instance, one might be offended by the possibility that white, upper-middle-class elementary-age children would enjoy more rights than their less advantaged peers if a standard of competence is the determinant. Therefore, it might be argued that an age-graded per se rule should be used, with the threshold age for competence to consent set high enough that children from diverse backgrounds would be psychologically as well as legally competent to exercise rights. Alternatively, it might be argued that, given evidence that repeated experience in exercising choices might socialize a sense of entitlement (Melton, 1983; Tapp & Melton, 1983), the threshold age for per se competence to consent should be set low so that disadvantaged youngsters might have opportunities to acquire a sense of entitlement, arguably a prerequisite for full use of legal prerogatives. The basic point is that advocates should be careful to distinguish empirical findings from personal normative judgments in discussions of social facts that may be crucial to legal analyses.

Practical Problems in Use of the Courts

Even if paradigm problems in application of psychological research can be overcome, there are still substantial practical problems to overcome in attempts to use the judicial system to foster or solidify social change on behalf of children and families. Most notably, litigation is expensive and time-consuming. For example, some of the key right to treatment suits of the early seventies (e.g., *"Willowbrook"*[13]) are still in the courts. Civil litigation typically is subject to lengthy delays and when complex institutional change is involved there inevitably is an additional lengthy implementation process even after adjudication of the initial issues raised by the plaintiffs. Sustaining legal action over such a period may require substantial monetary resources. Moreover, where there is any likelihood of legislative response, direct legislative action often may be less time-consuming. Of course, judicial action to fulfill basic rights is likely to come only when legislatures or administrators are unable or unwilling to act (cf. Johnson, 1976). Hence, the movement to the courts as instruments of change is apt to occur only when there is inaction by the other branches of government. The point nonetheless is that litigation as a practical matter probably should be reserved for last-resort efforts simply because of the time and expense involved. In that context, the *threat* of litigation may serve as an impetus to negotiation given that opponents also are likely to wish to avoid protracted litigation. Where, for example, states realize that the condition of their institutions is intolerable, they may be willing to enter consent decrees to improve these facilities and avoid lengthy litigation when the result is clear beforehand.

Besides the time and expense involved in using the courts to obtain relief, there also are practical constraints on courts themselves. Where orders will involve substantial institutional change, courts may have difficulty forcing the other branches of government to develop the financial and human resources to implement orders. Moreover, courts generally do not have the resources or often the expertise to monitor compliance; they simply were not intended to

---

[13]N.Y.S. Ass'n for Retarded Children, Inc. v. Rockefeller, *supra* note 3.

supervise the day-to-day management of schools and hospitals. It also is difficult for courts to obtain the political clout to obtain compliance. On the surface, judges have less legitimacy in undertaking such administrative efforts than do the executive and legislative branches. Consequently, if their actions are unpopular, judges' "activism" can be attacked as a usurpation of power even if judicial intervention is a matter of last resort when other authorities have not acted to guarantee legal rights to all. Although not dealing directly with the latter problem, judges can act to avoid some of the problems of over-involvement in managerial tasks by delegating authority to masters or court-appointed experts,[14] a tactic undertaken, for example, in the Boston desegregation case.[15] When it became clear that broad systemic change was necessary to counter inertia and outright resistance by the Boston School Committee, Judge Garrity appointed a panel of community leaders as masters and secured the expertise of the deans of the School of Education at Boston University in order to undertake the kind of administrative and programmatic reorganization necessary to make desegregation work in the Boston schools. The result was a network of innovative "magnet schools" and of pairings of individual schools with Boston's universities and businesses. Such specific intervention probably would have been beyond the ken of the court alone.

Even if it appears that the courts do offer the best avenue of advocacy and if resources are available to sustain the legal action, there still may be significant practical obstacles to use of the legal system to protect the rights of children. Indeed, children may lack a means of entry into the system. Even while the center of legal disputes, children often lack standing in the adjudication of these disputes. On an individual level, for example, children in the midst of custody disputes typically lack standing; if they are represented at all, it is likely to be by a guardian ad litem who may be uncertain about the parameters of the role (e.g., whether to advocate the child's own wishes or to argue for what appears to the guardian to be in the child's best interests). Similarly, on a class level children may not be able to establish themselves as parties to litigation. Perhaps the best example is *Wisconsin v. Yoder,*[16] a case involving Amish parents' removal of their children from school before they attained the age at which they could drop out legally. As will be discussed in more detail in the following section, the United States Supreme Court declined to consider the wishes of the Amish children themselves. Because the

[14]FED. R. CIV. P. 53.
[15]Morgan v. Kerrigan, *supra* note 1.
[16]406 U.S. 205 (1972).

parents were the ones risking legal liability for keeping their children out of
school, the Court assumed that the parents—not the children—had key interests at stake. Another case recently before the Supreme Court also raises questions concerning minors' access to the courts. In a case concerning local school
board censorship of library materials,[17] an initial issue was the standing of high
school students to contest this action.

Finally, there is no guarantee that the "test" issues will be reached even
if all of the other problems mentioned thus far are overcome. It is of course
not uncommon for courts to reach only narrow technical issues and thereby,
in the interest of parsimony, to avoid more fundamental substantive issues.
For example, one recent case before the Supreme Court raised numerous
important constitutional questions about standards for termination of parental rights and attracted the attention of diverse amici curiae.[18] The interest
of these child advocacy groups ultimately was for naught, however, as the case
was dismissed by the Supreme Court on jurisdictional grounds. A similar
example is *Kremens v. Bartley*,[19] the case that first raised the issue of whether
parents constitutionally could commit their children to mental hospitals without a hearing. Although the issue ultimately was decided several years later,[20]
the Supreme Court initially sidestepped the issue by remanding on mootness
grounds for redefinition of the class after Pennsylvania revised its statute to
treat minors aged 14 and older as adults for purposes of admission to mental
hospitals.

In short, the problems of using the legal system for advocacy on behalf of
children should not be minimized. There are significant paradigmatic problems in the application of developmental research in legal disputes affecting
children. Still more generally, the practical problems in civil rights litigation
are formidable.

CHANGES WROUGHT BY THE COURTS

Although this chapter thus far has dealt primarily with problems in litigation on behalf of children (particularly insofar as there is a need to apply

[17]Board of Education, Island Trees Union Free School District No. 26 v. Pico,—U.S.—, 102 S.Ct.
2799 (1982).
[18]Doe v. Delaware, 450 U.S. 382 (1981).
[19]Kremens v. Bartley, 431 U.S. 119 (1977).
[20]Secretary of Public Welfare v. Institutionalized Juveniles, 442 U.S. 640 (1979) (upholding the
constitutionality of revised Pennsylvania statute governing admission of minors to mental hospitals). *See also* Parham v. J. R., 442 U.S. 584 (1979) (upholding the constitutionality of Georgia's admission procedures).

psychological research), the point should not be lost that there still is substantial potential impact of judicial decision making on the lives of children. Regardless of whether an advocate starts from a "kiddie-lib" or a "child-saving" orientation or some combination thereof, the courts offer the ultimate means of ensuring the rights of children. Moreover, by the construction that the courts give to these rights, there can be striking impact on the status of children. To illustrate this point, we will consider the history of litigation on the limits of liberty for minors (a topic of prime concern to kiddie-libbers) and on the right to treatment for troubled youngsters (a topic of broad concern to child-savers). It should be noted that this brief review is not intended as an encyclopedic study of "children and the law"; indeed, few topics of juvenile and family law will be discussed here. The reader interested in a broad overview might consult Mnookin's (1978a) casebook or Melton's (1982b) recent edited volume on current legal issues affecting the delivery of services to children, youth, and families.

Children and Liberty

The question of the limits of children's independent decision making is of largely recent origin. Until the mid-sixties it was not clear that children were "persons" within the meaning of the Fourteenth Amendment, which makes the Bill of Rights applicable to the states. As noted in Chapter 2, although there were several early twentieth-century "children's rights" cases decided by the United States Supreme Court,[21] each of these cases could be construed as a vindication of *parents'* liberty interest in childrearing as they saw fit (Melton, 1982a). In none of the early cases was there a clear indication of minors' possessing constitutionally protected fundamental liberties independent of their parents. Children were perceived as properly dependent upon their parents who possessed a "right of control" over them.[22] Although parents' rights in this regard are limited by the fact that they are not "free . . . to make martyrs of their children,"[23] this restriction emanated from the *state's* interest in the socialization of children.[24] Indeed, the Supreme Court had held that it "would hardly seem open to question" that the state could impinge on basic freedoms of minors (e.g., freedom of religion) in ways that would be clearly unconstitutional if the same restrictions were placed on adults.[25] Given

---

[21] *E.g.,* Pierce v. Society of Sisters, 268 U.S. 510 (1925); Meyer v. Nebraska, 262 U.S. 390 (1923).
[22] Meyer v. Nebraska, *id.* at 400.
[23] Prince v. Massachusetts, 321 U.S. 158, 170 (1944).
[24] *Id.* at 165.
[25] *Id.* at 169.

clear indications that both parents and the state as parens patriae could exercise control over minors, the question of the limits of children's *actual* competence to make personal decisions was moot. Simply put, minors were per se incompetent (i.e., incompetent on the basis of age alone) to exercise self-determination; no additional inquiry was necessary or even relevant.[26]

The question of children's competence initially became a clearly live issue in 1967 when the Supreme Court explicitly stated for the first time that "neither the Fourteenth Amendment nor the Bill of Rights is for adults alone."[27] In that landmark case (*In re Gault*[28]), the Court lambasted the juvenile court as a "kangaroo court"[29] and proclaimed that juveniles charged with delinquent offenses were entitled to procedural protections fundamental to due process of law (e.g., rights to notice of the charges, representation by counsel, confrontation and cross-examination of witnesses, and the privilege against self-incrimination). At the same time, however, the Court recognized that there were

> special problems ... with respect to waiver of the privilege [against self-incrimination] by or on behalf of children.... If counsel was not present for some permissible reason when an admission was obtained, the greatest care must be taken to assure that the admission was voluntary, in the sense not only that it was not coerced or suggested, but also that it was not the product of ignorance of rights or of adolescent fantasy, fright, or despair.[30]

Thus, while the Court reserved judgment as to whether respondents in delinquency proceedings were entitled to *all* of the same due process rights as adult defendants in criminal proceedings,[31] it did acknowledge that recognition of some constitutional rights for minors would raise some questions as to the limits of their competent exercise of these rights. Essentially, if children *generally* are persons with constitutionally protected liberty interests, what limits may be placed on the exercise of these rights by minors *because* they are minors and presumably not fully mature?

The Supreme Court continued its ambivalent treatment of children's

---

[26]Per se incompetence need not rely on lack of recognition of constitutionally protected liberty. In common law, minors generally are considered unable to make binding contracts except for "necessaries" such as food and lodging.

[27]In re Gault, 387 U.S. 1, 13 (1967).

[28]*Id.*

[29]*Id.* at 28.

[30]*Id.* at 55.

[31]*Id.* at 10–11. The Court did in fact later hold that juveniles were not entitled to jury trials. McKeiver v. Pennsylvania, 403 U.S. 528 (1971).

rights with two cases pertaining to the limits of freedom of expression by minors. In 1968 in *Ginsberg v. New York*[32] the Court held that states could constitutionally prohibit the sale to minors of material believed to be obscene on the basis of its prurient appeal to them regardless of whether the material would be obscene to adults. Interestingly, the Court left open the possibility that parents could purchase the materials for their children,[33] an example of the historic deference of the law to parents in matters of childrearing. In defending the limits placed on minors' liberty in this context, Justice Stewart (concurring) argued that liberty was contingent upon competence:

> I think a State may permissibly determine that, at least in some precisely delineated areas, a child—like someone in a captive audience—is not possessed of that full capacity for individual choice which is the presupposition of First Amendment guarantees. It is only upon such a premise, I should suppose, that a State may deprive children of other rights—the right to marry, for example, or the right to vote—deprivations that would be constitutionally intolerable for adults.[34]

Even one of the dissenters, Justice Fortas (who had written the majority opinion in *Gault*), agreed that "the State in the exercise of its police power—even in the First Amendment domain—may make proper and careful differentiation between adults and children."[35]

However, in 1969 in *Tinker v. Des Moines Independent School District,* the Court reaffirmed that "students in school as well as out of school are 'persons' under our Constitution. They are possessed of fundamental rights which the State must respect, just as they themselves must respect their obligations to the State."[36] Accordingly, the Court held that a school system that had suspended students for wearing black armbands in protest of the Vietnam war had impermissibly invaded the students' exercise of First Amendment rights. The Court seemed particularly concerned that the Des Moines school authorities had attempted to limit behavior akin to "pure speech," although, in the opinion for the Court, Justice Fortas made no effort to distinguish *Tinker* from *Ginsberg*.

In 1972 the Supreme Court decided another case (*Wisconsin v. Yoder*)[37] involving minors' First Amendment rights (in this case, freedom of religion). *Yoder* is particularly noteworthy in the present context because it is the only

[32]390 U.S. 629 (1968).
[33]*Id.* at 639.
[34]*Id.* at 649–650.
[35]*Id.* at 673.
[36]393 U.S. 503, 511 (1969).
[37]406 U.S. 205 (1972).

case in which a Supreme Court opinion—albeit in a lone dissent by Justice Douglas—included a citation of developmental research to support an assertion about children's capacities. In *Yoder* the Court ruled that Amish parents' First and Fourteenth Amendment rights were violated by a state law compelling their children's attendance in school until age 16, in contrast to the Amish practice of removing their children from school upon the completion of eight grade. The Court majority assumed that the clash of interests was between the state and the parents:

> [O]ur holding today in no degree depends on the assertion of the religious interest of the child as contrasted with that of the parents. It is the parents who are subject to prosecution here for failing to cause their children to attend school, and it is their right of free exercise, not that of their children, that must determine Wisconsin's power to impose criminal penalties on the parent.[38]

In an impassioned dissent, Justice Douglas argued that the key interests at stake were those of the Amish youth themselves:

> It is the future of the student, not the future of the parents, that is imperilled in today's decision. If a parent keeps his child out of school beyond the grade school, then the child will be forever barred from entry into the new and amazing world of diversity that we have today. The child may decide that that is the preferred course, or he may rebel. It is the student's judgment, not his parent's, that is essential if we are to give full meaning to what we have said about the Bill of Rights and of the right of students to be masters of their own destiny. If he is harnassed to the Amish way of life by those in authority over him and if his education is truncated, his entire life may be stunted and deformed. The child, therefore, should be given an opportunity to be heard before the State gives the exemption which we honor today.[39]

Accordingly, "where the child is mature enough to express potentially conflicting desires,"[40] Douglas argued that his or her views should be canvassed. In support of the assumption that Amish eighth graders could be expected to manifest such maturity, Douglas cited Piaget, Elkind, Kohlberg, Gesell, and other developmental authorities as holding that "the moral and intellectual maturity of the fourteen-year-old approaches that of the adult."[41] The validity of such a generalization to Amish youth may be questionable, but the Court majority did not recognize their having significant interests at stake in *Yoder,* so the issue never was reached.

[38]*Id.* at 230–231.
[39]*Id.* at 245–246.
[40]*Id.* at 242.
[41]*Id.* at 245, n.3.

The Court's Assumptions about Minors' Competence. Beyond the incidental discussion of minors' competence to exercise self-determination in *Yoder,* several Supreme Court decisions in recent years have appeared to rest on assumptions about minors' capacities, albeit without the attempt that Justice Douglas made to ascertain the current state of scientific knowledge on these points. The cases in which such issues have arisen have involved a number of contexts in which minors might exercise consent: "voluntary" admission to mental hospitals (*Parham v. J. R.*);[42] waiver of the privilege against self-incrimination (*Fare v. Michael C.*);[43] purchase of contraceptives (*Carey v. Population Services International*);[44] and requests for abortions (*Planned Parenthood of Central Missouri v. Danforth*[45]; *Bellotti v. Baird I;*[46] *Bellotti v. Baird II;*[47] *H. L. v. Matheson*).[48]

Parham and *Fare* are particularly interesting because the decisions in these two cases were announced on the same day in 1979—with apparently conflicting assumptions about developmental phenomena. In *Parham* the Supreme Court held that a formal due-process hearing was not constitutionally required before minors were "voluntarily" committed to mental hospitals by their parents or guardian. Chief Justice Burger's opinion for the Court was replete with largely unsupported empirical assumptions about the workings of the mental health system, interaction in families of disturbed children, and psychological effects of various procedural forms (Slobogin, 1980). Perhaps most basic to the opinion, however, was an assumption that children generally are incompetent and that parents, therefore, should have authority to make major life decisions in their behalf:

> Most children, even in adolescence, simply are not able to make sound judgments concerning many decisions, including their need for medical care or treatment. Parents can and must make those judgments.[49]

Accordingly, formal hearings were perceived by the Chief Justice to be merely "time-consuming procedural minuets"[50] unnecessary to protect minors' interests.

---

[42]442 U.S. 584 (1979).
[43]442 U.S. 707 (1979).
[44]431 U.S. 678 (1977).
[45]428 U.S. 52 (1976).
[46]428 U.S. 132 (1976).
[47]443 U.S. 622 (1979).
[48]450 U.S. 398 (1981).
[49]442 U.S. 584, 603.
[50]*Id.* at 605.

In *Fare* the Court considered the question of whether a 16-year-old boy's request to speak with his probation officer during police interrogation constituted an invocation of his *Miranda* rights.[51] Michael C. was described as immature, emotional, and poorly educated.[52] Moreover, he had declined an attorney apparently because he believed the offer was a police trick: "How I know you guys won't pull no police officer in and tell me he's an attorney?"[53] Michael C. had been instructed by his probation officer to call him for assistance if he ever got into trouble again, and Michael apparently trusted his probation officer to give him good advice. Nonetheless, in a 5–4 decision, the Court held not only that a request for a probation officer did not constitute a per se invocation of the Fifth Amendment, but also that, within the "totality of the circumstances," Michael had made a valid waiver of his rights. The Court ignored both its own recognition of "special problems" with confessions by minors in *Gault* and a large body of decisions by lower courts indicating the need for special attention to the competency of minors to make independent judgments (without parents or counsel) concerning waivers of Fifth and Sixth Amendment rights. Apparently the Court's assumption in *Parham* of minors' incompetence "to make sound judgments" did not extend to the police station, presumably because of the Burger Court's desire to limit *Miranda* applications rather than a careful analysis of minors' capacities in various contexts.

Abortion Cases Concerning Minors. The most extensive, albeit fuzziest, discussion by the Supreme Court of the contingency of minors' constitutional rights on competence has come in a series of cases concerning privacy in decision making about sexual matters (i.e., abortions and contraceptives). In the first of these cases *Planned Parenthood of Central Missouri v. Danforth),*[54] the Court held that a Missouri statute requiring parental consent before minors could obtain an abortion was unconstitutional because it imposed the possibility of "an absolute, and possibly arbitrary, veto [by a third party] over the decision of the physician and his patient to terminate the patient's pregnancy."[55] The Court made clear, however, that "our holding . . . does not suggest that every minor, regardless of age or maturity, may give effective consent for termination of her pregnancy."[56] No standards were sug-

[51]442 U.S. 707.
[52]*Id.* at 733 (Powell, J., dissenting).
[53]*Id.* at 711.
[54]428 U.S. 52.
[55]*Id.* at 74.
[56]*Id.* at 75.

gested for circumstances under which a requirement of parental consent might be permissible or even necessary. That is, "maturity" was left undefined.

The Court in *Danforth* left open the question of whether parental notice or consultation, short of parental consent, might be required before a minor obtained an abortion. There were suggestions, however, that the Court would find such a requirement constitutional. Four justices dissented in *Danforth*. Justice White, joined by Chief Justice Burger and Justice Rehnquist, argued that a requirement of parental consent was justifiable in order to protect minors "from their own immature and improvident decisions."[57] In a separate dissent, Justice Stevens also supported a parental consent requirement as a means of ensuring "that the decision be made correctly and with full understanding of the consequences of either alternative."[58] Moreover, two justices in the majority (Stewart and Powell) indicated that the Missouri law was unconstitutional only because it allowed an *absolute* parental veto of a minor's abortion decision. They concluded that a consultation requirement might be permissible because of many adolescents' immaturity:

> There can be little doubt that the State furthers a constitutionally permissible end by encouraging an unmarried pregnant minor to seek the help and advice of her parents in making the very important decision whether or not to bear a child. That is a grave decision, and a girl of tender years, under emotional stress, may be ill-equipped to make it without mature advice and emotional support. It seems unlikely that she will obtain adequate counsel and support from the attending physician at an abortion clinic, where abortions for pregnant minors frequently take place.[59]

Succeeding cases have concerned the constitutionality of state statutes that involved a parental notice or consultation requirement, following the suggestions made by Justice Stewart in *Danforth*. In 1979 the Court considered a case *(Bellotti v. Baird)*[60] challenging the constitutionality of a Massachusetts law that required parental consent for abortions by minors, but allowed minors who had been denied such consent to appeal to a superior court judge. In the opinion for the Court in *Bellotti,* Justice Powell echoed the logic of the concurring opinion of Justice Stewart that he had joined in *Danforth*. Powell asserted again that parental consultation prior to an abortion decision often is desirable "as immature minors often lack the ability to

[57]*Id.* at 95.
[58]*Id.* at 103.
[59]*Id.* at 91.
[60]443 U.S. 622.

make fully informed choices that take account of both immediate and long-range consequences."[61] He seemed particularly concerned that minors might not make a competent selection of a physician, irrespective of the wisdom of the abortion decision itself.[62] Nonetheless, Powell argued that the Massachusetts statute went too far in limiting minors' options in abortion decisions. If parents refused consent, they might block the minor's access to the court. Powell concluded that the minor must have access to the court without the necessity of first seeking parental consent. Then the court would be required to authorize the abortion if she established either "that she is mature and well-informed enough to make intelligently the abortion decision on her own" or that the abortion would be in her best interest.[63]

The most recent Supreme Court decision concerning the restrictions that a state may place on abortions by minors was handed down in 1981 *(H. L. v. Matheson)*.[64] *Matheson* involved a test of the constitutionality of a Utah statute that requires physicians to "notify, if possible," the parents or guardian of a minor upon whom an abortion is to be performed. The Court decided the case on narrow grounds. Specifically, it held that H. L. had not established that she or any member of the class that she represented was mature or emancipated. In a 6–3 decision, the Court then held that, as applied to an immature, unemancipated girl living with and dependent upon her parents, the statute serves important state interests and is constitutionally drawn. In the opinion for the Court, Chief Justice Burger asserted that the statute served to preserve family integrity, to protect adolescents, and to provide an opportunity for parents to supply "essential medical and other information to a physician."[65] (As the dissenters pointed out, Burger gave no indication of what information a parent might provide that the adolescent could not.[66]) Burger further asserted that the risks of an abortion are grave:

> The medical, emotional, and psychological consequences of an abortion are serious and can be lasting; this is especially so when the patient is immature.[67]

Burger also made a rather ridiculous assertion that, "if the pregnant girl elects to carry her child to term, the *medical* decisions to be made entail few—per-

[61] *Id.* at 640.
[62] *Id.* at 641, n.21.
[63] *Id.* at 643–644.
[64] 450 U.S. 398.
[65] *Id.* at 411.
[66] *Id.* 443.
[67] *Id.* 411.

haps none—of the potentially grave emotional and psychological consequences of the decision to abort."[68]

The Court reserved judgment on the issue of whether a parental notice
requirement was constitutional when the minor is mature. There were indications, however, that the Court would find such a requirement unconstitutional. Justice Powell, joined by Justice Stewart, reaffirmed in a concurring
opinion his view, previously expressed in *Bellotti,* that a mature minor must
have access to an independent decision maker without the burden of parental
notice. The three dissenters, of course, regarded any notice requirement as an
unconstitutional interference with the minor's right to privacy. Thus, as then
constituted, a majority of the Court would appear to view a blanket parental
notice requirement as unconstitutional. It remains to be seen how the replacement of Justice Stewart by Sandra O'Connor will tip the balance.

Most importantly, the Court again gave little guidance as to the meaning
of "mature." In the opinion for the Court, Chief Justice Burger seemed almost
to equate maturity with emancipation (i.e., independence from parents of
domicile and livelihood), but such an equation was never explicitly stated.
The dissenters indicated that they viewed the mature minor rule adopted in
Danforth as applying to pregnant minors who are "capable of appreciating its
[an abortion's] nature and consequences."[69] Even the dissenters, however,
gave no clues as to the kinds and amount of knowledge about the abortion
procedure that are necessary before a minor may consent independently of her
parents.

Conclusions. Although it is clear that children now are considered to
be entitled to fundamental constitutional rights, it also is clear that the
breadth of these rights, at least as construed by the Supreme Court, is significantly narrower than for adults. Shortly after the Court's landmark decision
in *Gault,* Judge Lindsay Arthur (1968), a well-known traditionalist on the
juvenile bench, asked rhetorically, "Should Children Be as Equal as People?"
The Supreme Court seems to have answered, "Not quite." Nonetheless, by
proclaiming minors to be "persons" within the meaning of the Constitution,
the Court has opened the door to consideration of the circumstances under
which minors rationally might be extended the freedom or protection of constitutional rights.

Examination of the key Supreme Court cases involving children over the
past 15 years suggests that the Court's assessment of minors' "maturity" in

[68]*Id.* at 412–413.
[69]*Id.* at 450, n.49.

making decisions lies heavily in their determinations of the degree to which minors may exercise the rights accorded to adults. It also seems clear that the majority of the current members of the Court (particularly the "conservative" justices who have joined the Court during Burger's tenure as chief justice) have little faith in minors'—even adolescents'—competence to make informed decisions. Moreover, in forming this judgment, the Court appears to have relied exclusively on the "pages of human experience"[70] without any attempt to ascertain the current state of knowledge about children's decision-making prowess.

At the same time, it should be noted that the Court's view of children has not been so uniform as to result in the clear adjudication of social facts by judicial notice. That is, the Court has not stated its assumptions about children's capacities clearly and consistently enough to give these statements of social fact compelling precedential value. Indeed, it has appeared at times that the psychological assumptions that the Court has drawn have represented derivations of an "is" from an "ought." Frequently the Court seems to have based its assumptions about child development on a concept of how such processes should operate rather than an examination of how they in fact do. The conflicting assumptions in *Parham* and *Fare* are exemplary. The view of minors as generally incompetent in *Parham* seemed to have been derived from an idyllic view of family life and medical authority and, perhaps, a belief that disturbed adolescents should do what's good for them. On the other hand, the apparently inflated perception of minors' ability to conceptualize and maneuver through police interrogation (cf. Grisso, 1981) in *Fare* probably resulted from the Burger Court's skeptical approach to *Miranda* doctrine, perhaps combined with the sort of belief articulated by Arizona's Supreme Court in *Gault* that "confession is good for the child as the commencement of the assumed therapy of the juvenile court process"[71] Other examples of conflicting psychological assumptions by the Court (apparently based on a desire to reach different results) have come in discussions of child–parent relations in circumstances where family strife might be expected: when the parents seek to institutionalize a child[72] and when the child seeks to have an abortion without parental consent.[73]

Moreover, the Court has yet to make clear in any context what it means

---

[70]Parham v. J.R., 442 U.S. 584, 602 (1979).
[71]387 U.S. at 51, *citing* Application of Gault, 407 P.2d 760, 767–768 (1965).
[72]Parham v. J. R., 442 U.S. 584 (1979); *see especially* pp. 602–603, 610.
[73]Planned Parenthood of Central Missouri v. Danforth, 428 U.S. 52, 75 (1976).

by "mature." Even in the abortion area where the Court has expressly pro-
mulgated a mature minor rule, the Court has yet to indicate the standards by
which maturity is to be assessed, much less to address the subtleties of the
process by which consent should be obtained (cf. Saks, 1983). Such ambiguity,
absent clear statutory or ethical guidelines, makes professional practice ten-
uous and, in particular, probably results in deprivation of services to minors
who might in fact be "mature" because professionals do not wish to risk liability for working with minors who might not be able to give a valid consent.
(In fields where minors do not clearly have a constitutionally protected right
to privacy, ambiguity in statutes or regulations concerning minors' consent
may of course have similar effects; see Melton, 1981b.) Lack of specific substantive standards for competence to consent also makes difficult attempts to
provide evidence as to minors' abilities, both as individuals and as a class, to
meet various tests for competence. At present, advocates must rely on careful
analysis of what standards could be (see Weithorn, 1983) rather than what
they are.

   Although the Court's conflicting assumptions and the vacuum it has left
in standards concerning maturity are clearly problematic, this ambiguity at
least leaves open the possibility that social scientists might inform the Court
(and legislators) as to developmental trends in children's competencies insofar as standards are based on psychological assumptions. Even if such research
does not influence the formulation of standards, it might help to increase intellectual honesty and assumptions about the values and assumptions underlying
the policies that are selected to regulate the lives of children, youth, and their
families. In short, although the current Supreme Court is skeptical of children's capacity to make reasonable decisions, there is sufficient ambiguity
(and contradiction) in its positions to leave the door open for advocates to
assert children's liberty interests, especially where a right to privacy is potentially implicated.

Children and the Right to Treatment

   Of course the courts' involvement in issues pertaining to children's rights
potentially extends beyond issues of self-determination for children. The legal
system also is involved in protecting the nurturance rights of children, particularly those with special needs. In this regard, issues relating to the "right to
treatment" are exemplary although, as will become clear from the discussion
to follow, the original meaning of this term was substantially narrower than
a notion of broad entitlements to care and treatment for troubled persons,

including children. (For a detailed history of the right to treatment, see Golann & Fremouw, 1976).

The right to treatment originally was proposed by Morton Birnbaum (1960), a physician–lawyer, in the *American Bar Association Journal* and quickly endorsed by the editors of that journal (Editorial, 1960). It originally was conceptualized as a substantive due-process right for involuntarily committed persons. The proposal was based on a deceptively simple argument that, if the state deprives individuals of liberty for the purpose of providing treatment, then it must provide that treatment. To do otherwise is to invade fundamental rights without a rational, much less compelling, state purpose.

As the right to treatment has developed in law, it has taken on a variety of meanings in different legal contexts. Most commonly, it has rested on one of two constitutional theories. First, some judges have followed Birnbaum's quid pro quo theory and have found a right to treatment for civilly committed persons in the due-process clause of the Fourteenth Amendment. The prime example of such an approach is the opinion of Judge Johnson in *Wyatt v. Stickney*,[74] one of the earliest and most far-reaching right to treatment cases. Minimally acceptable "treatment" under this theory has been held to subsume both affirmative efforts to provide mental health treatment[75] and simply the provision of a humane environment (e.g., physical facilities in good repair; regular laundry; nutritious meals) for institutionalized persons.[76] Thus, although prescribing standards for minimum therapeutic efforts, right to treatment cases under the quid pro quo theory also have resulted in the establishment of minimum standards for the physical environment of institutions and for what amounts to purely custodial care.

Second, where patients are institutionalized "voluntarily" (as is often the case with institutionalized mentally retarded persons), some judges have found the quid pro quo theory inapplicable and have found not a right to treatment per se but rather a right to be *protected from harm*. In the leading application of the latter theory *("Willowbrook")*,[77] Judge Judd argued that when retarded persons are placed in an environment so inhumane and bereft

[74]324 F. Supp. 781 (M.D. Ala. 1971), *enforced,* 344 F. Supp. 373 (M.D. Ala. 1972) *and* 344 F. Supp. 387 (M.D. Ala. 1972), *modified sub nom.* Wyatt v. Aderholt, 503 F.2d 1305 (5th Cir. 1974).

[75]*See* Wyatt v. Stickney, 344 F. Supp. 373 (M.D. Ala. 1972).

[76]*Id.*

[77]N.Y.S. Ass'n for Retarded Children, Inc. v. Rockefeller, 357 F. Supp. 752 (E.D.N.Y. 1973), *enforced sub nom.* N.Y.S. Ass'n for Retarded Children, Inc. v. Carey, 393 F. Supp. 715 (E.D.N.Y. 1975) *and* 409 F. Supp. 606 (E.D.N.Y. 1976), *aff'd,* 596 F.2d 27 (2d Cir. 1979), *enforced,* 492 F. Supp. 1099 (E.D.N.Y. 1980).

of habilitative programs as to resemble penal confinement or worse, those conditions violate the Eighth Amendment prohibition of "cruel and unusual punishment" and the Fourteenth Amendment. Although the protection against harm standard is theoretically a narrow one distinguished from a true right to treatment, it has in fact served as the basis for orders that institutions must provide habilitative services in order to prevent regression among institutionalized residents.[78] Indeed an argument can be made that large institutions are so inherently harmful to residents that the state must make efforts to place residents in programmatically sophisticated community based programs (Halpern, 1976).

However, the applicability of the Eighth Amendment protection from harm standard to mental health and mental retardation facilities is not a settled matter, in part because of the doubtful applicability of the Eighth Amendment to noncorrectional settings. The Eighth Amendment well may be applicable to juvenile correctional facilities, however, and may provide a basis both for curbing abusive practices in such facilities and for establishment of standards for treatment, especially where state statutes identify the purpose of the juvenile justice system as treatment. There have in fact been several successful right to treatment (as distinguished from "protection from harm") suits based in part on Eighth Amendment claims challenging physical abuse and lack of treatment in facilities for delinquents.[79]

With regard to mental health institutions, even the due-process theory (Fourteenth Amendment) has yet to be validated by the Supreme Court, which thus far has explicitly reserved judgment on the issue.[80] The Supreme Court did recently hold that, at a minimum, mentally retarded residents of state institutions have rights to conditions of reasonable care and safety and to whatever training is necessary to maintain bodily safety and freedom from restraint. The Court once again did not reach the issue of whether there is a more general constitutionally based right to treatment or habilitation for institutionalized persons.[81]

Regardless of the existence of a constitutional right to treatment, how-

---

[78]N.Y.S. Ass'n for Retarded Children, Inc. v. Carey, 393 F. Supp. 715 (E.D.N.Y. 1975).

[79]*E.g.,* Nelson v. Heyne, 491 F.2d 352 (7th Cir. 1974), *cert.denied,* 417 U.S. 976 (1974); Morales v. Turman, 383 F. Supp. 52 (E.D. Tex. 1974), *rev'd on other grounds,* 535 F.2d 864 (5th Cir. 1976), *rev'd per curiam,* 430 U.S. 322 (1977), *rehearing denied,* 430 U.S. 988 (1977), *remanded,* 562 F.2d 993 (5th Cir. 1977); Martarella v. Kelley, 349 F. Supp. 575 (S.D.N.Y. 1972).

[80]O'Connor v. Donaldson, 442 U.S. 563, 573 (1975).

[81]Youngberg v. Romeo,—U.S.—, 102 S.Ct. 2452 (1982).

ever, it is clear that states may take on such an obligation by statute. Indeed, the first right to treatment case relying essentially on Birnbaum's logic *(Rouse v. Cameron)*[82] was actually based on a construction of the mental health statute of the District of Columbia, not the Constitution. Since then, many states have included at least a qualified right to treatment in their mental health statutes.[83] Judge Bazelon, the author of the District of Columbia Circuit Court of Appeals opinion in *Rouse,* seemed to predict the adoption of such obligations in an article that he wrote in the *University of Chicago Law Review* shortly after the *Rouse* decision:

> We should ultimately ground the right to treatment not in our duty to help the mentally ill person as a quid pro quo for confining him, but in our duty to help him as a troubled human being in our midst. As a human being, I have no doubt of the existence of this duty. As a judge, it would be wholly inappropriate for me to predict the ways in which this more basic right to treatment may take root in the law. Certainly the law approaches more closely every day the realization that individuals have definite entitlements that they may claim rather than request. We no longer regard the welfare client as a supplicant who must accept our bounty with whatever degrading conditions we choose to attach. We may soon realize that the necessities of life are a matter of personal right and societal duty, and not a bounty at all. Mental health is the most basic of these necessities. We owe it to every man. (Bazelon, 1969, pp. 753–754)

The trend toward statutory guarantees of a right to treatment that Bazelon foresaw may be be particularly significant for children, in view of the historic parens patriae duty of the state with respect to children. As already suggested, right to treatment suits brought on behalf of state training schools for delinquents have rested in part on statements of therapeutic purpose within juvenile codes.[84] Given such a purpose for juvenile justice systems, it is argued, it would be an arbitrary exercise of state power to deprive juveniles of liberty without providing treatment (a variant of Birnbaum's quid pro quo theory). More generally, given the state's duty—often expressly stated by statute—to act in the best interests of its wards, children who are in the state's care are arguably entitled to whatever treatment is necessary to ameliorate disorders to which they may be subject.[85] Not to provide such treatment would be tantamount to child neglect by the state itself.

Although the parens patriae obligations of the state apply to dependent

---

[82]373 F.2d 358 (D.C. Cir. 1966).

[83]*E.g.,* NEB. REV. STAT. § 83-1066(2) (Reissue 1976).

[84]*E.g.,* Nelson v. Heyne, *supra* note 79; Morales v. Turman, *supra* note 79.

[85]A statutory duty for guardians to act in their ward's best interests does not of course necessarily translate into such action. *See* Parham v. J. R., 442 U.S. 584, 637–638 (1979) (Brennan, J., dissenting in part).

children generally (although most directly to children in the state's own care), it is important to note that the discussion thus far has been largely limited to the right to treatment for *institutionalized* persons. Moreover, this right actually has been applied in large part to alleviate intolerable conditions of living in state institutions[86] rather than as an affirmative effort to enrich "treatment" to an optimal level. Thus, as developed in case law, the "right to treatment" generally does *not* have relevance to a right of *access* to treatment for children living at home. The problem of access to treatment (i.e., the opportunity to obtain needed treatment) actually subsumes two specific issues: (a) the right to education or habilitation for exceptional children, as established by some broad "entitlement" programs (e.g., Pub. L. 94–142),[87] and (b) the right of children to consent to treatment independently of their parents (see Melton, 1981a, b). The former approach may effectively result in a right to treatment for handicapped children, whether living at home or in institutional settings.[88] Indeed, Pub. L. 94–142 creates a right to educational services necessary to meet a child's special needs (including, where necessary, "related services" such as psychotherapy), with the provision of these services in the least restrictive environment.

Given such statutory guarantees, reliance on a constitutionally based theory of a right to treatment probably is not the most effective means of obtaining necessary treatment for minors, even those residing in state institutions. Nonetheless, it is still useful for our purposes to sketch some of the problems raised by major right to treatment suits such as *Wyatt* and *Willowbrook*. These problems illustrate that "winning the case" in litigation does not necessarily bring about the results sought. Rather, as noted at several other points in this volume, making a successful argument is not enough. Child advocates also must be concerned with avoiding undesirable side effects of a decision and with ensuring that favorable judgments are implemented. In fact, in protracted right to treatment litigation the latter purposes have proven at least as difficult—probably more difficult—to achieve as initially winning the case.

There are of course conceptual problems with defining treatment. Mental health professionals themselves disagree as to what constitutes therapeutic

---

[86]*See* Johnson (1976) for a graphic account of the conditions he has encountered as a federal judge hearing such cases.

[87]Education for All Handicapped Children Act, 20 U.S.C. §§ 1401–1461.

[88]Such a right may also rest on constitutional equal protection grounds, given states' obligations to provide public education. That is, once states have accepted the duty of providing education, they must provide it to all, arguably without regard to handicap. *See* PARC v. Pennsylvania, 334 F. Supp. 1257 (E.D. Pa. 1971) *and* 343 F. Supp. 279 (E.D. Pa. 1972).

behavior and courts cannot be expected to do better in defining "good" treatment. Even more basically, however, courts have yet to deal with the knotty fundamental problem of the appropriate standard to be used in evaluating whether treatment meets constitutional muster. For example, do patients have a right to *effective* treatment, to the *best* (most effective) treatment, to *a* treatment (regardless of whether effective), or simply to *care* that is humane and protects their physical health and safety? If effectiveness is to be considered, how is it to be measured? What constitutes adequate treatment for a patient whose treatability is a "legal fiction," a patient for whom no effective treatment is known? These conceptual issues have been avoided thus far because right to treatment suits typically have been brought in facilities in which everyone—including the defendants—agrees that conditions are intolerable. Consequently, the exact terms of the order usually are then worked out in a consent decree by the parties and rubber-stamped by the court. (Stickney, 1976, provides an interesting account of these negotiations in *Wyatt*.) Thus, although the authority of the court provides the impetus for the ultimate decree, the parties frequently agree upon minimum standards for treatment themselves. Thus, the court need not journey too far into the conceptualization of minimally acceptable treatment. It may of course participate indirectly in the negotiations, however, through court-appointed masters, who may be chosen for their expertise in mental health administration.

These conceptual problems aside, perhaps the most fundamental problem underlying the implementation of a right to treatment is that resources are finite. Assuming scarce resources, very specific and relatively high standards are likely to result in a diversion of resources away from other programs, which also may be funded at intolerably low levels. This reallocation may be a misallocation at times. For example, given the dearth of mental health professionals in Alabama at the time *Wyatt* was brought, resources might better have been spent on community programs relying primarily on paraprofessional staff. Moreover, even if funds theoretically are available, the judge enforcing a right to treatment ultimately is dependent on the action of the legislature to appropriate the funds necessary to carry out the order. In Alabama, for example, Judge Johnson encountered a recalcitrant Mental Health Board, legislature, and governor, thus creating a stalemate for a time with the commissioner of mental health in the middle (Stickney, 1976).

If orders are fully implemented, a potential undesirable side effect is that service delivery will be locked into a hospital-based model of treatment. Furthermore, the more specific that orders are, the less likely is there to be experimentation in mode of service delivery. To a certain extent, the particular staffing pattern and design requirements for physical facilities ordered will predetermine the kinds of treatment to be offered.

Dealing with staff unrest and fitting the orders to civil service strictures also may be problems. The two leading cases on institutional change as part of a right to treatment (i.e., *Wyatt* and *"Willowbrook"*) both have involved significant personnel issues. *Wyatt* in fact originally was brought by employees of Bryce Hospital in Alabama who had been laid off because of budget cutbacks.[89] They added patients to the class to buttress their argument that their dismissal jeopardized treatment at Bryce. Ultimately Judge Johnson's order provided for more mental health professionals than were then present in the entire state. Recruitment efforts proved largely unsuccessful and resulted in conflict between "old" and "new" staff:

> As to the recruitment of professional staff, the experimental evidence shows at least in the short run that advertising and money won't do it. For almost a year before I was fired as Commissioner, the Department advertised in all the leading professional journals and sent recruiting posters to the professional schools. Salaries were described as "open and on the rise," for at that time the staff expected adequate funding through court action or federal money. The results from all this advertising were extremely disappointing. When a trickle of new people did respond, putting their salaries at a new, higher level could and did alienate long-term employees. The latter could not receive raises because of . . . [a] wage freeze. (Stickney, 1976, pp. 39–40)

Similar issues of the status of "old" employees were raised in *"Willowbrook."* New York officials went back into court to ensure that one aspect of the consent decree (turning over the operation of several buildings at Willowbrook to a private agency) did not violate state civil service law or the state's contract with the civil service employees' union.[90]

Finally, if the state does prove recalcitrant or unable to comply with the court's orders, it is unclear what remedies are available on a practical basis. Simply releasing ("dumping") patients without alternative services seems to be a victory for no one. Under a quid pro quo theory, however (see Birnbaum's, 1960, original exposition of this theory), release would be the most logical remedy, at least for involuntarily committed patients, for failure to provide treatment. Moreover, one side effect of right to treatment litigation in some states may be that the state (even without such an order) simply shuts down programs in order to avoid the cost of acceptable ones.

Another alternative would be to rely on the civil liability of individual

---

[89]Wyatt v. Stickney, 325 F. Supp. 781, 782 (M.D. Ala. 1971).
[90]N.Y.S. Ass'n for Retarded Children, Inc. v. Carey, 456 F. Supp. 85 (1978).

hospital administrators and clinicians. However, establishing individual liability for not providing treatment[91] might make state hospitals an even less desirable place for professionals to work. Moreover, insofar as the real problem is a lack of resources, suits directed at hospital staff are likely to do little to remedy the basic problem. Ultimately courts may have to rely on moral suasion to convince state legislatures (who *do* have some control over the resources available to state institutions) to fulfill their obligations. In any case, it is difficult to imagine a federal judge using the sanction of contempt of court to force legislators to comply with orders to appropriate the necessary funds. In some instances, however, legislators actually may use the court as a buffer between themselves and their constituencies to provide a rationale for "liberal" reform (Johnson, 1976). Similarly, hospital administrators may welcome suits against themselves as a means of extracting additional funds.

CONCLUSIONS

As should be clear from this discussion, achieving social change through the judicial process is a complex matter. Even favorable judgments sometimes may result in unintended effects or in essentially no effect at all. Nonetheless, it is important to note that, where states have reneged on their duty to protect their dependent citizens, the courts may both clearly establish the existence of such duties in law and eventually create substantial change. Judge Johnson's account of changes in Alabama's mental retardation facility is exemplary. Partlow State School was, at the start of the *Wyatt* suit, a "shocking" place where conditions were "barbaric and primitive," so much so that several residents had died as a result of abuse and neglect. Although not without controversy, conditions had improved markedly in four years as a result of the *Wyatt* decree:

> During the past several years conditions at the Partlow State School for the retarded have improved markedly. It was pleasing to read in a Montgomery newspaper that members of the State Mental Health Board (the *Wyatt* defendants) recently met at Partlow and agreed that "what they saw was a different world" compared to four years ago; that "things are now unbelievably better," with most students "out in the sunshine on playground swings or tossing softballs . . . responding to a kind word or touch with smiles and squeals of delight"; and that "enrollment has been nearly cut in half, down from 2,300 to just under 1,300 while the staff has tripled from 600 to 1,800." (Johnson, 1976, pp. 909–910)

---

[91]State hospital officials are liable for monetary damages if they knowingly or maliciously violate patients' rights. O'Connor v. Donaldson, 422 U.S. 563, 577 (1975).

The reduction in enrollment was significant in view of the state's admission that 70% of the residents should never have been committed at all.[92]

By the same token, although decisions about minors' status as "persons" often have been ambivalent or unclear, the courts still have the potential to recognize the *actual* competencies of older children and adolescents and to respect their privacy. The revolution in juvenile procedure after *Gault* is illustrative of the possibilities that the courts hold for child advocates who seek the further recognition of children's personhood. Moreover, as suggested earlier in this chapter, psychologists and other specialists in the behavior of children may contribute to a policy based on data rather than supposition.

In short, although the problems of social change through litigation on behalf of children should not be taken lightly, child advocates should be informed about the potential for use of the legal process. At the same time, efforts must not stop in the courtroom or in the pretrial bargaining session. Attention also must be given to dissemination and implementation of legal reforms.

[92]Wyatt v. Aderholt, 503 F.2d 1305 (5th Cir. 1976).

CHAPTER 9

Concepts of Childhood

IMPLICATIONS FOR CHILD ADVOCACY[1]

In Chapter 1 the competing and often contradictory theories of child advocacy were reviewed. It was noted that the policies advocated sometimes will differ dramatically, depending upon whether the self-styled child advocate seeks to "save" or to "liberate" children. Assuming that both child savers and kiddie libbers sincerely strive to better the welfare of children, it is clear that their underlying premises about the nature of childhood differ. Child savers tend to perceive children as vulnerable and in need of special protections and entitlements. On the other hand, kiddie libbers tend to perceive children as more alike, than different from, adults, at least with respect to their basic status as citizens of the community. Moreover, those who seek to liberate children, although not denying that maturation is accompanied by increasing competence, tend to argue that children's lack of competence often may be the result of their being deprived of opportunities for the exercise of responsibility and accordingly for socialization into self-determination (cf. Bersoff, 1983). Of course, there are others who perceive children as properly being deprived of such opportunities on political/economic (i.e., they don't pay their own way) as well as psychological grounds.

The importance of this analysis lies in the fact that, regardless of whether the intent is to save or to liberate children, significant change in policies governing children may first require change in public attitudes toward children and, indeed, restructuring of the cognitive construct of "childhood." In addition, attempts to elucidate individual and group differences in the understand-

---

[1]This chapter was coauthored by James Faubion, Department of Philosophy, University of Virginia, Charlottesville, Virginia.

ing of this concept may help to provide the framework for attempts to mediate disputes among competing groups of child advocates.

Perhaps some notion of the degree of relativity of the concept of childhood can be imparted by recognition of the fact that childhood and, to an even greater extent, adolescence have undergone striking evolution even within our own culture. Analysis both of historical archives (e.g., Kett, 1977) and of trends in census data (Modell, Furstenberg, & Hershberg, 1976) suggests that "growing up, as a process, has become briefer, more normful, bounded, and consequential" (Modell et al., 1976, pp. 30–31). Indeed, despite psychoanalytic (e.g., Blos, 1962) and (now passé) evolutionary (Hall, 1904) views of adolescent sturm und drang as the necessary correlates of pubertal changes, there is evidence that adolescence, as a separate stage, was not "invented" until the late 19th century (Bakan, 1971). In the early days of our nation, speakers interchangably spoke of "children," "youth," and "young men" (Kett, 1977). As Kett (1977) has summarized,

> if adolescence is defined as the period after puberty during which a young person is institutionally segregated from casual contacts with a broad range of adults, then it can scarcely be said to have existed at all [in the early nineteenth century], even for those young people who attended school beyond age 14. (p. 36)

Thus, childhood as a real social phenomenon—and as a concept—has varied markedly even within relatively recent history, even if basic maturational laws have been relatively constant.

In short, although "the child" necessarily stands at the center of the discourse on child advocacy, the child nevertheless does not represent an object whose nature is immediately or transparently available to the observer, nor does childhood represent a concept with applications that are self-evident or determinable a priori. Rather, the child is a largely undefined point of reference, around which three ancillary discourses coalesce. One, political, would organize the institutions involved with child management. Another, prescriptive, would determine the ethical status of children, their rights and obligations. Still another, empirical or interpretational, would determine the child's being, or essence. The last is in some sense the most basic. Children's participation in the moral community is contingent at least in part on the level of intentionality of which they are assumed to be capable. The relatively nascent science of developmental psychology may be informative in that regard (cf. Lickona, 1976a). On the other hand, a discourse on the ethical status of children also obviously involves normative assumptions beyond the purview of social-scientific investigation. Nonetheless, the concern here is not to attempt to understand "childhood" through psychological investigation; indeed, the point is that the concept bears a social reality apart from the "objective" reality of developmental processes. Rather, the focus here is on understanding the variations in the concept of childhood.

As suggested earlier in this chapter, examination of individual and group differences in the conceptualization of childhood may assist in the clarification of underlying philosophical differences among child advocates and negotiation among competing groups. Even more basically, the nature of the cultural and historical relativity of the concept of childhood suggests that the conflicts implicit within the concept itself (e.g., self-directedness versus dependence) are deeply embedded in societal concepts of authority relations. To the extent that "childhood" is indeed a product of broader social and economic structures and assumptions, attitudes toward advocacy on behalf of children may be relatively resistant to change, in part because the often may be based on assumptions that are so much a part of the social fabric that they usually remain unarticulated. If this thesis is valid, child advocates may have to address very basic social concerns before substantial reform will occur on behalf of children.

As an initial effort at understanding the forces determining concepts of childhood, this chapter represents an examination of variations in such concepts from multiple disciplinary perspectives: philosophy, anthropology, history, and psychology. Study of childhood in historical and cultural perspective may place the child advocacy movement in context and suggest a basic agenda for such efforts. We trust that the richness of this multidisciplinary examination, although inevitably complex and abstract, will help to identify the significance of the concept of childhood in developing a conceptual framework for child advocacy. A closer look at the social meaning of the label of "child" across time and space may help advocates to understand conflicts resulting from variations in assumptive worldviews. Whether child savers or kiddie libbers, advocates might well examine for what social values they speak when they purport to speak on behalf of children, as well as for what values those of differing ideologies speak.

CHILDHOOD IN THE CONTEXT OF MODERN PHILOSOPHY

Given the complexity of the concept of childhood, it is unsurprising that the discourse on child advocacy frequently is a scene of controversy. We have already noted the clash between those favoring a paternalistic stance and those supporting institutionalization of self-determination rights (see also

Morton & Dubanoski, 1980; Worsfold, 1979). In addition, the discourse often is laden with the more fundamental ethical inquiry of whether the child is a partially or fully endowed moral person with inherent moral privileges of its own (compare Farson, 1974, with Baumrind, 1980). Beneath even this question, however, is the problem of the child's identity and character. This ontological problem has formal consequences for the child's ethical categorization as well as for the political policy of which the child is the legitimate heir. Consequently, it is unsurprising that this question of the nature of the child continues to underlie the discourse on child advocacy as a whole.

Analyses of this problem have tended to pursue a peculiar path. Analyses of the child's identity generally have avoided descriptions of the invariant of characteristic features of the child. Rather, such analyses have tended to appear as sets of weighted, quasiontological principles that specify the child's most important tangible qualities. Taken together, these analyses tend to fall more or less straightforwardly under one pole of a wide ranging dichotomy. As we have already noted, some philosophers (e.g., Henley, 1979) conclude that the child is a dependent being who cannot meet basic material needs and who cannot independently formulate coherent principles of actions or suitable goals. Others (e.g., Houlgate, 1979) conclude that the child is essentially autonomous and capable of independent thought and responsible self-direction. This dichotomy is in part generated by some moral philosophers' quest to determine the child's capacity to act as a rational agent because of the implications that this determination would have for assigning the possibility of moral action to the child (Locke, 1690/1960, Second Treatise, Chapters 2 and 6; Rawls, 1971, pp. 395–424). Thus, children are believed to be autonomous to the extent to which they can make valid judgments concerning the results of action and calculate the relation between means and ends. From such a persepective, dependency flows from an inability to perform such rational judgments. Ethical theory may therefore stimulate the collection of particular evidence deemed relevant to the determination of the child's being; it similarly may influence the adoption of autonomy and dependence as qualities defining the nature of this being.

Ethical theory is of course not solely responsible for this dualistic conceptualization of the child. Historically, it extends to the era preceding the French Revolution, perhaps to the Jesuit colleges of the sixteenth century (Ariès, 1960). Contemporaneously, it is a dichotomy raised throughout the social sciences, particularly within developmental theory itself (cf. Skolnick, 1975). Rousseau (1762/1974), for example, recognized in the child an inherent predisposition to act according to urges and laws that always were good, but he still did not conclude that children should be free to act as they might

wish. Similarly, although psychoanalytic theorists, particularly recent ego analysts (e.g., Erikson, 1963), attribute explicit directions and goals to the child,
the nonetheless are careful to urge the necessity of parental managment and
control. Conversely, in modern developmental theories generally, although
the child (at least the young child) is conceptualized as largely undifferentiated cognitively and affectively, he or she still is thought to be capable of
often acting independently and making adaptations to the demands of others
and the nature of the world. These dualistic concepts doubtlessly flow from
empirical observation. Nonetheless, the particular weights assigned to the
poles of the dichotomy often may operate not so much as a hypothesis but as
a presupposition in thought and in direction of research. Indeed, it is arguable
that the dualistic concept of childhood is a construct that is formed, to a certain extent, before the facts and is tied to the circumstances of historical
moment rather than the processes of a single mind. In short, this dualism
assumes meaning both as a cultural value and as a social rule.

Such an argument is consistent with Ariès's (1960) justly celebrated history of children in Europe since the medieval period. In his view, the point in
history in which childhood began to be viewed as a distinct stage in life apart
from infancy and adulthood was coincident with more general transforma-
tions in the organization of social life, particularly in terms of authority and
power (see also Donzelot, 1977; Foucault, 1975, 1978). This moment is
marked intellectually by the revision of the concept of humankind (Foucault,
1973, especially Part II, Chapter 9). This concept is no longer to be understood as a distinctive role and position in a divinely preordained nature.
Rather, the meaning of humankind becomes transcendental; in a conceptual
transformation that receives its most detailed transformation in Kant's *First
Critique,* "the self" comes to signify a purely abstract possibility left open by
the rational order of the world (Kant, 1781/1978, especially pp. 409–415).
At the same time, the analysis of humanity becomes essentially practical, a
calculus of action. If it goes without saying that human beings are agents of
their behavior with characters and wills of their own, it is nevertheless possible to raise a new question: Can people act not only according to their own
motivations but also in deference to and with respect for the motivations of
others (see Ariès, 1960, pp. 265–297; Foucault, 1975, Part III)? Whether
given in Hobbesian or anti-Hobbesian terms and based upon empirical or a
priori evidence, the answers to this question constitute an intellectual
dilemma that remains largely unresolved and perhaps unresolvable.

This is not to say, however, that the question has not been decided for
particular classes of persons, with or without justification. For children, as for
other groups denied full privileges of citizenship (e.g., criminals and the men-

tally disordered), the decision has been largely negative. As a result of their immaturity, children are to some degree socially undisciplined, unable to meet the requirements of a social order that, regardless of its "artificiality," "corruption," or "repressiveness," comes to be viewed (most notably by Rousseau, 1762/1974) as a necessary and irreducible aspect of the best of human life. The question of discipline thus appears to provide the rationale for both a practical program of classification and a legislative program of social policy. Discipline does not distinguish persons qua persons, but only persons as members of civil society. If children can neither perfectly understand nor consistently recognize the necessities of civil life, they remain human beings all the same. The deviance of the madman, the criminal, or the child does not constitute the basis of a distinction between what is human and what is not. Rather, it constitutes the basis of a distinction between those who are fully citizens and those who are not. Empirical considerations are not irrelevant: the mentally disordered will be treated differently from the criminal, and the child differently from these, precisely because the nature of their deviance varies. But many of the social ramifications are similar; the undisciplined are to be removed from the ordinary course of social life. Whether this segregation is imposed in the name of rehabilitation, reform, or training, its general manifestations—state-sanctioned institutions and special legal provisions—are to be remarkably stable and constant within the European history of the last 200 years (Ariès, 1960, Foucault, 1978).

Although the dualistic concept of childhood and the beginnings of age-grading (i.e., age-based segregation) thus can be traced to the revolutions in social and intellectual life that occurred around the time of the French and American Revolutions, marked age-grading is a still more recent phenomenon, again associated with more general social changes, apart from actual "discoveries" of objective phenomena of human development. Most of the institutions that have segregated youth from the rest of the community—compulsory education, child labor laws, the juvenile court, youth religious, and secular organizations—arose at the end of the nineteenth or the the beginning of the twentieth century. These institutions appear to have resulted as a response to industrialization and the accompanying wave of immigrants. As Kett (1977) has cogently shown, much of the special treatment of youth seemed to be aimed at inculcating middle-class values in the face of increasing heterogeneity within the society. Kett's analysis of the beginning of Sunday schools is exemplary:

> [F]ear of the metropolis provided the emotional thrust behind the organization of young people's societies. Evangelicals feared great cities. The metropolis was too

heterogeneous to allow the sort of moral oversight possible in villages and towns. In the eyes of evangelical Protestants, a combination of immigrants and the liquour interest dominated cities. In the Gilded Age, metropolitan wet populations repeatedly beat back efforts of town and village abstainers to impose prohibition. Prohibition became the symbolic issue over which differences in the cultural and moral values of the native and immigrant populations were fought out. The young people's movement, dry as a stone, was in large measure a response of the native Protestant population to the challenge of the city, but a response which aimed less at elevating the moral tone of the metropolis than at building a moat around villages and towns, the places in which evangelical strength was rising rather than declining. (p. 192)

Even more on point is the fact that the *intellectual* analyses of the nature of childhood and adolescence were heavily affected by these social pressures. G. Stanley Hall's (1904) work which is sometimes credited with the invention of "adolescence" was heavily influenced by his own religious and social beliefs (see Kett, 1977, especially pp. 204–210). His view of adolescence as a wiping clean of primitive life (akin to primitive societies) and a recapitulation of the quest for civilized life was a highly ethnocentric attempt to place the social changes surrounding him into a pseudoscientific, biological framework. Kett's (1977) analysis of the impact of these conceptual changes is again illuminating:

To speak of the "invention of the adolescent" rather than of the discovery of adolescence underscores a related point: adolescence was essentially a conception of behavior imposed on youth, rather than an empirical assessment of the way in which young people actually behaved. The architects of adolescence used biology and psychology (specifically, the "storm and stress" thought to be inherent in youth), to justify the promotion among young people of norms of behavior that were freighted with middle-class values. One of these norms was conformity, whether in the inculcation of "school spirit" in secondary schools or in the implanting of "loyalty" and "hero worship" in the team sports of boys' clubs. Another was hostility to intellectuality, evident both in the *Cardinal Principles of Secondary Education* and in the muscular Christianity which imbued movements like scouting. A third norm was passivity, although the rhetoric of boys–workers might appear at first to belie this. But if boys–workers praised aggressiveness (the "pugilistic" instinct), they insisted at the same time that it be directed only against other boys inthe context of highly regulated team sports. (p. 243)

The lesson seems clear: "Childhood" as a phenomenon is a product of particular value systems. Rather than an invariant concept, it has been subject to striking modifications over the past 200 years, particularly within the last century. Moreover, these changes in conceptualization of the child (and treatment of the child as a special kind of person) appear to be the product of more general changes in social organization and social thought.

THE ETHNOLOGY OF THE CHILD

The fact that the concept of childhood appears to be subject to historically variable determinations does not prove the argument, offered by some contemporary commentators, that childhood is a mere invention. The same fact, on the other hand, indicates that such a proposal is to be taken seriously. If the concept of childhood is underdetermined by physiological criteria, what criteria additionally come into play to complete its determination? This question cannot be answered rigorously within the context of a single historical tradition. It is, of course, an open question whether a program of ethnological research might be able to determine a pattern in the variations to which childhood is liable, if any such pattern exists. If, nevertheless, we may follow the suggestions of Ariès and his successors, it is likely that an ethnology of childhood must address at least two broad mechanisms of social organization. On the one hand, it must consider patterns of socialization and social control. Our historical review suggests that childhood tends to be increasingly articulated as a social category as a society places greater stress on behavioral propriety. Consequently, it is probable that the conditions that determine variations in such emphasis also influence the relevance, the salience, and the precision of the concept of childhood itself. On the other hand, an ethnology of childhood must consider systems of belief. Childhood is as much a concept as a role, and it would be incredible if an ideology of childhood did not specifically reflect the character of this role.

The Child and Authority

It is hardly conceivable that the child, in any society, is ever completely outside the demands of authority, whether this authority functions by means of a cosmological justification system, rules of descent, or the structure of family and community organization. Indeed, it is very likely that the child serves as the focal point of a fairly formalized pattern of nurturance in every culture at the moment of its birth (Barry & Paxson, 1971). Usually, but not always, infants receive surprisingly constant sets of material and emotional supports from those most closely bound to them by kinship. Almost always, if healthy, they enjoy more permissiveness, indulgence, and protection than at any other period of life. In general, this pattern is predictable enough: the very real physical and psychological incapacities of the young infant are ecological facts for which every self-maintaining culture must make some provision, and the heightened threat of death during the infancy period is a very real pressure with which every culture must cope, however limited its repertoire of knowledge might be. It is thus unsurprising that infant nurturance is more or less a cultural universal, and that its quality apparently is largely undetermined by cultural and social factors that more clearly influence other aspects of child managment and care. Nonetheless, it is still evident that with nurturance patterns, as with most other cultural configurations, a wide degree of variation in content and style is displayed. In particular, the environment of the nuclear family plays no particularly special role in child nurturance worldwide. At least one recent anthropological study (Ritchie & Ritchie, 1979) suggests that neither the intensity of the mother–child relationship nor the primacy of the nuclear home is crucial per se to the development of emotionally stable and instrumentally competent personalities in adulthood.

Patterns of infant nurturance generally place fewer demands and obligations upon the child than they do upon the adults or older children designated as educators or caretakers. This does not mean that the child is free, even during the infancy period, from direct and coercive mechanisms of control and demands for conformity of one sort or another. The content of these demands, however, is not always what the content of some of the more self-conscious practices of infant management in the West may lead us to expect. For example, although the child is universally expected to be weaned, training usually does not begin before the infancy period comes to an end around age two (Barry & Paxson, 1971; Whiting & Child, 1953). The onset of training in elimination control varies somewhat more greatly, but Western society in any case begins its training at a much earlier age than do most other societies. It is even unclear that weaning and training in elimination control, in spite of their universality and again in spite of Western practices, represent or constitute a closely integrated system of management. The correlation between the onset of the two is unimpressive, and elimination training is, with respect to its onset and severity, more clearly linked than weaning to other aspects of child management, such as the inculcation of modesty and independence (Barry & Paxson, 1971). It is thus likely that, although variations in weaning patterns are more intimately connected with such ecological or quasi-environmental variables as diet and food surplus, variations in elimination control patterns correspond to variations in socialization practices in general.

In fact, though there are significant cross-cultural variations in the rigor and elaboration of the child's subjection to authority, and wide cross-cultural variations in the degree to which the child is a focus of institutionalized authority, there is a much less intracultural variation of the same order. Although one culture may be lenient in the control and care of its children and another quite strict, the different institutions of child management within the boundaries of a single culture tend to display the same degree of leniency or strictness throughout, regardless of number or diversity. This interinstitutional correspondence is apparent, though perhaps not very markedly, in sets of practices that intuitively are quite disparate. The intensity of nurturance, for example, is correlated positively with the earliness and consistency of training in self-guidance and independence, in spite of the child's contrary role as object of attention in the former and and object of coercion in the latter (Barry & Paxson, 1971). The same relation also is apparent in practices associated with personality development (Barry, Josephson, Lauer, & Marshall, 1980).

Practices and Rigor: Theories of Causal Circumstances

In a recent essay, Ogbu (1981) has proposed that the criteria that define human competency are based upon two variable pressures: the pressure of the physical environment, which affects the design of economy and social organization, and the pressure of culture, which determines the assignment of crucial tasks, such as the "subsistence tasks of a given population," to particular social roles. Ogbu consequently proposes that the same pressures influence the structure of the transition from childhood to adulthood and at least one aspect of child management. They influence the structure of development to the extent that competency itself marks the stages of life. As Ogbu put it, "child categories and instrumental competencies eventually develop into adaptive adult categories and instrumental competencies" (p. 417). The pressures of physical environment and culture influence the content of child management to the extent that "child-rearing techniques serve only as a mechanism for inculcating and acquiring certain culturally defined instrumental competencies and are, in fact, shaped largely by the nature of these particular competencies" (p. 417). Following J. W. Berry (1971, 1977), Ogbu further suggests that the content of socialization practices may directly affect socialization style. Thus, he repeats Berry's idea that "harsh, restrictive methods of socialization" probably do not appear in societies that encourage independence and self-reliance in their children and, conversely, that permissive and expansive socialization methods probably are absent in societies that encourage conformity.

Ogbu's model of competency implicates an economic factor as the explanation of the variations that occur in the relation between the child and authority. There is indeed considerable evidence that economic factors substantially affect the content of socialization practices generally. Barry, Child, and Bacon's (1959) classic review of child-rearing practices in 104 societies reported striking relationships between character training and dominant economies of subsistence. For example, Barry et al. noted highly significant correlations between the predominance of agriculture and training in responsibility ($r = +.74$, for boys) as well as the inculcation of obedience ($r = +.50$, for boys). The predominance of agriculture is, on the other hand, strongly inversely related to rewards for achievement ($r = -.60$, for boys).

It is important to recognize, however, that Barry et al.'s study does not fundamentally compare character training with economic form. Rather, it compares such training with economic organization, specifically with the degree to which food resources are cared for and accumulated in advance of their actual consumption. Barry et al. place at one extreme those societies in which agriculture and animal husbandry provide the predominant means of subsistence because, in those societies, constant tendance of resources is paramount to the future availability of the food supply. Given then that adherence to strict routines may ensure the protection and maintenance of food resources, it might be expected that agrarian societies would value traits such as obedience and responsibility more highly than creativity and self-initiative. Barry et al. conceptualize hunting societies as lying at the other extreme, where "individual initiative and development of high skill seem to be at a premium. Where each day's food comes from that day's catch, variations in the energy and skill exerted in food-getting lead to immediate reward and punishment. Innovation, moreover, seems unlikely to be so generally feared" (p. 52). If the results of Barry et al.'s study must be understood then to refer only inferentially to subsistence economy as such, they nevertheless clearly indicate that economic organization is perhaps the most influential of any single cultural element in the determination of the content of socialization practices. The correlation between pressure toward compliance and the accumulation of food is not only extraordinarily high ($r = +.94$, for societies at extremes of accumulation; $r = +.92$, for societies in the middle range), it also is higher than the correlation between compliance pressure and nine other cultural variables (including cultural complexity, settlement size, social stratification, descent rules, and residence patterns). Thus, Barry et al. concluded that "accumulation of resources is indicated as a probable underlying variable responsible for the relationship found between socialization and subsistence economy" (p. 61).

Anthropological research therefore suggests that the mechanisms of authority that control the child of any culture are, in both substance and degree, expressive of the wider mechanisms that control adult character and interaction. The child/authority relation is thus symbolic of the culture's general norms for acceptable behavior and of the relative weight and coerciveness of the social order. The child appears to be subject to the most extensive and elaborately designed controls in societies that are relatively rigid and precise in their organization; the child's character appears to be modified in one way or another according to the importance that given traits possess in relation to primary economic roles. In general, where economic relations are largely unascribed, children seem to learn to be more independent, aggressive, and self-reliant; where organization is based upon relations of kinship or some other ascribed categorical status, children seem to learn to be more obedient and restrained.

The Ideology of Childhood

If child control functions sociologically to shape children into what they must become, it also functions to distinguish the child from other categories of persons. Given the tendencies and variations indicated by cross-cultural comparisons, it would be surprising if childhood did not in some sense represent a special economic role. To the degree that it represents a characteristic set of practices or duties, childhood is not, contrary to what evidence from our own society might indicate, always markedly distinct from adulthood. Although children rarely are incorporated fully into adult life, they are nevertheless frequently responsible for a variety of adult tasks, economic and sometimes even ceremonial, especially after age 7 or 8. It is not at all uncommon for children to work alongside their parents in agricultural and pastoral societies. Such situations are not unique to agrarian societies, however. Data from the Human Relations Area Files (HRAF) indicate that children may perform the duties and tasks of adults whatever these duties and tasks may be. Economic type does not correlate significantly with the incorporation of children into adult occupations (Barry, Josephson, Lauer, & Marshall, 1980).

To the degree that childhood does represent a set of values, economic factors seem to play a more clearly relevant role (see Arnold, Bulatao, Buripaki, et al., 1975, for a study of the values placed upon children in six urbanized societies; cf. Hoffman, Thornton, & Manis, 1978, for such a study of American parents). Though it is rare to find a society in which children are only slightly wanted or desired, people in most societies seem particularly to value the child because of economic utility ascribed to children. Not surprisingly, the child's ability to contribute to.the economic well-being of the family or household is more frequently cited by people of non-Western cultures as a reason to have and to want children; but even in America, the same feature of the child is cited by parents, usually in rural areas, with the highest fertility desires (Hoffman et al., 1978). The HRAF sample indicates, furthermore, that although only about 8% of world societies regard the child as only slightly worthwhile at best, about 87% of these societies direct these negative attitudes more strongly toward girls (Barry et al., 1980). The fact that none of these societies are matrilineal and that some, particularly the most complex, are strongly patrilineal (Murdock & Wilson, 1980), suggests that girls are less valued in societies for which the system of resource distribution is largely determined by a male-based system of inheritance. In over half of these societies, such conventionally masculine activities as warring and hunting (both of which have fairly straightforward economic precipitants) are foci of patterns of attainment of personal status and prestige (Murdock & Morrow, 1980; Tuden & Marshall, 1980). Thus, the structure of classification within the culture, which may be relatively independent of economic conditions, may contribute to the negative value placed on girls in these societies.

Though the economic utility of the child constitutes cross-culturally the most common motive to have and to want children, other motives of course appear. Among Americans, children are most frequently valued as a source of affection and stimulation (Hoffman et al., 1978); this value is expressed as frequently as economic utility in other highly industrialized, urbanized societies (Arnold et al., 1975). People may see the child as a means of self-expansion, as a means of personal achievement or immortality. They may view the child as a symbol of their own adulthood or as a symbol of the fulfillment of a moral duty. Data indicate that the child may be valued for an extraordinary variety of reasons, but there seems to be no indication that children are valued because of the ability to be independent and fully functional members of society. In particular, though children are widely valued for their economic utility, this value is sustained only insofar as their activities contribute to the well-being of the families or households of which they are a part and only insofar as their status remains subordinate to some manager, usually a parent.

Indeed, even where children are not primarily valued and desired as economic producers, childhood seems generally to be a category of social and economic impotence. Clearly, in most societies, the child's status has little to do with its practical incompetence, real or imaginary. Most societies in fact perceive children as capable of fulfilling many instrumental tasks and indeed expect such labor. The same attitudinal ambivalence that appears in the Western understanding of childhood thus appears in the understandings of most other cultural traditions as well. If the child is a physically and cognitively able being in many respects, moral and social independence is nevertheless not to be granted on this basis. If children are capable, physiologically and psychologically, of acting on their own, they do not, by this fact alone, prove themselves to be complete persons in the eyes of the community.

The child's economic utility may explain much of this ambivalence. It may explain why children generally are not granted independence from their economic superiors. It is perhaps not too strong to claim that the child tends to remain a child so long as his or her services are necessary to the economic unit into which he or she is born or in which he or she is reared. Of course, this is but part of the story. If economic factors appear to affect both the social institutions and ideological valuations of childhood, these factors still comprise only part of the reality of childhood itself.

CONCLUSIONS: AN AGENDA FOR ADVOCACY

What can be concluded from our brief historical and anthropological reviews? It seems clear that the concept of childhood is both historically and culturally relative and that it is deeply embedded in broader authority relations within a society. Thus, although cultures have to respond to the clear dependency of infants on adults for survival, relations to older children and adolescents seem founded on economic needs and broader societal values. Indeed, it seems clear that, apart from whatever universals there are in developmental processes, childhood has a largely symbolic character which shifts with major changes in social organization more than with changes in the repertoire of knowledge about child development.

The distinctions between childhood in the West and childhood in non-Western cultures can in fact be understood within such a framework. There seem to be two basic distinctions. First, since the turn of the century children in the West (particularly within the United States) have been removed from, and indeed legally forbidden from, participation in most forms of economic production. Second, within the last 15 years or so, children in the United States and some other Western countries have become objects of a social movement that would endow them with a legal status equal to—or, more precisely, similar to—that of adults. Putatively, such features appear to undermine the basis of an ethnological comparison between Western and non-Western childhood and, consequently, to undermine the basis of any general conclusion concerning the concept of childhood itself. Closer examination, however, suggests that these features are in fact quite consistent with the conclusions we have reached. If it is to be admitted that the establishment of child labor laws removes the Western child from the realm of economic utility, it is nevertheless clear that the same laws codify and stabilize the child's dependency even more effectively than the direct threat of punitive parental authority. Indeed, as Bronfenbrenner (1974b) has sensitively argued, these changes toward increasing age-grading in responsibilities, rights, and institutions have served to alienate youths further, both sociologically and psychologically. Moreover, it is arguable that these changes were largely economically determined (by the needs to generate a skilled labor force and to inculate the conformist values of a bureaucratized life).

Similarly, if indeed advocates of child liberation may wish to recognize legal rights for children, they still remain, for the most part, within the conceptual domain of the dualism to which childhood has been subject since the end of the Ancien Regime. Indeed, this social movement is coincident historically with movements to liberate other disadvantaged groups which, as with racial minorities, have been denied equal protection of the law for generations. In that context, the dualism with respect to children is reminiscent of the ambivalence of policy in recent years with respect to the degree to which the mentally disordered are to remain legally dependent.

The point is that substantial changes in the status of children may require fundamental changes in the way in which childhood is understood, which in turn may require changes in underlying cultural rules concerning social classification. This implicit logic often may be separate from conscious attitides concerning policies affecting children and remain essentiallly unarticulated. Moreover, these basic perceptions of children may become increasingly well entrenched as economic conditions tighten and the climate for liberal social change becomes less hospitable. The image presented by Shore's (1981) invited address to the Section on Clinical Child Psychology of the American Psychological Association may be an accurate reflection of the times: "Returning to Abraham and Issac: Child Advocacy in the Time of Shrinking Resources."

Lest this analysis sound too pessimistic, one implication is that child advocates need to be alert to individuals' and groups' concepts of the nature of childhood. These basic assumptions may need to be addressed before specific reforms may be undertaken. Thus, although we have argued that concepts of childhood well may be before the facts and relatively unrelated to empirical knowledge, psychological research still may be informative. Basic research on the meaning ascribed to the concept of childhood and the abilities and disabilities ascribed to various age groups may illuminate individual and group differences in the degree to which such concepts are held. Such research might be useful, then, in pinpointing advocates' agenda and targets. In some sense, we return in the end to the themes that have permeated this book. First, advocates need to go beyond polemics and to analyze carefully the interests at stake in child–family–state conflicts and to determine the theories that underlie policies affecting children. Second, advocates should be alert to the empirical evidence that (a) suggests the nature of the effects of various policies, or (b) indicates the validity of the theories justifying various policies, or (c) provides guidance as to the techniques that are likely to be effective in achieving change on behalf of children. Although the issues discussed in this volume inevitably involve ideology, their importance demands that advocates go beyond ideology to rigorous analysis of the import of the changes they would undertake.

APPENDIX

Children's Rights Interview

The research described in Chapters 1 and 2 (see Melton, 1980a, for statistical analyses) consisted of semistructured interviews of children in grades 1, 3, 5, and 7 in selected schools in the Boston area. The interviews consisted of two parts: (a) some general questions about children's understanding of the meaning of a "right" and to whom it applies, and (b) responses to vignettes about situations in which a child might assert a right. In each instance, the child's reasons for his or her answer and the conditions (e.g., age) he or she would apply to it were pursued.

The general questions asked in Part 1 of the interview were as follows:

1. What is a right?
2. Who has rights?
3. Do children have rights? What rights?
4. Should children have rights? What rights?

The remainder of the interview was devoted to the children's responses to the vignettes. Besides usefulness for research purposes, these vignettes are also useful foci for discussion in rights education classes for children (see Melton, 1982c). The vignettes included in the interview were as follows:

1. Joe knows that he has a chart in the school office, and he wants to know what it says about him. The teacher told Joe that he is not allowed to see his own chart. Should there be a rule or a law that the teacher can keep Joe from seeing his own chart? Why?
2. Mary's parents are getting a divorce. Her mother wants Mary to live with her, but her father wants Mary to live with him. Should there be a rule or a law that Mary could decide by herself with whom she will live? Why?
3. In Jane's school, everyone has to take a reading class. Jane doesn't like reading, though, and she thinks that she shouldn't have to take it. Should there be a rule or a law that Jane can take any subject she wants to? Why?
4. Joan went to the doctor, and he told her that she should take a shot. Joan said that she would not take one. Should there be a rule or a law that the doctor can make Joan take a shot even if she doesn't want to? Why?
5. Jim hurt himself while playing ball, and he was taken to the hospital. The people at the hospital said that they couldn't help him because his parents

didn't have enough money to pay for his care. Should there be a rule or a law that a doctor would have to help Jim even though is parents couldn't pay for it? Why?

6. Mark wrote a story for the school newspaper. In his story he said that he didn't like the school rules. The principle told him that he couldn't print his story. Should there be a rule or law that the principal can decide if Mark's story will go into the newspaper? Why?

7. David and Mike are both 6 years old. They were playing catch and some 10-year-old kids came by. The bigger kids told David and Mike that they would have to leave because they weren't old enough to play. Should there be a rule or a law that David and Mike can stay? Why?

8. Some people think that there should be a law that kids could vote for President. Do you think that there should be such a law? Why?

9. Linda wanted to work in Mr. Smith's grocery store. Mr. Smith said that she was not old enough to have a job. Should there be a rule or a law that kids like Linda can't work in a job? Why?

10. Betty kept a diary, and she said that no one else could read it, not even her parents. Should there be a rule or a law that Betty's parents can see her diary, even though she wants to keep it secret from everyone? Why?

11. Larry got into a fight at school. The teacher said that he would have to stay after school. Larry said, "Wait! You have to hear my side of it first." Should there be a rule or a law that the teacher can punish Larry even if he hasn't had a chance to tell his side of it? Why?

12. John wanted to go to a doctor to talk about some things that were bothering him, but his parents would not let him. Should there be a rule or a law that John could go to a doctor for help even if his parents didn't want him to? Why?

References

Aiken, M., & Hage, J. Organizational interdependence and intra-organizational structure. *American Sociological Review*, 1968, *6*, 912–930.

Akerley, M. S. The politics of definitions. *Journal of Autism and Developmental Disorders*, 1979, *9*, 222–231.

Allen, G. J., Chinsky, J. M., Larcen, S. W., Lochman, J. E., & Sellinger, H. E. *Community psychology and the schools: A behaviorally oriented multi-level preventive approach*. Potomac, Md.: Erlbaum, 1976.

American Psychological Association. Ethical principles of psychologists. *American Psychologist*, 1981, *36*, 633–638.

Anderson, K. A., & Anderson, D. E. Psychologists and spanking. *Journal of Clinical Child Psychology*, 1976, *5*(2), 46–49, 70.

Ariès, P. *L'enfant et la vie familie*. Paris: Libraire Plon, 1960. (Published in English as *Centuries of childhood: A social history of family life*. New York: Alfred A. Knopf, 1962.)

Arnold, F., Bulatao, R. A., & Buripaki, C., et al. *The value of children: A cross-national survey*. Honolulu: East–West Center, 1975.

Arthur, L. G. Should children be as equal as people? *North Dakota Law Review*, 1968, *45*, 204–221.

Bakan, D. Adolescence in America: From idea to social fact. In J. Kagan & R. Coles (Eds.), *Twelve to sixteen: Early adolescence*. New York: Norton, 1971.

Baker, R. G., & Gump, P. H. *Big school, small school*. Stanford, Calif.: Stanford University Press, 1964.

Barrett, C. L., Hampe, I. E., & Miller, L. C. Research on child psychotherapy. In S. L. Garfield & A. E. Bergin (Eds.), *Handbook of psychotherapy and behavior change: An empirical analysis* (2nd ed.). New York: Wiley, 1978.

Barry, H., III, & Paxson, L. M. Infancy and early childhood: Cross-cultural codes 2. *Ethnology*, 1971, *10*, 466–508.

Barry, H., III, Child, I. L., & Bacon, M. K. Relation of child training to subsistence economy. *American Anthropologist*, 1959, *61*, 51–63.

Barry, H., III, Josephson, L., Lauer, E., & Marshall, C. Traits inculcated in childhood: Cross-cultural codes 5. In H. Barry III & A. Schlegel (Eds.), *Cross-cultural samples and codes*. Pittsburgh: University of Pittsburgh Press, 1980.

Baumrind, D. Reciprocity: Development of prosocial behavior in children. *Educational Perspectives*, 1980, *19*(4), 3–9.

Bazelon, D. L. Implementing the right to treatment. *University of Chicago Law Review*, 1969, *36*, 742–754.

Bergin, A. E., & Garfield, S. L. (Eds.). *Handbook of psychotherapy and behavior change: An empirical analysis.* New York: Wiley, 1971.

Bergin, A. E., & Suinn, R. E. Individual psychotherapy and behavior therapy. *Annual Review of Psychology,* 1973, *24,* 509–556.

Bergmann, T., & Freud, A. *Children in the hospital.* New York: International Universities Press, 1965.

Berlyne, D. E. *Conflict, arousal, and learning.* New York: McGraw-Hill, 1960.

Berlyne, D. E. Exploratory and epistemic behavior. In S. Koch (Ed.), *Psychology: A study of science* (Vol. 5). New York: McGraw-Hill, 1963.

Berlyne, D. E. Emotional aspects of learning. *Annual Review of Psychology,* 1964, *15,* 115–142.

Berry, J. M. *Lobbying for the people: The political behavior of public interest groups.* Princeton, N. J.: Princeton University Press, 1977.

Berry, J. W. Ecological and cultural factors in spatial perceptual development. *Canadian Journal of Behavioral Science Review,* 1971, *3,* 324–337.

Berry, J. W. *Human ecology and cognitive style: Comparative studies in cultural and psychological adaptations.* New York: Halsted, 1972.

Bersoff, D. N. Children as participants in psychoeducational assessment. In G. B. Melton, G. P. Koocher, & M. J. Saks (Eds.), *Children's competence to consent.* New York: Plenum Press, 1983.

Bersoff, D. N., & Prasse, D. Applied psychology and judicial decision making: Corporal punishment as a case in point. *Professional Psychology,* 1978, *9,* 400–411.

Bibring, E. Mechanism of depression. In P. Greenacre (Ed.), *Affective disorders.* New York: International Universities Press, 1953.

Bikson, T. K. The status of children's intellectual rights. *Journal of Social Issues,* 1978, *34*(2), 69–86.

Billingsley, A. Bureaucratic and professional orientation patterns in casework. *Social Service Review,* 1964, *38,* 400–407.

Bing, S. R., & Brown, J. L. The juvenile court: Ideology of pathology. In G. P. Koocher (Ed.), *Children's rights and the mental health professions.* New York: Wiley, 1976.

Birnbaum, M. The right to treatment. *American Bar Association Journal,* 1960, *46,* 499–505.

Blau, P. M. Orientation toward clients in a public welfare agency. *Administrative Science Quarterly,* 1960, *5,* 341–361.

Blau, T. H. Quality of life, social indicators, and criteria of change. *Professional Psychology,* 1977, *8,* 464–473.

Bloom, B. S. *Stability and change in human characteristics.* New York: Wiley, 1964.

Blos, P. *On adolescence: A psychoanalytic interpretation.* New York: Free Press, 1962.

Boling, L., & Brotman, C. A fire-setting epidemic in a state mental health center. *American Journal of Psychiatry,* 1975, *132,* 946–950.

Brandt, S. F. *A layman's guide to lobbying without losing your tax-exempt status.* Arlington, Va.: National Mental Health Association, 1976.

Brandt, S. F. *Legislative action at the state level: Action guidelines.* Arlington, Va.: National Mental Health Association, 1980.

Brehm, J. W. *A theory of psychological reactance.* New York: Academic Press, 1966.

Brigham, T. A. Some effects of choice on academic performance. In L. C. Perlmuter & R. A. Monty (Eds.), *Choice and perceived control.* Hillsdale, N. J.: Lawrence Erlbaum, 1979.

Brim, O. G., Jr. Macro-structural influences on child development and the need for childhood social indicators. *American Journal of Orthopsychiatry,* 1975, *45,* 516–524.

Bronfenbrenner, U. Developmental research, public policy, and the ecology of childhood. *Child Development,* 1974, *45,* 1–5. (a)

Bronfenbrenner, U. The origins of alienation. *Scientific American,* 1974, *231*(2), 53–61. (b)

Bronfenbrenner, U. Lewinian space and ecological substance. *Journal of Social Issues,* 1977, *33,* 199–212.

Brooks, R. B. The impact of 94–142 on the child-clinician: Problems and challenges. *Division of Child and Youth Services Newsletter,* 1980, *3*(4), 4–6.

Brown, B. S. Invited address presented at the meeting of the American Association of Psychiatric Services for Children, Chicago, November 1979.

Bush, M., & Gordon, A. C. Client choice and bureaucratic accountability: Possibilities for responsiveness in a social welfare bureaucracy. *Journal of Social Issues,* 1978, *34*(2), 22–43.

Caplan, G. *Support systems and community mental health: Lectures on concept development.* New York: Behavioral Publications, 1974.

Children's Defense Fund. EPSDT in practice: What's happening in the field? *American Journal of Orthopsychiatry,* 1978, *48,* 77–95.

Cochran, M. M., & Brassard, J. A. Child development and personal social networks. *Child Development,* 1979, *50,* 601–616.

Congressional Quarterly. The Washington lobby (3rd ed.). Washington, D. C.: Author, 1979.

Cowen, E. L., Trost, M. A., Lorion, R. P., Dorr, D., Izzo, L. D., & Issacson, R. V. *New ways in school mental health: Early detection and prevention of school maladaptation.* New York: Human Sciences, 1975.

Crouch, R. E. An essay on the critical and judicial reception of *Beyond the Best Interests of the Child. Family Law Quarterly,* 1979, *13,* 49–103.

Cutler, C. L., & Schwach, H. J. *Juveniles and the law.* Middletown, Conn.: Xerox Educational Publications, 1975.

Danet, B., & Gurevitch, M. Presentation of self in appeals to bureaucracy: An empirical study of role specificity. *American Journal of Sociology,* 1972, *77,* 1165–1190.

Danet, B., & Hartman, H. Coping with bureaucracy: The Israeli case. *Social Forces,* 1972, *51,* 7–22.

Danish, S. J., & Smyer, M. A. Unintended consequences of requiring a license to help. *American Psychologist,* 1981, *36,* 13–21.

Davidson, W. S., & Rapp, C. A. Child advocacy in the justice system. *Social Work,* 1976, *21,* 225–232.

Davidson, W. S., & Saul, J. A. Youth advocacy in the juvenile court: A clash of paradigms. In G. B. Melton (Ed.), *Legal reforms affecting child and youth services.* New York: Haworth, 1982.

Deakins, J. *The lobbyists.* Washington, D. C.: Public Affairs Press, 1966.

Deffenbacher, K. A., Platt, G. J., & Williams, M. A. Differential recall as a function of socially induced arousal and retention interval. *Journal of Experimental Psychology,* 1974, *103,* 809–811.

Des Lauriers, A. M. Ego psychology and the definition of behavior disorders. In H. Rie (Ed.), *Perspectives in child psychopathology.* Chicago: Aldine-Atherton, 1971.

Dibner, S. S., & Dibner, A. S. *Integration of segregation for the physically handicapped child?* Springfield, Ill.: Charles C Thomas, 1973.

Donzelot, J. *La police des familles.* Paris: Les Editions de Minuit, 1977.

Dumont, M. P. The unbuilding of bureaucracy: Bureaucracy, democracy, and existential despair. *Psychotherapy and Social Science Review,* 1972, *6*(12), 21–25.

Edelman, M. W. Who is for children? *American Psychologist,* 1981, *36,* 109–117.

Editorial. A new right. *American Bar Association Journal,* 1960, *46,* 516–517.

Ehrenreich, N. S., & Melton, G. B. Ethical and legal issues in the treatment of children. In C. E. Walker & M. C. Roberts (Eds.), *Handbook of Clinical child psychology.* New York: Wiley, in press.

Ellis, N. R. The *Partlow* case: A reply to Dr. Roos. *Law and Psychology Review,* 1979, *5,* 15–49.

Erikson, E. H. *Childhood and society* (2nd ed.). New York: Norton, 1963.

Erikson, E. H. *Insight and responsibility.* New York: Norton, 1964.

Erskine, H., & Siegel, R. L. Civil liberties and the American public. *Journal of Social Issues,* 1975, *31*(2), 13–30.

Eysenck, H. J. The effects of psychotherapy: An evaluation. *Journal of Consulting Psychology,* 1952, *16,* 319–324.

Farson, R. *Birthrights.* New York: Macmillan, 1974.

Feagin, J. R. We still believe that God helps those who help themselves. *Psychology Today,* 1972, *6*(6), 101–110, 129.

Ferguson, L. R. The competence and freedom of children to make choices regarding participation in research: A statement. *Journal of Social Issues,* 1978, *34*(2), 114–121.

Feshbach, N. D., & Feshbach, S. Punishment: Parent rights versus children's rights. In G. P. Koocher (Ed.), *Children's rights and the mental health professions.* New York: Wiley, 1976.

Feshbach, S., & Feshbach, N. D. Child advocacy and family privacy. *Journal of Social Issues,* 1978, *34*(2), 168–178.

Foucault, M. *Surveiller et punir: Naissance de la prison.* Paris: Editions Gallimard, 1975.

Foucault, M. *The history of sexuality. Vol. I: An introduction* (R. Hurley, trans.). New York: Parthenon Books, 1978.

Foundation for Child Development. *National survey of children.* Unpublished paper, 1977.

Fried, R. C. *Performance in American bureaucracy.* Boston: Little, Brown, 1976.

Friedman, L. M. The idea of right as a social and legal concept. In J. L. Tapp & F. J. Levine (Eds.), *Law, justice, and the individual in society.* New York: Holt, Rinehart & Winston, 1977.

Friedrich, C. J. Some observations on Weber's analysis of bureaucracy. In R. K. Merton, A. P. Gray, B. Hockey, & H. C. Selvin (Eds.), *Reader in bureaucracy.* New York: Free Press, 1952.

Fuchs, R. F. Development and diversification in administrative rule making. *Northwestern University Law Review,* 1977, *72,* 83–110.

Garbarino, J. The price of privacy in the social dynamics of child abuse. *Child Welfare,* 1977, *56,* 565–575.

Garbarino, J., & Bronfenbrenner, U. The socialization of moral judgment and behavior in cross-cultural perspective. In T. Lickona (Ed.), *Moral development and behavior: Theory, research, and social issues.* New York: Holt, Rinehart & Winston, 1976.

Garbarino, J., & Crouter, A. Defining the community context for parent–child relations: The correlates of child maltreatment. *Child Development,* 1978, *49,* 604–616.

Garbarino, J., & Sherman, D. High-risk neighborhoods and high-risk families. The human ecology of child maltreatment. *Child Development,* 1980, *51,* 188–198.

Garbarino, J., Gaboury, M. T., Long, F., Grandjean, P., & Asp, E. Who owns the children? An ecological perspective on public policy affecting children. In G. B. Melton (Ed.), *Legal reforms affecting child and youth services.* New York: Haworth, 1982.

Garfield, S. L., & Bergin, A. E. (Eds.). *Handbook of psychotherapy and behavior change: An empirical analysis.* New York: Wiley, 1978.

Gartner, A., Kohler, M. C., & Reissman, F. *Children teaching children.* New York: Harper & Row, 1971.

Geen, R. G. Effects of being observed on short- and long-term recall. *Journal of Experimental Psychology,* 1973, *100,* 395–398.

Gelles, R. J., & Straus, M. A. Violence in the American family. *Journal of Social Issues,* 1979, *35*(2), 15–39.

Gellhorn, W. *Ombudsmen and others: Citizens' protectors in nine countries.* Cambridge, Mass.: Harvard University Press, 1966.

Golann, S., & Fremouw, W. J. (Eds.). *The right to treatment for mental patients.* New York: Irvington, 1976.

Goldenberg, I. I. *Build me a mountain: Youth, poverty, and the creation of new settings.* Cambridge, Mass.: MIT Press, 1971.

Goldstein, J., Freud, A., & Solnit, A. J. *Beyond the best interests of the child.* New York: Free Press, 1973.

Goldstein, J., Freud, A., & Solnit, A. J. *Before the best interests of the child.* New York: Free Press, 1979.

Gomes-Schwartz, B., Hadley, C. W., & Strupp, H. H. Individual psychotherapy and behavior therapy. *Annual Review of Psychology,* 1978, *29,* 435–471.

Gouldner, A. W. On Weber's analysis of bureaucratic rules. In R. K. Merton, A. P. Gray, B. Hockey, H. C. Selvin (Eds.), *Reader in bureaucracy.* New York: Columbia University Press, 1952.

Gotts, E. E. *Distinguishing characteristics of Appalachian children and families: Some findings and needs for further study.* Paper presented at the First Annual Conference on Appalachian Children and Families, Institute, West Virginia, June 1980.

Greenstein, F. D. *Children and politics.* New Haven: Yale University Press, 1965.

Greenwald, C. S. *Group power: Lobbying and public policy.* New York: Praeger, 1977.

Griggs, J. W., & Bonney, M. E. Relationship between "casual" orientation and acceptance of others, "self-ideal self" congruency and mental health changes for fourth and fifth grade children. *Journal of Educational Research,* 1970, *63,* 471–477.

Grinder, R. E. *Adolescence* (2nd ed.). New York: Wiley, 1978.

Grisso, T. *Juveniles' waiver of rights: Legal and psychological competence.* New York: Plenum Press, 1981.

Grisso, T., & Pomicter, C. Interrogation of juveniles: An empirical study of procedures, safeguards, and rights waiver. *Law and Human Behavior,* 1977, *1,* 321–342.

Grisso, T., & Vierling, L. Minors' consent to treatment: A developmental perspective. *Professional Psychology,* 1978, *9,* 412–427.

Grodin, M. A., & Alpert, J. J. Informed consent and pediatric care. In G. B. Melton, G. P. Koocher, & M. J. Saks (Eds.), *Children's competence to consent.* New York: Plenum Press, 1983.

Hall, D. R. *Cooperative lobbying: The power of pressure.* Tucson: University of Arizona Press, 1969.

Hall, G. S. *Adolescence: Its psychology and its relations to physiology, anthropology, sociology, sex, crime, religion, and education.* New York: Appleton, 1904.

Halpern, C. R. The right to habilitation: Litigation as a strategy for social change. In S. Golann & W. J. Fremouw (Eds.), *The right to treatment for mental patients.* New York: Irvington, 1976.

Haney, C. Psychology and legal change: On the limits of a factual jurisprudence. *Law and Human Behavior,* 1980, *4,* 147–199.

Hartmann, H. *Ego psychology and the problem of adaptation.* New York: International Universities Press, 1958. (Originally published, 1939.)

Heinicke, C. M., & Strassman, L. H. Toward more effective research on child psychotherapy. *Journal of the American Academy of Child Psychiatry,* 1975, *14,* 561–568.

Henley, The authority to educate. In O. O'Neil & W. Ruddick (Eds.), *Having children.* New York: Oxford University Press, 1979.

Hess, R. D., & Torney, J. V. *The development of political attitudes in children.* Chicago: Aldine, 1967.

Hobbs, N. Helping disturbed children: Psychological and ecological strategies. *American Psychologist,* 1966, *21,* 1105–1115.

Hobbs, N. *The futures of children: Categories, labels, and their consequences.* San Francisco: Jossey-Bass, 1975.

Holt, J. *Escape from childhood: The needs and rights of children.* New York: E. P. Dutton, 1974.

Hoffman, L. W., Thornton, A., & Manis, J. D. The value of children to parents in the United States. *Journal of Population*, 1978, *1*, 91-131.

Houlgate, L. D. Children, paternalism, and rights to liberty. In O. O'Neil & W. Ruddick (Eds.), *Having children.* New York: Oxford University Press, 1979.

Hunt, J. McV. *Intelligence and experience.* New York: Ronald, 1961.

Hyde, J. N. *Family advocacy: Implications for the development of an integrated child health policy.* Paper presented at the meeting of the Society for Research in Child Development, San Francisco, March 1979.

Jackson, P. W. The student's world. *Elementary School Journal*, 1966, *66*, 345-357.

Johnson, F. M. The Constitution and the federal district judge. *Texas Law Review*, 1976, *54*, 903-916.

Joint Commission on Mental Health of Children. *Crisis in child mental health: Challenge for the 1970's.* New York: Harper & Row, 1970.

Kahn, A. J., Kamerman, S. B., & McGowan, B. G. *Child advocacy: Report of a national baseline study.* New York: Columbia University School of Social Work, 1972.

Kahn, R. L., Katz, D., & Gutek, B. Bureaucratic encounters: An evaluation of government services. *Journal of Applied Behavioral Science*, 1976, *12*, 178-198.

Kamerman, S. B., & Kahn, A. J., eds. *Family policy: Government and families in 14 countries.* New York: Columbia University Press, 1978.

Kant, I. *The critique of pure reason* (N. Kemp-Smith, trans.). London: Macmillan Ltd., 1978. (Originally published, 1781.)

Katkin, D., Bullington, B., & Levine, M. Above and beyond the best interests of the child: An inquiry into the relationship between social science and social action. *Law and Society Review*, 1974, *8*, 669-687.

Katz, D., Gutek, B. A., Kahn, R. L., & Barton, E. *Bureaucratic encounters: A pilot study in the evaluation of government services.* Ann Arbor, Mich.: Institute for Social Research, 1975.

Katz, E., & Danet, B. (Eds.). *Bureaucracy and the public: A reader in official-client relations.* New York: Basic Books, 1973. (a)

Katz, E. & Danet, B. Communication between bureaucracy and the public: A review of the literature. In W. Schramm, I. Pool, N. Maccoby, E. Parkes, & F. Frey (Eds.), *Handbook of bureaucracy.* Chicago: Rand McNally, 1973. (b)

Keith-Spiegel, P. Children's rights as participants in research. In G. P. Koocher (Ed.), *Children's rights and the mental health professions.* New York: Wiley, 1976.

Kempe, R. S., & Kempe, C. H. *Child abuse.* Cambridge, Mass.: Harvard Press, 1978.

Keniston, K. How community mental health stamped out the riots (1968-78). *Trans-action*, 1968, *5*(8), 21-29.

Keniston, K. *All our children: The American family under pressure.* New York: Harcourt Brace Jovanovich, 1977.

Kett, J. The history of age grouping in America. In J. S. Coleman et al. (Eds.), *Youth: Transition to adulthood.* Chicago: University of Chicago Press, 1974.

Kett, J. F. *Rites of passage.* New York: Basic Books, 1977.

Kilman, P. R., Henry, S. E., Scarbro, H., & Laughlin, J. E. The impact of affective education on elementary school under-achievers. *Psychology in the Schools*, 1979, *16*, 217-224.

Kirst, M. W., Garms, W., & Opperman, T. State services for children: An exploration of who benefits, who governs. *Public Policy*, 1980, *28*, 185-206.

Kittrie, N. N. *The right to be different.* Baltimore: Penguin, 1971.

Kleinsmith, L. J., & Kaplan, S. Paired-associate learning as a function of arousal and interpolated interval. *Journal of Experimental Psychology*, 1963, *65*, 190–193.

Kleinsmith, L. J., & Kaplan, S. Interaction of arousal and recall interval in nonsense syllable paired-associate learning. *Journal of Experimental Psychology*, 1964, *67*, 124–126.

Knitzer, J. Advocacy and the children's crisis. *American Journal of Orthopsychiatry*, 1971, *41*, 799–806.

Knitzer, J. Child advocacy: A perspective. *American Journal of Orthopsychiatry*, 1976, *46*, 200–216.

Knitzer, J. Responsibility for delivery of services. In J. S. Mearig (Ed.), *Working for children: Ethical issues beyond professional guidelines*. San Francisco: Jossey-Bass, 1978.

Kohlberg, L. Stage and sequence: The cognitive-developmental approach to socialization. In D. A. Goslin (Ed.), *Handbook of socialization theory and research*. New York: Rand McNally, 1969.

Kohlberg, L. Moral stages and moralization: The cognitive-developmental approach. In T. Lickona (Ed.), *Moral development and behavior: Theory, research, and social issues*. New York: Holt, Rinehart & Winston, 1976.

Kohlberg, L. (Ed.). *Recent research in moral development*. New York: Holt, Rinehart & Winston, in preparation.

Kohlberg, L., & Turiel, E. Moral development and moral education. In G. S. Lesser (Ed.), *Psychology and educational practice*. Glenview, Ill.: Scott, Foresman, 1971.

Kohn, M. L. *Class and conformity: A study in values* (2nd ed.). Chicago: University of Chicago Press, 1977.

Koocher, G. P. A bill of rights for children in psychotherapy. In G. P. Koocher (Ed.), *Children's rights and the mental health professions*. New York: Wiley, 1976. (a)

Koocher, G. P. An introduction: Why children's rights? In G. P. Koocher (Ed.), *Children's rights and the mental health professions*. New York: Wiley, 1976. (b)

Koocher, G. P. Child advocacy and mental health professionals. In P. A. Vardin & I. N. Brody (Eds.), *Children's rights: Contemporary perspectives*. New York: Teachers College Press, 1979.

Koocher, G. P., & Pedulla, B. M. Current practices in child psychotherapy. *Professional Psychology*, 1977, *8*, 275–286.

Korte, C. D. The quality of life in rural and urban America. In A. W. Childs & G. B. Melton (Eds.), *Rural psychology*. New York: Plenum Press, 1983.

Kozol, J. *The night is dark and I am far from home*. Boston: Houghton Mifflin, 1975.

Latané, B., & Darley, J. M. Group inhibition of bystander intervention in emergencies. *Journal of Personality and Social Psychology*, 1968, *10*, 215–221.

Lefstein, N., Stapleton, V., & Teitelbaum, L. In search of justice: *Gault* and its implications. *Law and Society Review*, 1969, *3*, 491–537.

Lenrow, P., & Cowden, P. Human services, professionals, and the paradox of institutional reform. *American Journal of Community Psychology*, 1980, *8*, 463–484.

Lerner, M. J. *The belief in a just world: A fundamental delusion*. New York: Plenum Press, 1980.

Levine, M. Should the Surgeon General require that some government agencies carry a label warning that dealing with them may be dangerous to your mental health? *American Psychological Association Division of Community Psychology Newsletter*, 1978, *11*(2), 1–3. (a)

Levine, M. Even when you win, you don't win. *American Psychological Association Division of Community Psychology Newsletter*, 1978, *11*(3), 1–2. (b)

Levine, M., & Levine, A. *A social history of helping services: Court, clinic, school, and community*. New York: Appleton-Century-Crofts, 1970.

Levitt, E. E. The results of psychotherapy with children: An evaluation. *Journal of Consulting Psychology*, 1957, *21*, 186–189.

Levitt, E. E. Research on psychotherapy with children. In A. E. Bergin & S. L. Garfield (Eds.), *Handbook of psychotherapy and behavior change: An empirical analysis.* New York: Wiley, 1971.

Levonian, E. Attention and consolidation as factors in retention. *Psychonomic Science,* 1966, *6,* 275–276.

Levonian, E. Retention of information in relation to arousal during continuously-presented material. *American Educational Research Journal,* 1967, *4,* 103–116.

Levonian, E. Short-term retention in relation to arousal. *Psychophysiology,* 1968, *4,* 284–293.

Levonian, E. Retention over time in relation to arousal during learning: An explanation of discrepant results. *Acta Psychologia,* 1972, *36,* 290–321.

Lewis, C. E. Decision-making related to health: When could/should children act responsibly? In G. B. Melton, G. P. Koocher, & M. J. Saks (Eds.), *Children's competence to consent.* New York: Plenum Press, 1983.

Lickona, T. *Moral development and behavior: Theory, research, and social issues.* New York: Holt, Rinehart & Winston, 1976. (a)

Lickona, T. Research on Piaget's theory of moral development. In T. Lickona (Ed.), *Moral development and behavior: Theory, research, and social issues.* New York: Holt, Rinehart & Winston, 1976. (b)

Liebschutz, S. F., & Niemi, R. G. Political attitudes among black children. In R. G. Niemi (Ed.), *The politics of future citizens.* San Francisco: Jossey-Bass, 1974.

Locke, J. *Two treatises of government* (P. Laslett, Ed.). Cambridge: Cambridge University Press, 1960. (Originally published, 1690.)

Long, B. E. An approach for mental health education. In E. M. Bower (Ed.), *Orthopsychiatry and education.* Detroit: Wayne State University Press, 1971.

Looff, D. H. *Appalachia's children: The challenge of mental health.* Lexington, Ky.: University of Kentucky Press, 1971.

Marris, P. *Loss and change.* New York: Pantheon, 1974.

Massimo, J. L., & Shore, M. F. The effectiveness of a vocationally oriented psychotherapy. *American Journal of Orthopsychiatry,* 1963, *33,* 634–643.

McCord, J. A thirty-year follow-up treatment effects. *American Psychologist,* 1978, *33,* 284–289.

McGowan, B. G. Strategies in bureaucracies. In J. S. Mearig (Ed.), *Working for children.* San Francisco: Jossey-Bass, 1978.

McLean, P. D. Induced arousal and time of recall as determinants of paired-associate recall. *British Journal of Psychology,* 1969, *60,* 57–62.

Melody, W. H. *Children's television: The economics of exploitation.* New Haven: Yale University Press, 1973.

Melton, G. B. The psychologist as clinician-advocate: Issues in practice and training. *Journal of Clinical Child Psychology,* 1977, *6*(1), 27–29. (a)

Melton, G. B. "What if I couldn't?": Impact of a museum exhibit depicting special needs of the handicapped. *Journal of Clinical Child Psychology,* 1977, *6*(3), 89–90. (b)

Melton, G. B. Children's right to treatment. *Journal of Clinical Child Psychology,* 1978, *7,* 200–202. (a)

Melton, G. B. The psychologist's role in juvenile and family law. *Journal of Clinical Child Psychology,* 1978, *7,* 189–192. (b)

Melton, G. B. More on mainstreaming. *American Journal of Orthopsychiatry,* 1979, *49,* 386, 551.

Melton, G. B. Children's concepts of their rights. *Journal of Clinical Child Psychology,* 1980, *9,* 186–190. (a)

Melton, G. B. Preparing normal children for mainstreaming. *Journal for Special Educators,* 1980, *16,* 198–204. (b)

Melton, G. B. Children's participation in treatment planning: Psychological and legal issues. *Professional Psychology,* 1981, *12,* 246–252. (a)

Melton, G. B. Effects of a state law permitting minors to consent to psychotherapy. *Professional Psychology*, 1981, *12*, 647–654. (b)

Melton, G. B. Psycholegal issues in juveniles' competency to waive their rights. *Journal of Clinical Child Psychology*, 1981, *10*, 59–62. (c)

Melton, G. B. Children's rights: Where are the children? *American Journal of Orthopsychiatry*, 1982, *52*, 530–538. (a)

Melton, G. B. (Ed.). *Legal reforms affecting child and youth services*. New York: Haworth, 1982. (b)

Melton, G. B. Teaching children about their rights. In J. S. Henning (Ed.), *Children and the law: Empirical and theoretical approaches to children's rights*. Springfield, Ill.: Charles C Thomas, 1982. (c)

Melton, G. B. Decision making by children: Psychological risks and benefits. In G. B. Melton, G. P. Koocher, & M. J. Saks (Eds.), *Children's competence to consent*. New York: Plenum Press, 1983.

Melton, G. B. *Minors and privacy: Are legal and psychological concepts compatible?* Manuscript in preparation.

Melton, G. B., & Lind, E. A. Procedural justice in family court: Does the adversary model make sense? In G. B. Melton (Ed.), *Legal reforms affecting child and youth services*. New York: Haworth, 1982.

Melton, G. B., Koocher, G. P., & Saks, M. J. (Eds.). *Children's competence to consent*. New York: Plenum Press, 1983.

Meltsner, A. J. *Policy analysts in the bureaucracy*. Berkeley: University of California Press, 1976.

Mercer, J. R. *Labeling the mentally retarded*. Berkeley: University of California Press, 1973.

Merton, R. K. Bureaucratic structure and personality. In R. K. Merton, A. P. Gray, B. Hockey, & H. C. Selvin (Eds.), *Reader in bureaucracy*. New York: Free Press, 1952.

Milbrath, L. W. *The Washington lobbyists*. Westport, Conn.: Greenwood, 1963.

Milbrath, L. W., & Goel, M. L. *Political participation: How and why do people get involved in politics?* (2nd ed.). Chicago: Rand McNally, 1977.

Miller, D. R., & Swanson, G. E. *The changing American parent*. New York: Wiley, 1958.

Mladenka, K. R. Citizen demand and bureaucratic response: Direct dialing democracy in a major American city. *Urban Affairs Quarterly*, 1977, *12*, 273–290.

Mnookin, R. H. Child-custody adjudication: Judicial functions in the face of indeterminancy. *Law and Contemporary Problems*, 1975, *39*, 226–290.

Mnookin, R. H. (Ed.). *Child, family, and state: Problems and materials on children and the law*. Boston: Little, Brown, 1978. (a)

Mnookin, R. H. Children's rights: Beyond kiddie libbers and child savers. *Journal of Clinical Child Psychology*, 1978, *7*, 163–167. (b)

Mnookin, R. H., & Kornhauser, L. Bargaining in the shadow of the law: The case of divorce. *Yale Law Journal*, 1979, *88*, 950–997.

Modell, J., Furstenberg, F., Jr., & Hershberg, T. Social change and transitions to adulthood in historical perspective. *Journal of Family History*, 1976, *1*, 7–33.

Montero, D. Support for civil liberties among a cohort of high school graduates and college students. *Journal of Social Issues*, 1975, *31*, 123–136.

Moos, R. H. *The human context: Environmental determinants of behavior*. New York: Wiley, 1976.

Moos, R., & Trickett, E. J. *Classroom Environment Scale manual*. Palo Alto, Calif.: Consulting Psychologist Press, 1974.

Morin, S. F., & Schultz, S. J. The gay movement and the rights of children. *Journal of Social Issues*, 1978, *34*(2), 137–148.

Morse, A. E., Hyde, J. N., Newberger, E. H., & Reed, R. B. Environmental correlates of pediatric social illness: Preventive implications of an advocacy approach. *American Journal of Public Health*, 1977, *67*.

Morse, S. J. Law and mental health professionals: The limits of expertise. *Professional Psychology*, 1978, *9*, 389–399.

Morton, T., & Dubanoski, R. A. Children's rights: Attitudes and perceptions. *Educational Perspectives*, 1980, *19*(4), 24–27.

Murdock, G. P. & Morrow, D. O. Subsistence economy and supportive practices: Cross-cultural codes 1. In H. Barry III & A. Schlegel (Eds.), *Cross-cultural samples and codes*. Pittsburgh: University of Pittsburg Press, 1980.

Murdock, G. P., & Wilson, S. F. Settlement patterns and community organization: Cross-cultural codes 3. In H. Barry III & A. Schlegel (Eds.), *Cross-cultural samples and codes*. Pittsburgh: University of Pittsburgh Press, 1980.

Nader, L., & Todd, H. F., Jr. (Eds.). *The disputing process: Law in 10 societies*. New York: Columbia University Press, 1978.

Nader, R. Ombudsmen for state governments. In D. C. Rowat (Ed.), *The ombudsman: Citizen's defender* (2nd ed.). London: George Allen & Unwin, 1968.

Nader, R., Petkas, P. J., & Blackwell, K. (Eds.). Whistle blowing: *The report of the Conference on Professional Responsibility*. New York: Grossman, 1972.

National Academy of Sciences. *Toward a national policy for children and families*. Washington, D. C.: Author, 1976.

National Education Association. *The status of the American family: Policies, facts, opinions, and issues*. Washington, D. C.: Author, 1979.

Novaco, R., & Monahan, J. Research in community psychology: An analysis of work published in the first six years of the *American Journal of Community Psychology*. *American Journal of Community Psychology*, 1980, *8*, 131–145.

Ogbu, J. U. Origins of human competence: A cultural-ecological perspective. *Child Development*, 1981, *52*, 413–429.

Ojemann, R. H. Investigations on the effects of teacher understanding and appreciation of behavior dynamics. In G. Caplan (Ed.), *Prevention of mental disorders in children*. New York: Basic Books, 1961.

Oliver, D. W., & Newman, F. M. *Rights of the accused: Criminal procedure and public security*. Middletown, Conn.: Xerox Educational Publications, 1975.

O'Neill, P. Cognitive community psychology. *American Psychologist*, 1981, *36*, 457–469.

Paul, J. L., Turnbull, A. P., & Cruickshank, W. M. *Mainstreaming: A practical guide*. Syracuse, N.Y.: Syracuse University Press, 1977.

Pearson, C., & Cutler, C. Liberty under law: *Case studies of the basic principles of the Bill of Rights*. Middletown, Conn.: Xerox Educational Publications, 1975.

Pelton, L. H. Child abuse and neglect: The myth of classlessness. *American Journal of Orthopsychiatry*, 1978, *48*, 608–617.

Perlmuter, L. C., & Monty, R. A. (Eds.). *Choice and perceived control*. Hillsdale, N.J.: Lawrence Erlbaum, 1979.

Piaget, J. *The moral judgment of the child*. New York: Free Press, 1965. (Originally published, 1932.)

Platt, A. M. *The child savers: The invention of delinquency* (2nd ed.). Chicago: University of Chicago Press, 1977.

Polier, J. W. Professional abuse of children: Responsibility for the delivery of services. *American Journal of Orthopsychiatry*, 1975, *45*, 357–362.

Prothro, J. W., & Grigg, C. W. Fundamental principles of democracy: Bases of agreement and disagreement. *Journal of Politics*, 1960, 22, 276–294.

Rappaport, J. *Community psychology: Values, research, and action*. New York: Holt, Rinehart & Winston, 1977.

Rawls, J. *A theory of justice*. Cambridge, Mass.: Harvard University Press, 1971.

Reiss, D. Varieties of consensual experience. I. A theory for relating family interaction to individual thinking. *Family Process*, 1971, *10*, 1–28.

Reppucci, N. D. Implementation issues for the behavior modifier as institutional change agent. *Behavior Therapy*, 1977, *8*, 594–605.

Reppucci, N. D., & Saunders, J. T. Social psychology of behavior modification: Problems of implementation in natural settings. *American Psychologist*, 1974, *29*, 649–660.

Ricks, D., Umbarger, C., & Mack, R. A measure of increased temporal perspective in successfully treated adolescent boys. *Journal of Abnormal and Social Psychology*, 1964, *69*, 685–689.

Ritchie, Jane, & Ritchie, James. *Growing up in Polynesia*. Sydney, Australia: George Allen & Unwin, 1979.

Robertson, T. S., & Rossiter, J. R. Children and commercial persuassion: An attribution theory analysis. *Journal of Consumer Research*, 1974, *1*, 13–20.

Rogeness, G. A., Bednar, R. A., & Diesenhaus, H. The social system and children's behavior problems. *American Journal of Orthopsychiatry*, 1974, *44*, 497–502.

Rogers, C. M., & Wrightsman, L. S. Attitudes toward children's rights: Nurturance or self-determination. *Journal of Social Issues*, 1978, *34*(2), 59–68.

Roos, P. Custodial care for the "subtrainable": Revisiting an old myth. *Law and Psychology Review*, 1979, *5*, 1–14.

Rosen, A. C., Rekers, G. A., & Bentler, P. M. Ethical issues in the treatment of children. *Journal of Social Issues*, 1978, *34*(2), 122–136.

Rosen, C. E. The impact of an Open Campus program upon high school students' sense of control over their environment. *Psychology in the Schools*, 1977, *14*, 216–219.

Rossiter, J. R. Does TV advertising affect children? *Journal of Advertising Research*, 1979, *19*, 49–53.

Rousseau, J. J. *The Emile* (B. Foxley, trans.). New York: Dutton, 1974. (Originally published, 1762.)

Rowat, D. C. (Ed.). *The ombudsman: Citizen's defender* (2nd ed.). London: George Allen & Unwin, 1968.

Ryan, W. *Blaming the victim*. New York: Vintage, 1971.

Saks, M. J. *Jury verdicts: The role of group size and social decision rule*. Lexington, Mass.: Lexington Books, 1977.

Saks, M. J. Social psychological perspectives on the problem of consent. In G. B. Melton, G. P. Koocher, & M. J. Saks (Eds.), *Children's competence to consent*. New York: Plenum Press, 1983.

Saltzburg, S. A. The flow and ebb of constitutional criminal procedure in the Warren and Burger Courts. (Foreword to the 10th annual review of criminal procedure: United States Supreme Court and Courts of Appeals 1979–1980.) *Georgetown Law Journal*, 1980, *69*, 151–209.

Sarason, S. B. *The culture of the school and the problem of change*. Boston: Allyn & Bacon, 1971.

Sarason, S. B. *The creation of settings and the future societies*. San Francisco: Jossey-Base, 1972.

Sarata, B. P. V., & Reppucci, N. D. The problem is outside: Staff and client behavior as a function of external events. *Community Mental Health Journal*, 1975, *11*, 91–100.

Scarr, S. (Ed.). *Psychology and children: Current research and practice*. Special issue of *American Psychologist*, 1979, *34*(10).

Saunders, J. T., & Reppucci, N. D. The social identity of behavior modification. In M. Hersen, R. M. Eisler, & P. M. Miller (Eds.), *Progress in behavior modification* (Vol. 6). New York: Academic Press, 1978.

Seligman, M. E. P. *Helplessness: On depression, development, and death*. San Francisco: W. H. Freeman, 1975.

Selman, R. L. The relation of role-taking to the development of moral judgment in children. *Child Development*, 1971, *42*, 79–91.

Shimp, T. A., Dyer, R. F., & Divita, S. F. An experimental test of the harmful effects of premium-oriented commercials on children. *Journal of Consumer Research,* 1976, *3,* 1–11.

Shore, M. F. *Returning to Abraham and Issac: Child advocacy in the time of shrinking resources.* Invited address to the Section on Clinical Child Psychology, American Psychological Association, Los Angeles, August 1981.

Shore, M., & Massimo, J. Comprehensive vocationally oriented psychotherapy for adolescent delinquent boys: A follow-up study. *American Journal of Orthopsychiatry,* 1966, *36,* 609–616.

Shore, M. F., & Massimo, J. Five years later: A follow-up study of comprehensive vocationally oriented psychotherapy. *American Journal of Orthopsychiatry,* 1969, *39,* 769–774.

Shore, M. F., & Massimo, J. After ten years: A follow-up study of comprehensive vocationally oriented psychotherapy. *American Journal of Orthopsychiatry,* 1973, *43,* 128–132.

Shore, M. F., & Massimo, J. Fifteen years after treatment: A follow-up study of comprehensive vocationally oriented psychotherapy. *American Journal of Orthopsychiatry,* 1979, *49,* 240–245.

Shore, M. F., Massimo, J., Kisielawski, J., & Moran, J. K. Object relations changes resulting from successful psychotherapy with adolescent delinquents and their relationship to academic performance. *Journal of the American Academy of Child Psychiatry,* 1966, *5,* 93–104.

Shure, M. B., & Spivack, G. *Problem-solving techniques in child-rearing.* San Francisco: Jossey-Bass, 1978.

Siegel, D. M., & Hurley, S. The role of the child's preference in custody proceedings. *Family Law Quarterly,* 1977, *11,* 1–58.

Silverman, M. Beyond the mainstream: The special needs of the chronic child patient. *American Journal of Orthopsychiatry,* 1979, *49,* 62–68. (a)

Silverman, M. Reply to letter to the editor. *American Journal of Orthopsychiatry,* 1979, *49,* 551–552. (b)

Skinner, B. F. *Walden two.* New York: Macmillan, 1948.

Skinner, B. F. *Beyond freedom and dignity.* New York: Bantam, 1971.

Skolnick, A. The limits of childhood: Conceptions of child development and social contexts. *Law and Contemporary Problems,* 1975, *39,* 38–77.

Slobogin, C. "Voluntary" hospitalizations of children: A look at the *Parham* decision. *Division of Child and Youth Services Newsletter,* 1980, *3*(2), 3–4.

Sobel, S. B. Throwing the baby out with the bath water: The hazards of follow-up research. *American Psychologist,* 1978, *33,* 290–291.

Speier, M. *How to observe face-to-face communication: A sociological introduction.* Pacific Palisades, Calif.: Goodyear, 1973.

Spivack, G., & Shure, M. B. *Social adjustment of young children.* San Francisco: Jossey-Bass, 1974.

Spivack, G., Platt, J. J., & Shure, M. B. *The problem-solving approach to adjustment.* San Francisco: Jossey-Bass, 1976.

Stacey, F. *Ombudsmen compared.* Oxford: Clarendon Press, 1978.

Steiner, G. Y. *The children's cause.* Washington, D.C.: Brookings Institution, 1976.

Stickney, S. S. *Wyatt v. Stickney:* Background and postscript. In S. Golann & W. J. Fremouw (Eds.), *The right to treatment for mental patients.* New York: Irvington, 1976.

Stilwell, W. E. *Long-term effects of an affective-social educational program upon elementary school age children.* Paper presented at the Annual Meeting of the American Educational Research Association, Toronto, March 1978.

Takanishi, R. Childhood as a social issue: Historical roots of contemporary child advocacy movements. *Journal of Social Issues,* 1978, *34*(2), 8–28.

Tapp, J. J., & Levine, F. J. Legal socialization: Strategies for an ethical legality. *Stanford Law Review,* 1974, *27,* 1–72.

Tapp, J. L., & Melton, G. B. Preparing children for decision making: Implications of legal socialization research. In G. B. Melton, G. P. Koocher, & M. J. Saks (Eds.), *Children's competence to consent.* New York: Plenum Press, 1983.

Task Force on Children out of School. *The way we go to school: The exclusion of children in Boston.* Boston: Beacon Press, 1970.

Teele, J. E. *Evaluating school busing: Case study of Boston's Operation Exodus.* New York: Praeger, 1973.

Thain, G. Suffer the hucksters to come unto the little children?: Possible restrictions of television advertising to children under Section 5 of the Federal Trade Commission Act. *Boston University Law Review,* 1976, *56,* 651–684.

Thibaut, J., & Walker, L. A theory of procedure. *California Law Review,* 1978, *66,* 541–566.

Trickett, E. J. Toward a social-ecological conception of adolescent socialization: Normative data on contrasting types of public school classrooms. *Child Development,* 1978, *49,* 408–414.

Tuden, A., & Marshall, C. Political organization: Cross-cultural codes 4. In H. Barry III & A. Schlegel (Eds.), *Cross-cultural samples and codes.* Pittsburgh: University of Pittsburgh Press, 1980.

Urbain, E. S., & Kendall, P. C. Review of social-cognitive problem-solving interventions with children. *Psychological Bulletin,* 1980, *89,* 109–143.

Vickers, G. Institutional and personal roles. *Human Relations,* 1971, *24,* 433–447.

Wald, M. S. Legal policies affecting children: A lawyer's request for aid. *Child Development,* 1976, *47,* 1–5.

Walker, E. L., & Tarte, R. D. Memory storage as a function of arousal and time with homogeneous and heterogeneous lists. *Journal of Verbal Learning and Verbal Behavior,* 1963, *2,* 113–119.

Warren, R. L. Mental health planning and model cities: "Hamlet" or "Hellzapoppin." *Community Mental Health Journal,* 1971, *7,* 39–49.

Weber, M. *The theory of social and economic organizations* (A. M. Henderson & T. Parsons, trans.; T. Parsons, Ed.). Oxford: Oxford University Press, 1947.

Wechsler, H. (Ed.). *Minimum drinking-age laws: An evaluation.* Lexington, Mass.: Lexington Books, 1980.

Weeks, K. M. *Ombudsmen around the world: A comparative chart* (2nd ed.). Berkeley: Institute of Governmental Studies, University of California, 1978.

Weinstein, G., & Fantini, M. D. (Eds.). *Toward humanistic education.* New York: Praeger, 1970.

Weinstein, L. Project Re-Ed schools for emotionally disturbed children: Effectiveness as viewed by referring agencies, parents, and teachers. *Exceptional Children,* 1969, *35,* 703–711.

Weiser, J. C., & Hayes, J. E. Democratic attitudes of teachers and prospective teachers. *Phi Delta Kappan,* 1966, *47,* 476–481.

Weithorn, L. A. Involving children in decisions affecting their own welfare: Guidelines for professionals. In G. B. Melton, G. P. Koocher, & M. J. Saks (Eds.), *Children's competence to consent.* New York: Plenum Press, 1983.

Westman, J. C. *Child advocacy: New professional roles for helping families.* New York: Free Press, 1979.

Weyrauch, W. O. The "basic law" or "constitution" of a small group. In J. L. Tapp & F. J. Levine (Eds.), *Law, justice, and the individual in society: Psychological and legal issues.* New York: Holt, Rinehart & Winston, 1977.

White, R. W. Motivation reconsidered: The concept of competence. *Psychological Review,* 1959, *66,* 297–333.

Whiting, J. J. M., & Child, I. L. *Child training and personality: A cross-cultural study.* New Haven: Yale University Press, 1953.

Whyte, W. H., Jr. *The organization man.* New York: Simon & Schuster, 1956.

Wilson, W. C. Belief in freedom of speech and press. *Journal of Social Issues,* 1975, *31*(2), 69–76.

Wolfe, M. Childhood and privacy. In I. Altman & J. F. Wohlwill (Eds.), *Human behavior and environment: Advances in theory and research* (Vol. 3). New York: Plenum Press, 1979.

Worsfold, V. L. A philosophical justification for children's rights. *Harvard Educational Review,* 1974, *44,* 142–157.

Wright, B. A. *Physical disability: A psychological approach.* New York: Harper & Row, 1960.

Zalkind, S. S., Gaugler, E. A., & Schwartz, R. M. Civil liberties attitudes and personality measures: Some exploratory research. *Journal of Social Issues,* 1975, *31*(2), 77–92.

Zax, M., & Cowen, E. L. *Abnormal psychology: Changing conceptions* (2nd ed.). New York: Holt, Rinehart & Winston, 1976.

Zellman, G. L. Antidemocratic beliefs: A survey and some explanations. *Journal of Social Issues,* 1975, *31*(2), 31–54.

Zellman, G. L., & Sears, D. O. Childhood origins of tolerance for dissent. *Journal of Social Issues,* 1971, *27*(2), 109–136.

Ziegler, H., & Baer, M. *Lobbying: Interaction and influence in American state legislatures.* Belmont, Calif.: Wadsworth, 1969.

Zill, N., & Brim, O. G. *Childhood social indicators.* Unpublished paper, Foundation for Child Development, 1975.

Table of Cases

219

Author Index

Subject Index